PENGUIN MODERN CLASSICS

THE LETTERS AND JOURNALS OF KATHERINE MANSFIELD

Katherine Mansfield was born in Wellington, New Zealand, in 1888, and died at Fontainebleau in 1923. She came to England for the latter part of her education. Her first writing (apart from some early sketches) was published in *The New Age*, to which she became a regular contributor. Her first book, *In a German Pension*, was published in 1911. In 1912 she began to write for *Rhythm*, edited by John Middleton Murry, whom she married. For the next few years her writing was mainly experimental. In 1916 she wrote *Prelude*, and from that time onward she was master of her own style. She contracted tuberculosis in 1917, and thence-forward led a wandering life in search of health, and wrote under difficulties. Her second book of collected stories, *Bliss*, was not published until 1921. Her third collection, *The Garden Party*, appeared a year later. It was the last book to be published in her lifetime. After her death, two more collections of her stories were published; also her *Letters* and her *Journal*.

C. K. Stead is the author of three books of poems, a novel, a book on modern poetic theory (*The New Poetic: Yeats to Eliot*, which has been published in Penguins), and a number of short stories and critical articles. He has edited a collection of essays on *Measure for Measure* and an anthology of New Zealand short stories. He is Professor of English at the University of Auckland.

The Letters and Journals of Katherine Mansfield

A Selection

*

EDITED BY C. K. STEAD

PENGUIN BOOKS

PENGUIN BOOKS

Published by the Penguin Group
27 Wrights Lane, London W8 5TZ, England
Viking Penguin Inc., 40 West 23rd Street, New York, New York 10010, USA
Penguin Books Australia Ltd, Ringwood, Victoria, Australia
Penguin Books Canada Ltd, 2801 John Street, Markham, Ontario, Canada L3R 1B4
Penguin Books (NZ) Ltd, 182–190 Wairau Road, Auckland 10, New Zealand

Penguin Books Ltd, Registered Offices: Harmondsworth, Middlesex, England

Published in Penguin Books 1977
Reprinted 1979, 1981, 1985, 1988

Printed and bound in Great Britain by
Cox & Wyman Ltd, Reading
Set in Monotype Baskerville

This book is affectionately dedicated
to Celia and Cecil Manson

Contents

Introduction

When Katherine Mansfield died on 9 January 1923 at the age of thirty-four she had published three books of short stories. Of these the first, *In a German Pension* (1911), had been an immediate success, running quickly through three impressions, but it had gone out of print with the collapse of the publishing firm of Stephen Swift, and throughout the remaining twelve years of her life Katherine Mansfield resisted all efforts to persuade her to allow it to be republished. Her second book, *Bliss*, appeared in 1920 and her third, *The Garden Party*, in 1922. Both were favourably received. In 1923 Katherine Mansfield's husband, John Middleton Murry, issued the collection of stories she had been at work on before her death, *The Dove's Nest*. There followed one further book made up of uncollected and unfinished stories, *Something Childish* (1924), and a reissue of *In a German Pension*, making five books, a total of eighty-eight stories. In the fifty years since her death not one of these stories has ever been out of print[1] and the best of them seem to have a secure place in the history of the short story and in the development of modern British fiction.

In addition to her fiction Katherine Mansfield left a variety of writing of other kinds. She was a prolific correspondent, an irregular keeper of diaries and notebooks, a busy

1. U.K. publishers' figures for sales during the two decades from 1952 to 1972 show Constable's *Collected Stories* having sold 46 000 copies, Oxford's World's Classics' *Selected Stories* 67,000 copies, and Collins Classics' *Selected Stories* 24,000 copies (since 1957), while Penguin Books have kept sometimes two, sometimes three, of her titles in print, selling around 10,000 a year of each title. In a period when short stories have been described as virtually unsaleable these figures indicate a firmly established reputation.

reviewer and an occasional versifier. In a will dated 14 August 1922 she bequeathed 'all manuscripts notebooks papers letters' to her husband but she added 'I should like him to publish as little as possible and tear up and burn as much as possible he will understand that I desire to leave as few traces of my camping ground as possible.' A letter written a week earlier and left to be opened in the event of her death is less sweeping but still clear enough in its intention: 'All my manuscripts I leave entirely to you to do what you like with. Go through them one day, dear love, and destroy all you do not use. Please destroy all letters you do not wish to keep and all papers. You know my love of tidiness. Have a clean sweep . . . and leave all fair – will you?'

There is no evidence that Murry destroyed anything at all. On the contrary over a period of years he transcribed and published almost everything, however apparently insignificant or fragmentary, first using the pieces in his new periodical, *The Adelphi*, to which his late wife was for some years the most regular contributor, and then editing them and publishing them as books. In 1923 Katherine Mansfield's *Poems* appeared, in 1927 her *Journal*, in 1928 a two-volume selection of her letters, in 1930 *Novels and Novelists* (reprinting her reviews of fiction written for *The Athenaeum*) and in 1939 *The Scrapbook of Katherine Mansfield*. In 1951 the almost complete texts of her letters to Murry, a 700-page volume, replaced the 1928 selection of letters; and in 1954 there was a much enlarged 'definitive' edition of the *Journal*. A rough count suggests that in addition to her short stories Murry published something like 700,000 words of those papers he was instructed to tidy and leave fair. The 'camping ground' she hoped to conceal is now open to the public.

Murry's promotion of his wife's literary remains brought him royalties and opprobrium, and increased her fame. The good and the bad seem inextricably mixed in his work on her behalf. He transcribed, edited and wrote commentaries tirelessly but in a way which encouraged a sentimental, and sometimes a falsely mystical, interest in her talent. He could not keep himself out of the picture either, seeing the development of her art always in relation to the development of her feeling for him. He was accused of making capital out of her death. He antagonized many people previously well-disposed towards her writing and perhaps ensured something of a reaction against it at the same time that he was making it more widely known. Finally, by publishing more and more of his wife's private papers revealing tensions in the marriage, Murry cast himself publicly in the role of the husband who had failed her.

Worse might have been said of him had it been known that he was ignoring her instruction to 'tear up and burn as much as possible', and Murry must have been uneasy about it. He was fond of quoting (and misquoting) the last sentence of the letter posthumously received, in which she said 'I feel no other lovers have ever walked the earth together more joyfully – in spite of all.' But he never printed it all, and that can only have been because to do so would have revealed her wish that her 'camping ground' should not be exposed.

It must be admitted, however, that Murry's position was a difficult one. There was certainly bad taste in his manner of presenting his wife's work but it could not have been otherwise, he being the man he was, and there was no one else to do the job. He did his best; and if the financial rewards he earned were considerable[1] so too were the brickbats. Perhaps he published too much, and too soon; but at least, if he need not have published, it is difficult to see how he could have taken upon himself the decision of what to keep and what to destroy. In asking that, Katherine Mansfield was asking too much – and

1. Murry's official biographer describes how in 1923 Murry, about to be remarried, 'espied the house of his dreams', bid for it £925 he did not have, and 'by a crowning stroke of luck' received almost immediately £1000 in royalties on Katherine Mansfield's books. 'I felt Katherine's blessing was on our marriage', he wrote in an unpublished manuscript. In 1942 he was drawing about £500 a year on her royalties. Buying the farm where he and his fourth wife were to live he wrote in his journal 'It is Katherine who has bought this farm for us' (F. A. Lea, *John Middleton Murry*, London, 1959, pp. 124 and 300).

her manner of asking it (in the letter if not in the will) was ambiguous: 'destroy *all you do not use*' and 'destroy . . . *all you do not wish to keep*'. In these ambiguities he might have found a sort of justification for his own procedure.

That procedure was simply, over a period of years, to publish almost everything and let the public choose what it liked. The poems were reprinted once but interest in them was slight (as were most of the poems) and they were allowed to lapse. Her letters, on the other hand, were widely read and admired. And of the *Journal* Murry was able to say by 1939 that European opinion had received it as a 'minor classic'. Whether this would have pleased Katherine Mansfield or not we can only guess, but we can be certain it would have surprised her. She had more than once announced in letters to Murry that she was starting a journal with the idea of publishing it, but the resolve had always petered out shortly afterwards. On 15 September 1920, for example, she writes 'I've begun my journal book. I want to offer it to Methuen – to be ready this Xmas. Do you think that's too long to wait? It ought to be rather special – dead true . . .' Three weeks later she is writing 'The Journal – I have absolutely given up. I dare not keep a journal. I should always be trying to tell the truth'.

How was it, then, that versions of a '*Journal*' were published in 1927 and 1954, and a '*Scrapbook*' in 1939? From what manuscript sources were these derived? Even more puzzling, how did material from the *Scrapbook* come to be incorporated into the 1954 'definitive edition' of the *Journal*?

The answers to these questions might have been arrived at by anyone who pondered carefully on the publication facts, on the nature and variety of the writing in each volume, and on the description of manuscript material given by Murry in his Introduction to the *Scrapbook* and his Preface to the 1954 *Journal*.[1] But those answers were not arrived at, probably be-

1. '. . . notebooks – ordinary French school *cahiers* mostly – in which finished and unfinished stories, quotations, odd observations, intimate confessions, unposted letters and stray sentences are crammed up like

cause no one thought to ask the questions. It seems to have been generally assumed that Katherine Mansfield had kept two manuscript books, a '*Journal*' and a '*Scrapbook*', and that her husband had published most of the contents of both.

In 1957, on the death of Murry, the Alexander Turnbull Library in Wellington acquired from his estate all his Mansfield notebooks, manuscripts and papers. The first to look closely at these was Professor Ian A. Gordon, and his findings were first published in the quarterly *Landfall* in March 1959. Gordon found that there was only one collection of manuscripts from which all of the *Scrapbook* and the two versions of the *Journal* had been derived. This collection consisted of four ordinary and rather empty diaries for the years 1914, 1915, 1920 and 1922; about thirty notebooks containing fragments of stories, scenes, snatches of conversation, ideas, notes from reading, quotations, calculations of household finances, unposted letters; and, finally, about one hundred loose sheets of equally heterogeneous material. Out of this confusing pile of writing, much of it only barely legible, Murry had compiled the three separate editions of *Journal* material.

Professor Gordon seems to have been divided between admiration of Murry's 'brilliant ... editorial patchwork' which had shaped a minor classic out of such diverse and difficult material, and uncertainty about whether it was not also a brilliant piece of editorial deception. He reported that all the material in the published *Journal* and *Scrapbook* was authentic – Murry had invented nothing. He showed that Murry's transcription, dating and chronological ordering, though not without errors, were on the whole commendably accurate. But he was troubled by the fact that Murry seemed

---

some rich thievery ...' (Introduction to the *Scrapbook*, 1939). '... comments, confessions, and unposted letters, which she had a habit of writing in the same exercise books as those in which she wrote her stories; fragmentary diaries ...; brief and often difficult notes for stories; marginal comments in the books she had read ...' (Preface to the *Journal*, 1954).

to have taken the rough edges off the material so that the published versions do not accurately represent the notebooks they derive from, which are 'scrappier, less tidy'.

This discrepancy between the apparent scrappiness of the manuscript material and the coherence of the published *Journal* led Gordon to make one statement which his own account of the state of the papers does not seem to support. 'It is hardly too much to claim', he wrote 'that it [the *Journal*] is as much Murry's work as Katherine Mansfield's.' It seems a great deal too much to claim; yet one can see a sort of metaphysical puzzle here: How can Katherine Mansfield be 'author' of a book of which, as such, she was quite unaware? She is author of the fragments of which it is composed; but if the fragments hang together as beautifully as they do, this must surely be because of Murry's 'brilliant ... editorial patchwork'.

Such a conclusion, it seems to me, is understandable but false. Another disposition of the same material would, I feel sure, have hung together quite as well, and this is because of the essential unity of all Katherine Mansfield's writing in letters and notebooks. This writing is of considerable variety, yet it is all of a piece. Into the briefest notes and jottings just as into long letters something of the author's life is infused. She has the rare talent of being able to address herself intimately to anyone, or even to no one – to a blank page. ('She has the terrible gift of nearness,' Frieda Lawrence once wrote. 'She can come so close.') The particularity and vividness of the writing is an extension of the particularity and vividness of the personality, and it is everywhere present. That is why Murry had only to transcribe more or less at random to achieve a book coherent enough to become a 'minor classic' – and I hope the point will be illustrated also by the coherence achieved in the case of this present selection. The material has, it must be admitted, the fascination of a kitset which can be assembled in different ways to produce instant – and genuine – art.

In selecting from the great mass of correspondence and journals available I have been guided principally by the wish to represent Katherine Mansfield's writing at its best rather than to give a balanced biographical portrait. There are periods in her life when she suffers such deep anguish, or fear, or distrust that the quality of her letters seems to decline correspondingly. Where she is mistress of negative feelings and can give full-blooded expression to them (see for example her letter of 20 November 1919 on the subject of hate, or her journal entry of 15 December 1919 on the subject of death) the writing is often truly impressive. Where she seems defeated by such feelings (and the periods of defeat sometimes last for months on end) I have passed over material which is of importance biographically but is inferior as writing. What is meant by 'inferior as writing' is easy to recognize but difficult to explain. Perhaps it is sufficient to say that she is at her best when the writing is least deliberate, when it flows easily and naturally, governed by feeling and observation rather than by any apparent calculation of its effect.

But on the other hand, while letting the quality of the writing govern my choices, I have had to recognize that any such selection gives a portrait of the woman which will arouse biographical questions in the minds of readers not familiar with her life; and in order to satisfy this interest I have divided my selection into chapters according to where Katherine Mansfield was at the time of writing, and added biographical commentary sufficient to supply important facts not provided by the selected passages. Further, in putting the selection together I have alternated letters and notebook material according to chronology rather than keeping them apart under separate headings. This, I think, gives a broader and richer view of the development of Katherine Mansfield's style and her ideas.

If there is any bias in my selection it is probably away from the personal and towards the literary. I have, for example, more consistently reproduced the record of Katherine Mansfield's feelings about books and about her own stories than her feelings about her husband. But on the other hand I have not hesitated to use the most personal and private records if they seem to have merit in themselves, or to illuminate the development of her talent.

I must also – in outlining my principles of selection – admit to having found myself resistant, or at least cautious, in choosing from those passages for which in the past Katherine Mansfield may well have been most noted – the passages of 'sensibility'. This is not out of a distrust of emotional writing but rather out of the feeling that her emotion is often less genuine when she is being 'sensitive' than when she is being (for example) satirical, or bullying, or simply plain and factual.

Working on Katherine Mansfield's letters in 1950 Murry observed (in a letter to Violet Schiff preserved in the British Museum) 'It's indubitably true that she tended to assume a personality to please a correspondent. I suppose we all do it in some degree. But in her it was very pronounced.' This easy adoption of different masks, different voices, is one of the principal skills on which her success as a fiction writer rests, and it is not surprising to notice the way her recognition of the distinct character of each of her friends determines the persona she adopts in writing to them. She is always confidently herself, but it is a subtly different self for each friend. To Lady Ottoline Morrell and to Virginia Woolf she is witty, literary, professional, but just a little more fulsome than might have come naturally to her, and sometimes wary too. To her cousin 'Elizabeth' (the Countess Russell) she is inclined to be tremulous and lyrical. To Violet and Sydney Schiff she is intense, lady-like, even prim. To younger writers and painters (William Gerhardi and Richard Murry, for example) she is overwhelmingly kind, considerate, encouraging, and a bit more solemn than, no doubt, she felt. To her father she is practical and reassuring. To her Russian friend Koteliansky she is brilliant, enigmatic, dark, like a character out of a novel by Dostoyevsky. To her devoted companion Ida Baker ('L.M.') she is for the most part the practical, no-nonsense, slightly salty K.M. of everyday life. Perhaps she is most herself where she trusted most completely and where the relationship was free, sisterly and undemanding – and one sees this in letters to her American painter friend, Anne Estelle Rice. Here she appears relaxed, witty, honest, direct, intelligent, practical. Finally, of course, to her husband she is all these things and more by turns – a Cleopatra, at once lover, companion, editorial assistant, little sister, big sister, supporter, dependent, and (not least) remorseless critic.

'As to the poetical Character [Keats says in a letter of 1818] . . . it is not itself – it has no self – it is everything and nothing – it has no character . . . A poet is continually informing and filling some other Body.' Katherine Mansfield has this chameleon quality. She is always adopting a mask, changing roles, assuming the identity of the person she speaks to or the thing she contemplates. Yet through all these changes we are able to say that some roles suit her better than others, even that some are false, and this is because we retain a clear notion of what is permanently and indelibly 'Katherine Mansfield'. Only the firmly resolved character can so give itself to each experience, dare so far to lose itself in the impression of the moment, as to persuade itself that it has no character at all – something which worried Katherine Mansfield as it worried Keats. She is in fact finely confident in her letters, and it is a confidence both of personality and of talent, each serving and augmenting the other. However much illness and fear undermined her there was a sort of reassurance to be got from taking up a pen and addressing herself to a friend or to a notebook. In these letters and journals she is continually putting herself together again.

Suffering took its toll, however. Loneliness in foreign places to which she had gone in search of a cure for her tuberculosis, the pain of the disease itself, distress at the death of her brother, a feeling of having been deserted by her husband, fear of death – this suffering, which she bore on the whole with great fortitude, made her ashamed of her satirical self, afraid of inflicting pain on others. Suffering, she said, was the gift which had taught her to look on the world with love. And this in turn is said to be the foundation on which her best stories are built. Perhaps it is – but I am inclined to believe it is also the source of some of her weakest writing. That is why I say I find myself wary of her 'sensibility', the sensitive writing for which she has been widely praised. It is not quite natural to her personality or central to her talent. It is, rather, an accident of her disease augmented and fostered by the fashion of the day – and I think it is the real K.M. who tells Ida Baker brutally that 'yearning sentimental writing about a virginia creeper and the small haigh voices of tainy children is more than [she] can stick' (see the letter of 29 August 1921). Similarly in the stories – the K.M. who laughs and lightly caricatures her subjects seems to me to be writing more naturally and genuinely than the one who conscientiously trembles and pines at the sufferings of others. 'The Daughters of the Late Colonel', for example, which several reviewers called 'cruel' at the time of its publication, I find in every way superior to 'Miss Brill', which brought its author tender letters of thanks from numbers of readers.

She was susceptible, of course, to these responses, sensitive to the charge of cruelty and pleased to be told she had touched a reader's heart. But if she had retained her health she would undoubtedly have continued to follow the direction of that robust, anarchic intelligence apparent in all her best work, deeply committed to no social forms and niceties (in this she remained indelibly the colonial), seeing Nonsense everywhere (Male Nonsense especially), and enjoying her ability to represent it inflated to bursting point.

D. H. Lawrence, according to Frieda Lawrence's report, used to say that Katherine Mansfield's nearest literary relation was Dickens – the Dickens who pounces quick and sharp on funny details and by a slight (often satirical) exaggeration, and by the repetition of certain magically comic phrases, expands an insignificant scene or event until it becomes unforgettably significant. This, I think, places her correctly. Her talent was a comic talent. 'I don't think any-

one has ever made me laugh more than she did in those days,'
Leonard Woolf recalled in his autobiography, describing her
sitting upright on the edge of a chair telling stories 'with not
the shadow of a gleam of a smile on her mask-like face, the
extraordinary funniness of the story . . . increased by the
flashes of astringent wit'. This humour is nowhere more
beautifully apparent than in her letters, and it appears too,
occasionally, in the reviews when, with the same straight face,
she renders a book absurd simply by retelling its story. The
idea that she was some kind of mystic in search of Truth
through Love is very largely a fiction built on her last desperate efforts to stay alive, and sustained after her death by
her husband's critical commentaries. There was nothing
mystical about her that antibiotics would not have cured.

To read Katherine Mansfield's letters and journals is to be
struck again and again by the recognition that her talent was
larger than her actual achievement at the time of her death –
and to say that is not at all to imply that her achievement in
fiction is not both significant and durable. She has her place
in the development of the modern short story – and her place
on the *scene*, among an impressive cast of characters who were
making English literary history. But the immediacy of her
contact with the natural world and her facility in represent-
ing it, her extraordinary visual memory, the acuteness of her
ear both for speech and for indiscriminate sounds (like 'the
panting of a saw'), her subtlety in following the threads of
human feeling, the ease with which (even in her early
twenties) she could create and satirically manipulate con-
vincing dialogue – all these qualities together with an in-
definable all-pervasive freshness in her writing, as if every
sentence had been struck off first thing on a brilliant morning,
make her natural talents in fiction superior to those of all her
contemporaries except Lawrence. There is no reason why her
performance, had she lived, should not have outstripped that
of Forster and Woolf; and one is not in the least surprised to
discover that on hearing the news of her death Virginia
Woolf, who in the published version of her diary is only re-

corded throwing *Bliss* across the room exclaiming 'She can't write!', confided to the same diary 'I was jealous of her writing. The only writing I have ever been jealous of'.

Holding the various elements of her talent together, governing them, there is an artistic sense which is indistinguishable from a critical sense, is, in fact, simply the critical sense in action. As a reviewer of contemporary fiction Katherine Mansfield is interesting. But she worked, during the period of her reviewing, under great pressure and mainly on inferior novels; and she was unhappy about the conventions which required, for example, an editorial 'we' and encouraged picturesque rather than practical writing. There are remarks of great interest and value scattered through her reviews. But the real quality of her critical mind blazes forth most clearly in comments dashed down informally in letters and notebooks. One doesn't need to agree or disagree with her on the subject of Lawrence's *The Lost Girl*, for example (see the note attached to a letter to Murry written early in December 1920); but when she asks herself why the 'trill' Alvina feels 'in her bowels' is peculiarly offensive, and answers 'Because it is *not on this plane* that the emotions of others are conveyed to our imaginations', one feels the kind of flash, or shock, that only a critical insight of the very highest order can give. At another level her crisp notes on Murry's editing of *The Athenaeum* show the application of critical intelligence to practical day-to-day work.

A Note about Textual Sources

All extracts of journal material in this selection are derived from the 1954 edition of the *Journal*, edited by Middleton Murry, and these have not been checked against the manuscripts. As already indicated, Professor Gordon has reported (and other Katherine Mansfield scholars confirm) that if Murry is not an infallible editor he is certainly a very good and conscientious one, and one who had long familiarity with his wife's difficult handwriting as well as detailed knowledge of her life, her friends, and her habits of mind. Thus the selected extracts may reproduce some errors of transcription or of dating but it is unlikely that these will be numerous or significant.

In the case of the letters to Murry, these were selected in the first place from the *Letters to John Middleton Murry* published in 1951, but they have been checked and corrected against the manuscripts held in the Alexander Turnbull Library. This checking shows Murry's texts to be substantially sound, with few significant errors of transcription. His omissions have been chiefly of names of friends – or sometimes a name is altered to conceal an identity. To offer an example: in 'Dream II' appended to the letter of 1 November 1920, Murry's published version conceals the identity of Lady Ottoline Morrel (as does his transcription of the letter written two days previously). Sometimes Ottoline becomes 'M' (Morrel), sometimes 'H.L.' (Her Ladyship).

There are very few deletions of whole sentences from Murry's texts; but the sentence now restored to the letter of 20 November 1919 (beginning 'Her great fat arms . . .') is an example of one.

The principal (though not the sole) source for published letters to people other than Murry is the 1928 two-volume *Letters of Katherine Mansfield*, long since out of print. Here Murry's transcriptions also appear to have been fairly sound;

but his editorial method at that time, which was to delete all passages that were too personal or might be upsetting to friends, means in many cases the published letter is only a fragmented version of the original. I have checked and corrected the published texts of some of these letters against the manuscripts; others I have been unable to check (in some cases the manuscripts seem to have disappeared unrecorded into the hands of private collectors) but have nonetheless used. Since my own selection is one made up of fragments this reproduction of incomplete letters hardly matters; but the reader may wish to be aware of it.

The letters to Ida Baker, to S. S. Koteliansky, to Sydney and Violet Schiff, and some of those to the Countess Russell (Katherine Mansfield's cousin Elizabeth), have been checked against the manuscripts deposited in the British Museum. Some few letters (such as the extraordinary one of May 1916 to Koteliansky recounting a quarrel between the D. H. Lawrences) are here published for the first time.

Acknowledgements

My reading for this selection began during the first seven months of 1972 when I held the Winn–Manson Katherine Mansfield Fellowship in Menton, France. I am most grateful to the Winn–Manson Committee for the award of that fellowship, and to the town of Menton for its hospitality.

The bulk of the work that year, however, was done in the British Museum, and I acknowledge my debt to the Nuffield Foundation for providing accommodation in London for myself and my family. I am also grateful to my own university, the University of Auckland, for assisting me to carry out the checking of manuscripts in the Alexander Turnbull Library in Wellington.

My thanks are due to Miss Ida Baker ('L.M.') for her hospitality and helpfulness; to Miss Brigid Brophy for a pleasant exchange on the subject of Katherine Mansfield; to Dr E. H. McCormick for his comments and encouragement while we were both working at the British Museum; and to Mrs Margaret Scott, at present editing the collected Mansfield letters, for letters and conversations which were helpful and encouraging.

Acknowledgement is made to the Society of Authors and the Estate of Katherine Mansfield for permission to use material remaining in copyright.

C. K. Stead

New Zealand 1907–8

Kathleen Mansfield Beauchamp was born in Wellington, New Zealand, on 14 October 1888, the third daughter of Harold (later Sir Harold) Beauchamp, a successful merchant and banker. Two further children (a daughter and a son) were born after Kathleen, making her the middle one of five children. In 1893 the family moved to Karori, a few miles out of Wellington. The substance of some of Katherine Mansfield's finest fiction is drawn from memories of family life there, and the story 'Prelude' was so-named because it was to be prelude to a novel entitled Karori.

In 1898 the family moved back into Wellington. At the age of thirteen Kathleen fell in love with Arnold Trowell, a boy cellist who was shortly to travel to Europe on a scholarship. She began to take cello lessons from the boy's father, and for some years her ambition veered back and forth between music and literature.

Early in 1903 the whole Beauchamp family embarked for England to install the three eldest girls at Queen's College, Harley Street, London. Kathleen was fourteen. It was here that she wrote her first stories as 'Katherine Mansfield'. Among her friends at Queen's College was Ida Constance Baker, who was to figure again and again in her life (often referred to under the name she chose for herself: 'Lesley Moore', or simply 'L.M.').

The daughters were almost four years at school. By the end of 1906, when the Beauchamp parents returned to London to fetch them home, Kathleen was reluctant to go and determined to return soon. Back in New Zealand she was confirmed in her feeling that her own country could not offer the kind of life she wished to lead.

By 1908 she had badgered her parents into accepting that she was serious in her ambition to be a writer and that to pursue this ambition she must be allowed to live in London. The largest part of her journals

which have survived from this period in New Zealand are concerned
with a journey into the remote parts of the North Island.

Journal

[*1907*]

February   I am at the sea – at Island Bay in fact – lying flat
on my face on the warm white sand. And before me the sea
stretches.

To my right – shrouded in mist, like a fairy land – a dream
country, the snow mountains of the South Island; to my
left, fold upon fold of splendid golden hills. Two white
lighthouses, like great watching birds perched upon them.
A huge yellow dog lies by me. He is wet and ruffled, and I
have no boots or stockings on – a pink dress – a panama hat –
a big parasol. Adelaida, I wish that you were with me.

Where the rocks lie their shadow is thickly violet upon the
green blue – you know that peacock shade of water. Blue –
with the blueness of Rossetti; green – with the greenness of
William Morris. Oh, what a glorious day this is! I shall stay
here until after dark – walking along the beach – the waves
foaming over my feet – drinking a great deal of tea – and
eating a preposterous amount of bread and apricot jam at a
little place called the Cliff House.

Across the blue sea a boat is floating with an orange sail.
Now the Maori fishermen are sailing in – their white sail
bellying in the wind. On the beach a group of them – with
blue jerseys, thick trousers rolled to their knees. The sun
shines on their thick crisp hair, and shines on their faces so
that their skins are the colour of hot amber. It shines on their
bare legs, and firm brown arms. They are drawing in a little
boat called *Te Kooti*, the wet rope running through their
fingers and falling in a mystic pattern on the foam-blown
sand.

When New Zealand is more artificial, she will give birth
to an artist who can treat her natural beauties adequately.
This sounds paradoxical, but is true.

August 27 This morning we played Weber's Trio – tragic, fiercely dramatic, full of rhythm and accent. And then this afternoon I became frightened. I felt that I had nothing to play, that I could not touch the Concerti, that I had not improved. How horrible it was! Yet the sunlight lay on the music-room floor and my 'cello was warm to touch. He came, and in one instant we understood each other, and I think he was happy. O joyous time! It was almost inhuman. And to hear that 'Bravely done! You've a real grip of it all. Very good!' I would not have exchanged those words for all the laurel wreaths in existence. And to end with, a Weber Fugue passage, for first violin and then 'cello. It bit into my blood. Après, we had tea and currant buns in the smoking-room and ate to the accompaniment of the Fugue, and discussed marriage and music.

October 21 Damn my family! O Heavens, what bores they are! I detest them all heartily. I shall certainly not be here much longer. Thank Heaven for that!

[*November–December*]

Kaingaroa Plain On the journey the sea was most beautiful, a silver-point etching, and a pale sun breaking through pearl clouds.

There is something inexpressibly charming to me in railway travelling. I lean out of the window, the breeze blows, buffeting and friendly, against my face, and the child spirit, hidden away under a hundred and one grey city wrappings, bursts its bonds, and exults within me. I watch the long succession of brown paddocks, beautiful, with here a thick spreading of buttercups, there a white sweetness of arum lilies. And there are valleys, lit with the swaying light of broom blossom. In the distance, grey *whares*, two eyes and a mouth, with a bright petticoat frill of a garden, creeping round them.

On a white road once a procession of patient cattle wended their way, funeral-wise – and behind them a boy rode on a brown horse. Something in the poise of his figure, in the strong sunburnt colour of his naked legs reminded me of Walt Whitman.

Everywhere on the hills, great masses of charred logs, looking for all the world like strange fantastic beasts: a yawning crocodile, a headless horse, a gigantic gosling, a watch-dog – to be smiled at and scorned in the daylight – but a veritable nightmare in the darkness. And now and again the silver tree-trunks, like a skeleton army, invade the hills.

At Kaitoke the train stopped for 'morning lunch', the inevitable tea of the New Zealander. The F.T. and I paced the platform, peered into the long wooden saloon where a great counter was piled with ham sandwiches, and cups and saucers, soda cake and great billys of milk. We didn't want to eat and walked to the end of the platform, and looked into the valley. Below us lay a shivering mass of white native blossom – a little tree touched with scarlet – a clump of *toi-toi* waving in the wind, and looking for all the world like a family of little girls drying their hair.

Later in the afternoon we stopped at Jakesville. How we play inside the house while Life sits on the front door step and Death mounts guard at the back!

*

After brief snatches of terribly unrefreshing sleep, I woke, and found the grey dawn slipping into the tent. I was hot and tired and full of discomfort – the frightful buzzing of the mosquitoes – the slow breathing of the others – seemed to weigh upon my brain for a moment, and then I found that the air was alive with bird's song. From far and near they called and cried to each other.

I got up, and slipped through the little tent-opening on to the wet grass. All round me the willows still full of gloomy shades – the caravan in the glade a ghost of itself – but across the clouded grey sky, the vivid streak of rose colour – blazoned in the day. The grass was full of clover bloom. I caught up my dressing gown with both hands and ran down to the river – and the water flowed on – musically laughing, and the green willows suddenly stirred by the breath of the dawning day, swung softly together. Then I forgot the tent and was happy . . .

*

So we crept again through that frightful wire fence – which every time seemed to grow tighter and tighter, and walked along the white, soft road. On one side the sky was filled with the sunset, vivid, clear yellow and bronze green, and that incredible cloud shade of thick mauve.

Round us in the darkness, the horses were moving softly, with a most eerie sound. Visions of long dead Maoris, of forgotten battles and vanished feuds, stirred in me, till I ran through the dark glade on to a bare hill; the track was very narrow and steep, and at the summit a little Maori *whare* was painted black against the wide sky. Before it two cabbage trees stretched out phantom fingers, and a dog, watching me coming up the hill, barked madly.

Then I saw the first star, very sweet and faint, in the yellow sky, and then another and another, like little lilies, like primroses. And all round me in the gathering gloom, the woodhens called to each other with monotonous persistence. They seemed to be lost and suffering.

I reached the *whare* and a little Maori girl and three boys sprang from nowhere, and waved and beckoned. At the door a beautiful old Maori woman sat cuddling a cat. She wore a white handkerchief round her black hair, and a vivid green and black check rug wrapped round her body. Under the rug I caught a glimpse of a very full blue print dress, worn native fashion, the skirt over the bodice.

Then the rain fell heavily, drearily in to the river and the flax swamp, and the mile upon mile of dull plain. In the distance, far and away in the distance, the mountains were hidden behind a thick grey veil.

Monday The *manuka* and sheep country – very steep and bare, yet relieved here and there by the rivers and willows, and little bush ravines. It was intensely hot – We were tired, and in the evening arrived at Pohue, where Bodley has the Accommodation House, and his fourteen daughters grow peas. We camped on the top of a hill, mountains all round, and in the evening walked in the bush, to a beautiful daisy-pied creek – fern, *tuis*, and we saw the sheep sheds. Smell and sound, 12 Maoris – their hoarse crying – dinner cooking in the homestead, the roses, the Maori cook.

*

Thursday In the morning rain fast – the chuffing sound of the horses. We get up very early indeed, and at six o'clock, ready to start, the sun breaks through the grey clouds. There is a little dainty wind, and a wide fissure of blue sky. Wet boots, wet motor veil, torn coat, and the dew shining on the scrub. No breakfast. We start, the road grows worse and worse. We seem to pass through nothing but scrub-covered valleys, and then suddenly comes round the corner a piece of road. Great joy, but the horses sink right into it, the traces are broken; it grows more and more hopeless. The weather breaks and rain pours down. We lose the track again and again, become rather hopeless, when suddenly far ahead we see a man on a white horse. The men leave the trap and rush off. By and by through the track we met two men. Maoris in dirty blue ducks – one can hardly speak English. They are surveyors. We stop, boil the billy and have tea and herrings. Oh, how good! Ahead the purple mountains, the thin wretched dogs, we talk to them. Then we drive the horses off, but there is no water; the dark people, our conversation – *E ta, haeremai te kai* – it is cold. The crackling fire of *manuka*, walking breast high through the *manuka*.

Lily of the valley, the [*illegible*] We approach Galatea. We lunch by the Galatea River, there is an island in the centre, and a great clump of trees. The water is very green and swift. I see a wonderful huge horse-fly, the great heat of the sun, and then the clouds roll up.

*

Through the red gate there were waving fields and a fresh flax swamp – the homestead in the distance [*illegible*] a little field of sheep, willow and cabbage trees, and away in the distance the purple hills in the shadow – sheep in for shearing.

Here we drive in and ask for a paddock. Past the shearing shed – past the homestead to a beautiful place, with a little patch of bush trees – *tuis*, magpies – cattle – and water running through. But I know from bitter experience, that we shall be eaten with mosquitoes. Two Maori girls are washing; I go to talk with them. They are so utterly kids. While the dinner cooks I walk away – and lean over a giant log. Before me a perfect panorama of sunset – long, sweet, steel-like clouds, against the faint blue – the hills full of gloom – a little river with a tree beside it is burnished silver like the sea – the sheep, and a weird passionate abandon of birds.

*

... a *whare* on a hill, carved too; but no one is at home, though there is a suggestion of fire lately. From the saddle we look across mile upon mile of green bush, then burnt bush russet colour – blue distance and a wide cloud flecked sky. All the people must doubtless have gone shearing. I see none. Above the *whare* there is a grave, a green mound looking over.

And always through the bush this hushed sound of water running on brown pebbles. It seems to breathe the full deep bygone essence of it all. A fairy fountain of green moss. Then rounding a corner we pass several little *whares* deserted and grey. They look very old and desolate, almost haunted. On one door there is a horse collar and a torn and scribbled notice. Flowers in the garden, one clump of golden broom, one clump of yellow iris. Not even a dog greets us. All the *whares* look out upon the river and the valley and the bush-gloried hills. The trees smothered in [*illegible*] blossom.

*

So we journey from their *whare* to Waiotapu. A grey day and I drive. Long dust-thick road; and then before us, Tarawera, with the great white cleft – the poverty of the country – but the gorgeous blue mountains all round us in a great stretch of burnt *manuka*.

We lunch and begin to decide whether to go to the Whare-puni. The men folk go, but eventually come back and say that the walk is too long — also the heat of the day – but there is a great *pa*, one and a half miles away. There we go. The first view: a man on the side of the road, in a white shirt and brown pants, waits for us. Opposite is a thick Maori fence, in the distance across the paddock, several *whares* clustered together like snails on the green patch. And across the paddock a number of little boys from the ages of twelve to three, come straggling along, out at elbow, bare-footed, indescribably dirty. But some of them are almost beautiful, none of them very strong. There is one great fellow . . . who speaks English. Black curls clustering round his head band, rest, almost languor in his black eyes; a slouching walk, and yet there slumbers in his face passionate unrest and strength.

On Monday night we slept outside Warbrick's *whare* – – rather sweet. Mrs Warbrick such a picture in her pink dressing-gown. [*illegible*] Her hands are like carving. She gives us a great loaf of bread, leans swaying against the wire fence in the distance to see the niece Johanna walking up the garden with a white enamel teapot. She is a fat, well-made child in a blue pinafore, her hair plaited and most strange eyes. Then she milks the cows. Wahi (?) brings us a great bowl of milk and a little cup of cream: also a cup of lard.

She dines with us, teaches me Maori and smokes a cigarette. Johanna is rather silent, reads Byron and Shakespeare and wants to go back to school. W. teaches her fancy-work. At night we go and see her – the clean place, the pictures, the beds – Byron and the candle-like flowers in a glass – sweet – the paper and pens – photos of Maoris and whites too. Johanna stays by the door while we see her 'jewellery', her clothes. [*illegible*] There is something sad about it all; she is so lovely.

*

Monday All Sunday, the further she went from Rotorua, the happier she became. Towards evening they came to a great mountain. It was very rugged and old and grim, an ancient fighting *pa*. Here the Maoris had fought, and at the top of this peak a spring bubbled. In the blue evening it was grim, forbidding, silent, towering against the sky – an everlasting monument. Then rounding the corner, they saw the Waikato river, turbulent and wildly rushing below them.

The camp in a paddock down by the river – a wonderful spot . . . Before them a wide sheet of swift, smooth water – and a poplar tree, and a long straight line of pines . . . Just there, on the bank ahead of them – a *manuka* tree in full blossom leans towards the water. The paddock is full of *manuka*.

After dinner, they go through the gates – always there is a thundering sound from afar off – down the sandy path, and into a little pine avenue. The ground is red brown with needles – great boulders come in their path – the *manuka* has grown over the path. With heads bent, hands out, they battle through. And then suddenly a clearing of burnt *manuka*, and they both cry aloud. There is the river – savage, fierce, rushing, tumbling, madly sucking the life from the still, placid flow of water behind – like waves of the sea, like fierce wolves. The noise is like thunder. And right before them the lonely mountain outlined against a vivid orange sky. The colour is so intense that it is reflected in their faces, in their hair; the very rock on which they climb is hot with the colour. They climb higher.

The sunset changes, becomes mauve, and in the waning light all the stretch of burnt *manuka* is like a thin mauve mist around them. A bird, large and silent, flies from the river right into the flowering sky. There is no other sound except the voice of the passionate river.

They climb on a great black rock and sit huddled up there alone, fiercely, almost brutally thinking, like Wapi. Behind them the sun was faintly heliotrope – and then suddenly from behind a cloud a little silver moon shone through – the sudden exquisite note in the night. The sky changed, glowed again, and the river sounded more thundering, more deafening. They walked back slowly, lost the way – and found it – took up a handful of pine needles and smelt it greedily. And then in the distant paddock the tent shone like a golden poppy.

Outside, the stars and the utter spell – magic mist moving – mist over the whole world. Lying, her arms over her head – she can see faintly, like a grey thought, the moon and the mist. They are hardly distinguishable. She is not tired now – only happy. She can see the poplar tree mirrored in the water. The grass is wet. There is the faintest sound of crickets. As she brushes her hair, a wave of cold air strikes her – damp cold fingers about her heart.

The sun comes. The poplar is green now. The dew shines on everything – a little flock of geese and goslings float across the river. The mist becomes white, rises from the mountain ahead. There are the pines – and there just on the bank – the flowering *manuka* is a mass of white colour against the blue water. A lark sings, the water bubbles. She can just see ahead the gleam of the rapids. The mist seems rising and falling.

And now the day fully enters with a duet for two oboes. You *hear* it.

Sunshine – had there ever been such sunshine? They walked over the wet road through the pine trees. The sun gleamed golden, locusts crunched in the bushes. Through her thin blouse she felt it scorching her skin and was glad.

December 17 In the train. Has there ever been a hotter day. The land parched – golden with heat. The sheep are sheltering in the shadow of the rocks. In the distance the hills are shimmering with the heat. M. & I sit opposite each other. I look *perfectly charming*.

[*1908*]

May I have just finished reading a book by Elizabeth Robins, *Come and Find Me*. Really, a clever, splendid book; it creates in me such a sense of power. I feel that I do now realise, dimly, what women in the future will be capable of. They truly as yet have never had their chance. Talk of our enlightened days and our emancipated country – pure nonsense! We are firmly held with the self-fashioned chains of slavery. Yes, now I see that they *are* self-fashioned, and must be self-removed. Eh bien – now where is my ideal and ideas of life? Does Oscar – and there is a gardenia yet alive beside my bed – does Oscar now keep so firm a strong-hold in my soul? No; because I am growing capable of seeing a wider vision – a little Oscar, a little Symons, a little Dolf Wyllarde – Ibsen, Tolstoi, Elizabeth Robins, Shaw, D'Annunzio, Meredith. To weave the intricate tapestry of one's own life, it is well to take a thread from many harmonious skeins – and to realise that there must be harmony. Not necessary to grow the sheep, comb the wool, colour and brand it – but joyfully take all that is ready, and with that saved time, *go* a great way further. Independence, resolve, firm purpose, and the gift of discrimination, *mental clearness* – here are the inevitables. Again, Will – the realisation that Art is absolutely self-development. The knowledge that genius is dormant in every soul – that that very individuality which is at the root of our being is what matters so poignantly.

Here then is a little summary of what I need – power,

wealth and freedom. It is the hopelessly insipid doctrine that love is the only thing in the world, taught, hammered into women, from generation to generation, which hampers us so cruelly. We must get rid of that bogey – and then, then comes the opportunity of happiness and freedom.

2

Bavaria, 1909-10

Katherine Mansfield arrived back in London in August 1908, not yet twenty years old, with an allowance from her father of £100 a year and the determination to succeed as a writer. The three years which followed are the most confusing and tumultuous of her life in terms of 'experience' (which she sought recklessly and found painfully) and the least documented by her own letters and journals.

In 1908–9 she renewed her friendship with the young cellist, Arnold Trowell, fell in love with his brother, Garnet, a violinist, married a singing teacher, George Bowden (eleven years her senior), but stayed with him only a night, returned to Garnet Trowell and became pregnant by him (if she was not already), travelled to Wörishofen in Bavaria where she wrote a series of sketches that formed the basis of her first book and where the pregnancy miscarried. She returned to London, and in 1910 her German sketches began to appear in A. R. Orage's periodical The New Age. *In December 1911* In A German Pension *appeared and promised to be a great success until the publisher, Stephen Swift, went bankrupt.*

There were several other love affairs during this period and a second pregnancy which terminated either in miscarriage or abortion.

The MS. of the poem 'To Stanislaw Wyspianski' (below) is dated Wörishofen, 1910, and therefore seems to belong with the first of the German pension stories. It is written, however, as if from New Zealand, and might therefore be thought to have been drafted earlier (perhaps in 1907, at the time of Wyspianski's death while K.M. was still in New Zealand) if there were anything to suggest she knew of the Polish nationalist's poetry so early. The poem was not included in either of the collections of her verse published by her husband after her death but appeared first in an edition of 100 copies in 1938. It seems now to be generally accepted as her best poem.

Journal

[*1909*]

June 1909   It is at last over, this wearisome day, and dusk
is beginning to sift in among the branches of the drenched
chestnut tree. I think I must have caught cold in my beautiful exultant walk yesterday, for today I am ill. After I wrote
to you, I began to work but could not – *and* so cold. Fancy
wearing two pairs of stockings and two coats and a hot-water
bottle in June, and shivering . . . I think it is the pain that
makes me shiver and feel dizzy. To be alone all day, in a
house whose every sound seems foreign to you, and to feel
a terrible confusion in your body which affects you mentally,
suddenly pictures for you detestable incidents, revolting
personalities, which you only shake off to find recurring
again as the pain seems to diminish and grow worse again.
Alas! I shall not walk with bare feet in wild woods again.
Not until I have grown accustomed to the climate . . .

*

Some day when I am asked: 'Mother, where was I born?'
and I answer: 'In Bavaria, dear,' I shall feel again, I think,
this coldness – physical, mental – heart coldness, hand coldness, soul coldness. Beloved, I am not so sad tonight. It is
only that I feel so desperately the need of speech – the
conviction that you are *present* . . . That is all.

*

Sunday Morning   Yet another Sunday. What has this day
not brought us both? For me it is full of sweetness and
anguish. Glasgow – Liverpool – Carlton Hill – *Our House*. It
is raining again today – just a steady persistent rain that
seems to drift one from one memory to the other. When I
had finished my letter to you, I went down to supper, drank
a little soup, and the old Doctor next me suddenly said:
'Please go to bed *now*,' and I went like a lamb and drank

some hot milk. It was a night of agony. When I felt morning was at last come, I lighted a candle, looked at the watch, and found it was just a quarter to twelve! Now I know what it is to fight a drug. Veronal was on the table by my bed. Oblivion – deep sleep – think of it! But I didn't take any. Now I am up and dressed, propping . . .

To Stanislaw Wyspianski

From the other side of the world,
From a little island cradled in the giant sea bosom,
From a little land with no history,
(Making its own history, slowly and clumsily
Piecing together this and that, finding the patterns solving the
    problem,
Like a child with a box of bricks)
I, a woman with the taint of the pioneer in my blood
Full of a youthful strength that wars with itself and is lawless
I sing your praises, magnificent warrior; I proclaim your
    triumphant battle.
My people have had nought to contend with;
They have worked in the broad light of day and handled the
    clay with rude fingers;
Life – a thing of blood and muscle; Death – a shovelling
    underground of waste material.
What would they know of ghosts and unseen presences,
Of shadows that blot out reality, of darkness that stultified morn?
Fine and sweet the water that runs from their mountains;
How could they know of poisonous weed, of rotted and clogging
    tendrils?
And the tapestry woven from dreams of your tragic childhood
They would tear in their stupid hands,
The sad, pale light of your soul blow out with their childish
    laughter.
But the dead – the old – Oh Master, we belong to you there;
Oh Master, there we are children and awed by the strength of a
    giant;
How alive you leapt into the grave and wrestled with Death
And found in the veins of Death the red blood flowing

And raised Death up in your arms and showed him to all the
   people.
Yours a more personal labour than the Nazarene's miracles,
Yours a more forceful encounter than the Nazarene's gentle
   commands.
Stanislaw Wyspianski – Oh man with the name of a fighter,
Across these thousands of sea-shattered miles we cry and proclaim
   you;
We say 'He is lying in Poland, and Poland thinks he is dead;
But he gave the denial to Death – he is lying there, wakeful;
The blood in his giant heart pulls red through his veins'.

3
England and France, 1913–15

Katherine Mansfield met John Middleton Murry early in 1912. Murry, still an undergraduate at Oxford, had begun editing an elegant literary periodical which he called Rhythm. *During 1912 Murry left Oxford and, at K.M.'s invitation, moved into a room in her flat in London. They became lovers, and Katherine was made joint-editor of* Rhythm. *Her publisher, Stephen Swift, offered to act as publisher of* Rhythm, *but his bankruptcy followed almost immediately and left Murry and K.M. in financial difficulties. They continued with their periodical for a time, however, changing its name to* The Blue Review.*

The first of what was to become the voluminous collection of letters from K.M. to Murry were written from a cottage in Cholesbury which they took in the summer of 1913, K.M. staying there throughout the week while Murry went up to London, returning at the weekends.

There could be no marriage until Katherine secured a divorce from her first husband, and this was not in fact managed until 1918. In the meantime the Mansfield–Murry relationship passed through a great variety of phases, from intense love to virtual estrangement. The years from 1913 to 1915 were marked by a great deal of restless coming and going, sometimes together, sometimes apart. Some of K.M.'s wanderings during this period are charted in the letters and journal entries which follow.

To J. M. Murry
[Summer 1913]

This is just 'good morning' to you.

It has been a warm bright day here – very quiet. Immediately you had gone the house fell fast asleep, and it refuses to wake up or so much as smile in a dream until next Friday. I

feel that I have been here a long time – and that it's New
Zealand. I'm very happy, darling. But when you come into
my thoughts I refuse you, quickly, quickly. It would take me
a long time away from you before I could bear to think of you.
You see, when I am not with you, every little bit of you puts
out a flaming sword.

*

[Summer 1913]

Yes, Friday *will* be fun. I am beginning to 'pretend' that
you are a sailor – trading with all sorts of savages from Monday until Friday and that *The Blue Review* is your schooner
and Secker the Fish-Eyed Pilot. Could you not write a long –
complicated – extremely insulting – symbolical serial round
that idea with minute, obscene descriptions of the savage
tribes . . .?

Thank you for Pa's letter. He was cheerful and poetic, a
trifle puffed up, but very loving. I feel towards my Pa man
like a little girl. I want to jump and stamp on his chest and
cry 'You've *got* to love me'. When he says he does, I feel
quite confident that God is on my side.

It is raining again today, and last night the wind howled
and I gloomed and shivered, and heard locks being filed and
ladders balanced against windows and footsteps padding
upstairs . . . all the old properties jigged in the old way. I'm a
lion all day, darling, but with the last point of daylight I
begin to turn into a lamb and by midnight – mon Dieu! – by
midnight the whole world has turned into a butcher!

Yes, I like Boulestin very much. There's something very
sympathetic about him.

Goodbye for today, darling.

*

[Summer 1913]

The postman knocked into my dream with your letter and
the back door key. I had locked myself in 3 times 3 with Mrs
Gomm's key, but I am glad you sent me ours.

I have begun the story and mean to finish it this evening: it feels pretty good, to me.

Walpole's letter was a little too strenuous. (What is a beautiful picture?) But I prefer that to Gilbert's[1] one remark: 'Davies steeped in Bunyan'. Oh dear! I'm afraid Walpole is having his birthday cake far too soon – like all our young men (except Jack and Tig). What a surprise for them when we sit down at the heads of their tables – all among their cake crumbs and groaning little tummies – you, with a laurel wreath on your darling head, and me trailing a perfectly becoming cloud of glory.

Pride is a charming, sheltering tree: but don't think I'm resting in it. I'm only standing underneath with my eyes turned up, for a moment's grace.

Last night Mrs Gomm and I had a glass of dandelion wine, and over it I heard how Mrs Brown's petticoat had dropped off in the hurdle race 'King Edward's Coronation time'. Such goings on!

Goodbye for today. I love you. 'Not tomorrow, not the next day, but the next.' Tell me what train you are coming by. I cannot quite believe that you are coming back here. I feel – quite alone and as if I were writing to someone in the air – so strange.

*

[*Summer 1913*]

Am I such a tyrant, Jack dear – or do you say it mainly to tease me? I suppose I'm a bad manager, and the house seems to take up so much time if it isn't looked after with some sort of method. I mean . . . when I have to clear up twice over or wash up extra unnecessary things I get frightfully impatient and want to be working. So often this week, I've heard you and Gordon[2] talking while I washed dishes. Well, someone's got to wash dishes and get food. Otherwise – 'There's nothing in the house but eggs to eat'. Yes, I hate hate *hate* doing these

1. Gilbert Cannan.
2. Gordon Campell.

things that you accept just as all men accept of their women. I can only play the servant with a very bad grace indeed. It's all very well for females who have nothing else to do . . . and then you say I am a tyrant, and wonder because I get tired at night! The trouble with women like me is – they can't keep their nerves out of the job in hand – and Monday after you and Gordon and Lesley[1] have gone I walk about with a mind full of ghosts of saucepans and primus stoves and 'Will there be enough to go round?' . . . and you calling (whatever I am doing) '*Tig*, isn't there going to be tea? It's five o'clock' as though I were a dilatory housemaid.

I loathe myself, today. I detest this woman who 'superintends' you and rushes about, slamming doors and slopping water – all untidy with her blouse out and her nails grimed. I am disgusted and repelled by the creature who shouts at you. 'You might at least empty the pail and wash out the tea-leaves!' Yes, no wonder you 'come over silent.'

Oh, Jack, I wish a miracle would happen – that you would take me in your arms and kiss my hands and my face and every bit of me and say 'It's all right, you darling thing. I quite understand'.

All the fault of money, I suppose.

But I love you, and I feel humiliated and proud at the same time. That you *don't* see – that you *don't* understand and yet love me puzzles me . . .

Will you meet me on Wednesday evening at the Café Royal at about 10.30? If you can't be there, let me know by Wednesday morning . . . I'll come back and sleep at '57' if I may, even though I *don't* live there.

*

[*Summer 1913*]

I've nursed the epilogue to no purpose. Every time I pick it up and hear 'You'll keep it to six', I *can't* cut it. To my knowledge there aren't any superfluous words: I mean every line of it. I don't 'just ramble on' you know, but this

1. Lesley Moore (Ida Baker).

thing happened to just fit 6½ pages. You can't cut it without making an ugly mess somewhere. I'm a powerful stickler for form in this style of work. I hate the sort of licence that English people give themselves . . . to spread over and flop and roll about. I feel as fastidious as though I wrote with acid. All of which will seem, I suppose, unconvincing, and exaggeration. I can only express my sincerest distress (which I do truly feel) and send you the epilogue back. If you and Wilfred[1] feel more qualified for the job . . . oh, do by all means – but I'd rather it wasn't there at all than sitting in *The Blue Review* with a broken nose and one ear as though it had jumped into an editorial dog-fight.

Journal

[1914]

January. Paris 'Will you touch me with the child in my arms?' is no mere pleasantry. Change the 'will' into 'can' and it's *tief, sehr tief!* I was thinking just now . . . that I hardly dare give rein to my thoughts of J. and my longing for J. And I thought: if I had a child, I would play with it now and *lose myself in it* and kiss it and make it laugh. And I'd use a child as my guard against my deepest feeling.

When I felt: 'No, I'll think no more of this; it's intolerable and unbearable,' I'd dance the baby.

That's true, I think, of all, all women. And it accounts for the curious look of security that you see in young mothers: they are safe from any *ultimate* state of feeling because of the child in their arms. And it accounts also for the women who call men 'children'. Such women fill themselves with their men – gorge themselves really into a state of absolute heartlessness. Watch the sly, satisfied smile of women who say 'Men are nothing but babies!'

1. W. W. Gibson.

To J. M. Murry

[February 1914]

Everything here too 'is just the same'. The femme de ménage is singing in the kitchen – a most improbable song. It runs along – very blithe and nice – for about five notes and then it *drops* – any distance you like, but a little deeper each time. If the 'aspects' were not good that song would frighten me no end . . . *provided* that I was in a little house on the edge of the steppes with a mushroom-shaped cloud over it and no smoke coming out of the chimney etc., etc. But things being what they are, my romantic mind imagines a kind of 15th century French Provincial Ride-a-Cock-Horse – you know the business . . . dashing off on some one's knee to get a pound of butter and being suddenly 'tumbled into the gutter'. Which, after all, is a very pleasant place to fall. I wonder if Queens played this Disturbing Game with their youngest pages.

Journal

[1914]

March 19   Dreamed about New Zealand. Very delightful.
March 20   Dreamed about N.Z. again – one of the painful dreams when I'm there and hazy about my return ticket.

*

March 23   It's raining; I have a cold and my fire has gone out. Sparrows outside are cheeping like chickens. Oh heavens! what a different scene the sound recalls! The warm sun, and the tiny yellow balls, so dainty, treading down the grass blades, and Sheehan giving me the smallest chick wrapped in a flannel to carry to the kitchen fire.
March 24   Mother's birthday. I woke at 2 o'clock and got up and sat on the box of the window thinking of her. I

would love to see her again and the little frown between her brows, and to hear her voice. But I don't think I will. My memory of her is so complete that I don't think it will be disturbed.

*

April 2 I have begun to sleep badly again and I've decided to tear up everything that I've written and start again. I'm sure that is best. This misery persists, and I am so tired under it. If I could write with my old fluency for *one day*, the spell would be broken. It's the continual effort – the slow building-up of my idea and then, before my eyes and out of my power, its slow dissolving.

*

April 4 Won a moral victory this morning, to my great relief. Went out to spend 2s. 11d. and left it unspent. But I have never known a more hideous day. Terribly lonely. Nothing that isn't satirical is really true for me to write just now. If I try to find things lovely, I turn pretty-pretty. And at the same time I am so frightened of writing mockery for satire that my pen hovers and won't settle. Dined with Campbells and Drey. Afterwards to Café Royal. The sheep were bleating and we set up a feeble counterpart. Saw a fight. The woman with her back to me – her arms crooked sharp at the elbows, her head thrust out, like a big bird. D. is frightened.

*

April 7 The heavens opened for the sunset tonight. When I had thought the day folded and sealed, came a burst of heavenly bright petals . . . I sat behind the window, pricked with rain, and looked until that hard thing in my breast melted and broke into the smallest fountain, murmuring as aforetime, and I drank the sky and the whisper. Now who is to decide between 'Let it be' and 'Force it'? J. believes in the whip: he says his steed has plenty of strength, but it is idle and shies at such a journey in prospect. I feel, if mine does not gallop and dance at free will, I am not riding at all, but just swinging from its tail. For example, today . . . Tonight he's all sparks.

*

August 17 I simply cannot believe that there was a time when I cared about Turgeniev. Such a poseur! Such a hypocrite! It's true he was wonderfully talented, but I keep thinking what a good cinema play *On the Eve* would make.

In October 1914 K.M. and Murry took a cottage, again at Choles-bury, within walking distance of one occupied by the D. H. Lawrences with whom they were now close friends.

Journal

[*1915*]

January 9 J. went to town. I worked a little, chased the fowls. One brown fowl refused to leave the garden. Long after it *knew* there was no gap in the wire-netting, it kept on running up and down. I must not forget that nor how cold it was, nor how the mud coated my thin shoes. In the evening Lawrence and Koteliansky. They talked plans; but I felt *very* antagonistic to the whole affair. After they had gone, Jack and I lay in bed, deeply in love, strangely in love. Everything made plain between us. It was very wonderful. We gave each other our freedom in a strange way. I had such a longing to kiss Jack and say 'Goodbye, Love!' I don't know why exactly. I pressed his cheek against mine and he felt small, and I felt an anguish of love. Then I said suddenly 'what are you thinking?' and he said 'I was thinking that you had gone away and Campbell and Frieda came to tell me', and I was not a bit upset or surprised. (When Lawrence mentioned F.'s[1] name by chance tonight it cut me like a knife.)

January 10 Windy and dark. In the morning, Frieda suddenly. She had had a row with Lawrence. She tired me to death. At night we went to the Lawrences', leaving her here. It was a warm night with big drops of rain falling. I didn't mind the going, but the coming back was rather awful. I was unwell, and tired, and my heart could scarcely beat. But we made up a song to keep going. The rain splashed up to my knees, and I was frightened. L. was nice, very nice, sitting with a piece of string in his hand, on true sex.

*

January 15 Heard from Lesley and Lawrence. Today it was worse. A tremendous wind blew. The sky was like zinc. I tried to write to him, but my letter broke the bounds of my letters and I couldn't. So I told J. a *little*. In the evening we went to the Lawrences'. Frieda was rather nice. I had a difficulty in not telling her, so dreadful did I feel. Came home busy and tired with thought, but could not work, so went to bed immediately and dreamed of N.Z. Heard from Clayton.

*

January 16 Walked to Lawrences'! They were horrible and witless and dull.

*

January 19 Lawrences to dinner. They came late. Jack made a currant pudding. Lawrence arrived cross, but he gradually worked round to me. We talked of the war and its horrors. I have simply felt it closing in on me and my unhappy love, and all to no purpose. Wrote to him just a little note. Jack was horrid at times.

*

1. Francis Carco.

January 20   A man outside is breaking stones. The day is utterly quiet. Sometimes a leaf rustles and a strange puff of wind passes the window. The old man chops, chops, as though it were a heart beating out there. I waited for the post as of old today – but no letter.

In the afternoon there came a violent storm, but we walked over to the Cannans', dined with them and the Lawrences and the Smiths and had a play after. Late we went to the L's' to sleep; very untidy – newspapers and faded mistletoe. I hardly slept at all, but it was nice.

*

January 21   A stormy day. We walked back this morning. J. told me a dream. We quarrelled all the way home more or less. It has rained and snowed and hailed and the wind blows. The dog at the inn howls. A man far away is playing the bugle. I have read and sewed today, but not written a word. I want to to-night. It is so funny to sit quietly sewing, while my heart is never for a moment still. I am dreadfully tired in head and body. This sad place is killing me. I live upon old made-up dreams; but they do not deceive either of us.

Katherine Mansfield had been growing discontented with Murry during this period, and had been exchanging love letters with the French writer (also a Pacific colonial, born in Noumea) Francis Carco, who was then a soldier in the French army. In February 1915, encouraged by Carco, she left England and made a dash for the war zone to the town of Gray where he was stationed.

Journal

[*1915*]

February 20   The curious thing was that I could not concentrate on the end of the journey. I simply felt so happy that I leaned out of the window with my arms along the brass rail and my feet crossed and [*illegible*] the sunlight and the wonder-

ful country unfolding. At Châteaudun where we had to
change I went to the Buffet to drink. A big pale green room
with a large stove jutting out and a buffet with coloured
bottles. Two women, their arms folded, leaned against the
counter. A little boy, very pale, swung from table to table,
taking the orders. It was full of soldiers sitting back in their
chairs, swinging their legs and eating. The sun shone through
the windows.

The little boy poured me out a glass of horrible black coffee.
He served the soldiers with a kind of dreary contempt. In the
porch an old man carried a pail of brown spotted fish – large
fish, like the fish one sees in glass cases swimming through
forests of beautiful pressed seaweed. The soldiers laughed
and slapped each other. They tramped about in their heavy
boots. The women looked after them, and the old man stood
humbly waiting for someone to attend to him, his cap in his
hands, as if he knew that the life he represented in his torn
jacket, with his basket of fish – his peaceful occupation – did
not exist any more and had no right to thrust itself here.

The last moments of the journey I was very frightened. We
arrived at Gray, and one by one, like women going in to see a
doctor, we slipped through a door into a hot room completely
filled with two tables and two colonels, like colonels in comic
opera, big shiny grey-whiskered men with a touch of burnt-
red in their cheeks, both smoking, one a cigarette with a long
curly ash hanging from it. He had a ring on his finger.
Sumptuous and omnipotent he looked. I shut my teeth. I
kept my fingers from trembling as I handed the passport and
the ticket.

'It won't do, it won't do at all,' said my colonel, and looked
at me for what seemed an age in silence. His eyes were like
two grey stones. He took my passport to the other colonel,
who dismissed the objection, stamped it, and let me go. I
nearly knelt on the floor.

By the station stood F., terribly pale. He saluted and
smiled and said, 'Turn to the right and follow me as though
you were not following.' Then fast he went towards the

Suspension Bridge. He had a postman's bag on his back, and
a paper parcel. The street was very muddy. From the toll
house by the bridge a scraggy woman, her hands wrapped in
a shawl, peered out at us. Against the toll house leaned a
faded cab. 'Montez! vite, vite!' said F. He threw my suitcase, his letter bag and the parcel on to the floor. The driver
sprang into activity, lashed the bony horse, and we tore away
with both doors flapping and banging. 'Bon jour, ma
chérie'. said F. and we kissed each other quickly and then
clutched at the banging doors. They would not keep shut,
and F. who is not supposed to ride in cabs, had to try to hide.
Soldiers passed all the time. At the barracks he stopped a
moment and a crowd of faces blocked the window. 'Prends,
ça, mon vieux,' said F., handing over the paper parcel.

Off we flew again. By a river. Down a long strange white
street with houses on either side, very gay and bright in the
late sunlight. F. put his arm round me. 'I know you will
like the house. It's quite white, and so is the room, and the
people are, too.'

At last we arrived. The woman of the house, with a serious
baby in her arms, came to the door.

'It is all right?'

'Yes, all right. Bonjour, Madame.'

It was like an elopement.

We went into a room on the ground floor, and the door was
shut. Down went the suitcase, the letter bag, [*illegible*]
again. Laughing and trembling we pressed against each
other – a long long kiss, interrupted by a clock on the wall
striking five. He lit the fire. We stayed together a little, but
always laughing. The whole affair seemed somehow so
ridiculous, and at the same time so utterly natural. There
was nothing to do but laugh.

Then he left me for a moment. I brushed my hair and
washed and was ready when he came back to go out to
dinner. The wounded were creeping down the hill. They were
all bandaged up. One man looked as though he had two
red carnations over his ears; one man as though his hand was

covered in black sealing-wax. F. talked and talked and talked. 'When I was little I thought the sun was the most terrible thing in the world, but now it is quite pale.' [*An illegible sentence*].

Then the long, long dinner. I hardly said a word. When we came out, stars were shining, through wispy clouds, and a moon hung like a candle-flame. There was a tiny lamp on the table; the fire flickered on the white wood ceiling. It was as though we were on a boat. We talked in whispers, overcome by this discreet little lamp. In the most natural manner we slowly undressed by the stove. F. slung into bed. 'Is it cold?' I said. 'Ah, no, not at all cold. Viens, ma bébé. Don't be frightened. The waves are quite small.' With his laughing face, his pretty hair, one hand with a bangle over the sheets, he looked like a girl. [*illegible*]

The sword, the big ugly sword, but not between us, lying in a chair. The act of love seemed somehow quite incidental, we talked so much. It was so warm and delicious, lying curled in each other's arms, by the light of the tiny lamp – *le fils de Maeterlinck* – only the clock and the fire to be heard. A whole life passed in thought. Other people, other things. But we lay like two old people coughing faintly under the eiderdown and laughing at each other. We went to India, to South America, to Marseilles in the white boat, and then we talked of Paris. And sometimes I lost him in a crowd of people; and it was dark, and then he was in my arms again, and we were kissing. (Here he is. I know his steps.)

I remember how he talked of the sea in his childhood – how clear it was – how he used to lean over the pier and watch it and the fish and shells gleaming – and then his story: 'Le lapin blanc.' At last the day came and birds sang, and again I saw the pink marguerites on the wall. He was *très paresseux*, he lay on his stomach, and would not get up. Finally – one, two, three – and then he shivered and felt ill and had fever and a sore throat and shivers. All the same, he washed scrupulously and dressed, and at last I had the blue and red

vision again – dors mon bébé – and then a blurred impression
of him through the blind.

I did not feel happy again until I had been to the *cabinet* and
seen the immense, ridiculous rabbits. By the time he came at
12.30. I felt awfully happy. We went off to lunch at the same
little restaurant, and had eggs we dipped the bread in, and
pears and oranges. The soldiers there. The garden full of
empty bottles. The little boy – the same boy who had smoked
the long cigarette the night before.

*

*At the end of February Katherine Mansfield returned to Murry.
She went back to Paris in March, to write, and again in May.*

To J. M. Murry

Paris   [*19 March 1915*]

. . . Folkestone looked like a picture painted on a coffin lid
and Boulogne like one painted on a sardine tin. Between
them rocked an oily sea . . .

Paris   [*20 March 1915*]

I don't know what you think of yourself but I think you're a
little pig of a sneak. Not a letter – not a sign – not a copy of
the *Saturday Westminster* – plainly nothing. Why are you so
horrid? Or is it the post? I'll put it down to the post and
forgive you, darling. A baby in arms could play with me
today. The weather is so warm I'm sitting with the windows
wide open and nothing but a thin blouse on (in a way of
speaking). All the trees are popping and the air smells of
mignonette. Big open barges full of stones are being towed
by black and red beetles up the river. The steering men lean
idly, legs crossed – you know their way – and the water
froths against the bows. The carts passing make a merry
jingle and the concierge has put a pink hyacinth in her

window. Bogey (I'm a fool when I'm alone. I turn into a little child again), there is a woman on the opposite side of the river. She sits with her back against a tree, her legs stretched out in front of her, combing her long brown hair. To this side and to that she bends and then, with that charming weary gesture, she throws her head back and draws the comb all the length of it. If I were near enough I am sure I would hear her singing . . .

[*21 March 1915*]

Still no letter – perhaps I can be certain of one tomorrow. I walked to the post this morning and then finding neither light nor murmur there, I went to the Luxembourg gardens. About 3 of the biggest chestnut trees are really in leaf today – you never saw anything lovelier, with pigeons and babies adoring. I walked and walked until at last I came to a green plot with the back view of the head and shoulders of a pa-man rising out of an enormous stone urn – d'une forme d'une car-otte. Laughing with my muff as is my solitary habit, I sped to see his face and found that it was a statue of Verlaine. What extraordinary irony! The head seemed to me to be very lovely in its way – bashed in but dignified, as I always imagine Verlaine. I stayed a long time looking at that and then sunned myself off on a prowl. Every soul carried a newspaper. *L'Information* came out on orange sails. *La Patrie* lifted up its voice at the Métro stations. Nothing was talked of but the raid last night. (I'm trying to tell you about this raid but I'm sure I shan't be able to).

Oh, Jaggle, I was really rather fine. I came home late – I had been dining with B.[1] at the Lilas. It was a lovely night. I came in, made some tea – put out the lamp and opened the shutters for a while to watch the river. Then I worked until about one. I had just got into bed and was reading Kipling's

1. Beatrice Hastings, with whom K. M. had collaborated on *The New Age*. She was soon to become Modigliani's mistress and the subject of some of his paintings.

Simples Contes des Collines, Bogey, when there was a sharp quick sound of running and then the trumpets from all sides blaring *Garde à vous!* This went on, accompanied by the heavy groaning noise of the shutters opening and then a chirrup of voices. I jumped up and did likewise. In a minute every light went out except one point on the bridges. The night was bright with stars. If you had seen the house stretching up and the people leaning out! And then there came a loud noise like *doo-da-doo-da* repeated hundreds of times. I never thought of Zeppelins until I saw the rush of heads and bodies turning upwards, as the *Ultimate Fish* (see *The Critic in Judgment*) passed by, flying high, with fins of silky grey. It is absurd to say that romance is dead when things like this happen. And the noise it made – almost soothing, you know, steady and clear *doo-da-doo-da* – like a horn. I longed to go out and follow it, but instead I waited, and still the trumpets blared – and finally when it was over I made some more tea and felt that a great danger was past and longed to throw my arms round someone. It gave me a feeling of boundless physical relief like the aftermath of an earthquake . . .

To S. S. Koteliansky

[*22 March 1915*]

Write me a letter when you feel inclined to – will you? I am staying here for a while instead of at the rooms in London. I understood you that week-end at the Lawrences for I have been like that myself. It is a kind of paralysis that comes of living alone and to oneself and it is really painful. I was silly and unsympathetic, for Lawrence could not understand it because he has never felt it and I should have been wiser. But come quite alive again this Spring – will you? I do not know how it is in London just now but here the very fact of walking about in the air makes one feel that flowers and leaves are dropping from your hair and from your fingers. I could write you a long letter but I am afraid you cannot read my handwriting. Tell me if you can and then I will. Yes, write to me here.

The nights are full of stars and little moons and big Zeppelins – very exciting. But England feels far far away – just a little island with a cloud resting on it. Is it still there?

To J. M. Murry

[23 March 1915]

I walked on today and came to a garden behind Notre Dame. The pink and white flowering trees were so lovely that I sat down on a bench. In the middle of the garden there was a grass plot and a marble basin. Sparrows taking their baths turned the basin into a fountain and pigeons walked through the velvety grass, pluming their feathers. Every bench and every chair was occupied by a mother or a nurse or a grandfather, and little staggering babies with spades and buckets made mud pies or filled their baskets with fallen chestnut flowers or threw their grandfathers' caps on to the forbidden grass plot. And then there came a Chinese nurse trailing 2 babies. Oh, she was a funny little thing in her green trousers and black tunic, a small turban clamped to her head. She sat down with her darning and she kept up a long birdlike chatter all the time, blinking at the children and running the darning needle through her turban. But after I had watched a long time I realized I was in the middle of a dream. Why haven't I got a real 'home' – a real life – why haven't I got a Chinese nurse with green trousers and two babies who rush at me and clasp my knees? I'm not a girl – I'm a woman. I *want* things. Shall I ever have them? To write all the morning and then to get lunch over quickly and to write again in the afternoon and to have supper and *one* cigarette together and then to be alone again until bed-time – and all this love and joy that fights for outlet – and all this life drying up, like milk in an old breast. Oh I want life. I want friends and people and a house. I want to give and to spend (the P.O. savings bank apart, darling).

[*25 March 1915*

I had a great day yesterday. The Muses descended in a ring, like the angels on the Botticelli Nativity roof – or so it seemed to 'humble' little Tig, and I fell into the open arms of my first novel. I have finished a huge chunk, but I shall have to copy it on thin paper for you. I expect you will think I am a dotty when you read it, but, tell me what you think, won't you? It's queer stuff. It's the spring makes me write like this. Yesterday I had a fair wallow in it, and then I shut up shop and went for a long walk along the Quai – very far. It was dusk when I started, but dark when I got home. The lights came out as I walked, and the boats danced by. Leaning over the bridge I suddenly discovered that one of those boats was exactly what I want my novel to be. Not big, almost 'grotesque' in shape – I mean perhaps *heavy* – with people rather dark and seen strangely as they move in the sharp light and shadow; and I want bright shivering lights in it, and the sound of water. (This, my lad, by way of uplift.) But I *think* the novel will be alright. Of course, it's not what you could call serious – but then I can't be, just at this time of year, and I've always felt a spring novel would be lovely to write.

*

I have adopted Stendhal. Every night I read him now, and first thing in the morning.

[*8 May 1915*]

Last night I woke to hear torrential rain. I got up with a candle and made the shutters firm – and that awful line of Geo. Meredith's sang in my head. 'And Welcome Water Spouts that Bring Fresh Rain.' Then I dreamed that I went to stay with the sisters Brontë who kept a boarding house called the Brontë Institut – *pain*fully far from the railway station, and all the way there through heather. It was a sober place with linoleum on the stairs. Charlotte met me at the door and said, 'Emily is lying down'. Kot, I found, was also there, taking supper. He broke an orange into a bowl of bread and milk. 'Russian fashion,' said he. 'Try it. It's very good.' But I refrained.

Journal

[*1915*]

Sunday 16 May Paris . . . I bought a book by Henry James yesterday and read it, as they say, 'until far into the night'. It was not very interesting or very good, but I can wade through pages and pages of dull, turgid James for the sake of that sudden sweet shock, that violent throb of delight that he gives me at times. I don't doubt this is genius: only there is an extraordinary amount of pan and an amazing *raffiné* flash –

One thing I want to annotate. His hero, Bernard Longueville, brilliant, rich, dark, agile, etc., though a witty companion, is perhaps wittiest and most amused when he is alone, and preserves his best things for himself . . . All the attributive adjectives apart I am witty, I know, and a good companion – but I feel my case is exactly like his – the amount of minute and delicate joy I get out of watching people and things when I am alone is simply enormous – I really only have 'perfect fun' with myself. When I see a little girl running by on her heels like a fowl in the wet, and say 'My dear, there's a Gertie,' I laugh and enjoy it as I never would with anybody. Just the same applies to my feeling for what is called 'nature'. Other people won't stop and look at the things I want to look at, or, if they do, they stop to please me or to humour me or to keep the peace. But I am so made that as *soon* as I am with anyone, I begin to give consideration to

their opinions and their desires, and they are not worth half
the consideration that mine are. I don't miss J. at all now –
I don't want to go home, I feel quite content to live here, in a
furnished room, and watch. It's a pure question of weather,
that's what I believe. (A *terrific* Gertie has just passed.)
Life with other people becomes a blur: it does with J., but
it's enormously valuable, and marvellous when I'm alone,
the detail of life, the *life* of life.

To S. S. Koteliansky

[*17 May 1915*]

. . . There is a wharf not far from here where the sand barges
unload. Do you know the smell of wet sand? Does it make you
think of going down to the beach in the evening light after
a rainy day and gathering the damp drift wood (it will dry
on top of the stove) and picking up for a moment the long
branches of sea weed that the waves have tossed and listening
to the gulls who stand reflected in the gleaming sand, and
just fly a little way off as you come and then – settle again . . .

4
Bandol, December 1915–April 1916

In mid-1915 Murry and Katherine Mansfield moved to a house at 5 Acacia Road, St John's Wood, London. It was here that her brother, Leslie Heron Beauchamp ('Chummie'), who had come to England as a soldier, spent his last leaves with her before going to France. Their interminable recollections of childhood added to the store of material she had already begun to use in the first drafts of 'The Aloe' (later called 'Prelude'). Her brother, of whom she was passionately fond, was killed in France in October 1915. The shock of grief at his death made her feel she could not stay in London. She set out for the South of France. Murry accompanied her, but, feeling shut out by her preoccupation with her dead brother, left her in a hotel in Bandol and returned to London.

At the end of December, however, he returned to Bandol. They rented the Villa Pauline and during the months which followed they lived in perfect accord. 'It was, without doubt, the happiest time of our lives together' Murry wrote after her death. It was also among the most productive for both of them. During the hours set aside for work they sat opposite one another at the same table, he writing a book on Dostoyevsky, she writing 'The Aloe'. In the afternoons they walked about the hills or along the shore. In the evenings they would choose a subject and both write a poem about it. How much all this meant to K.M. is indicated, not so much in the extracts which follow, but in letters written two years later (see chapter 6) when she returned to the town alone and found everything changed.

It is worth noting that K.M.'s journal entries at this time contain a number of entries on Dostoyevsky, evidence of the fact that she read and discussed with Murry the books he was writing about. Ida Baker believes that some of Murry's most successful critical ideas emerged in his conversations with his wife.

To S. S. Koteliansky

Marseilles   [*19 November 1915*]

... On the mantelpiece in my room stands my brother's photograph. I never see anything that I like, or hear anything, without the longing that he should see and hear, too – I had a letter from his friend again. He told me that after it happened he said over and over 'God forgive me for all I have done' and just before he died he said, 'Lift my head, Katy, I can't breathe' –

To tell you the truth these things that I have heard about him blind me to all that is happening here – All this is like a long uneasy ripple – nothing else – and below – in the still pool there is my little brother ...

Journal

[*1915*]

November, Bandol, France   *Brother.* I think I have known for a long time that life was over for me, but I never realized it or acknowledged it until my brother died. Yes, though he is lying in the middle of a little wood in France and I am still walking upright and feeling the sun and the wind from the sea, I am just as much dead as he is. The present and the future mean nothing to me. I am no longer 'curious' about people; I do not wish to go anywhere; and the only possible value that anything can have for me is that it should put me in mind of something that happened or was when we were alive.

'Do you remember, Katie?' I hear his voice in the trees and flowers, in scents and light and shadow. Have people, apart from these far-away people, ever existed for me? Or have they always failed me and faded because I denied them reality? Supposing I were to die as I sit at this table, playing with my Indian paperknife, what would be the difference?

No difference at all. Then why don't I commit suicide? Because I feel I have a duty to perform to the lovely time when we were both alive. I want to write about it, and he wanted me to. We talked it over in my little top room in London. I said: I will just put on the front page: To my brother, Leslie Heron Beauchamp. Very well: it shall be done.

To J. M. Murry

[*9 December 1915*]

... I think the Oxford Book of English verse is *very* poor. I read it for hours this morning in bed. I turned over pages and pages and pages. But except for Shakespeare and Marvell and just a handful of others it seems to be a mass of falsity. Musically speaking, hardly anyone seems to. *even understand* what the middle of the note is – what that sound is like. It's not perhaps that they are even 'sharp' or 'flat' – it's something much more subtle – they are not playing on the *very note itself*. But when, in despair, I took up the French Book I nearly sautéd from the fenêtre with rage. It's like an endless gallery of French salon furniture sicklied o'er with bed canopies, candelabra, and porcelain cupids, all bow and bottom. Of course, there *are* exceptions. Victor Hugo, by the way, reminded me very much of our white bull taking a railway ticket – to Parnassus ...

[*23 December 1915*]

... The sailors in the sailing ships have been washing. They are all pegged out along the masts and spars. It's a very still, primrose and cowslip day. I am going to drive in a kerridge to that little Dürer town I told you of ...

Journal

[*24 December 1915*]

To sit in front of the little wood fire, your hands crossed in your lap and your eyes closed – to fancy you see again upon your eyelids all the dancing beauty of the day, to feel the flame on your throat as you used to imagine you felt the spot of yellow when Bogey held a buttercup under your chin . . . when breathing is such a delight that you are almost afraid to breathe – as though a butterfly fanned its wings upon your breast. Still to taste the warm sunlight that melted in your mouth; still to smell the white waxy scent that lay upon the jonquil fields and the wild spicy scent of the rosemary growing in little tufts among the red rocks close to the brim of the sea . . .

The moon is rising but the reluctant day lingers upon the sea and sky. The sea is dabbled with a pink the colour of unripe cherries, and in the sky there is a flying yellow light like the wings of canaries. Very stubborn and solid are the trunks of the palm trees. Springing from their tops the stiff green bouquets seem to cut into the evening air and among them, the blue gum trees, tall and slender with sickle-shaped leaves and drooping branches half blue, half violet. The moon is just over the mountain behind the village. The dogs know she is there; already they begin to howl and bark. The fishermen are shouting and whistling to one another as they bring in their boats, some young boys are singing in half-broken voices down by the shore, and there is a noise of children crying, little children with burnt cheeks and sand between their toes being carried home to bed . . .

I am tired, blissfully tired. Do you suppose that daisies feel blissfully tired when they shut for the night and the dews descend upon them?

January 22 Now, really, what is it that I do want to write? I ask myself, Am I less of a writer than I used to be? Is the need to write less urgent? Does it still seem as natural to me to seek that form of expression? Has speech fulfilled it? Do I ask anything more than to relate, to remember, to assure myself?

There are times when these thoughts half-frighten me and very nearly convince. I say: You are now so fulfilled in your own being, in being alive, in living, in aspiring towards a greater sense of life and a deeper loving, the other thing has gone out of you.

But no, at bottom I am not convinced, for at bottom never has my desire been so ardent. Only the form that I would choose has changed utterly. I feel no longer concerned with the same appearance of things. The people who lived or whom I wished to bring into my stories don't interest me any more. The plots of my stories leave me perfectly cold. Granted that these people exist and all the differences, complexities and resolutions are true to them – why should *I* write about them? They are not near me. All the false threads that bound me to them are cut away quite.

Now – now I want to write recollections of my own country. Yes, I want to write about my own country till I simply exhaust my store. Not only because it is 'a sacred debt' that I pay to my country because my brother and I were born there, but also because in my thoughts I range with him over all the remembered places. I am never far away from them. I long to renew them in writing.

Ah, the people – the people we loved there – of them, too, I want to write. Another 'debt of love'. Oh, I want for one moment to make our undiscovered country leap into the eyes of the Old World. It must be mysterious, as though floating. It must take the breath. It must be 'one of those islands . . .' I shall tell everything, even of how the laundry-basket squeaked at 75. But all must be told with a sense of mystery, a radiance, an afterglow, because you, my little sun of it, are set. You have dropped over the dazzling brim of the world. Now I must play my part.

Then I want to write poetry. I feel always trembling on the brink of poetry. The almond tree, the birds, the little wood where you are, the flowers you do not see, the open window out of which I lean and dream that you are against my shoulder, and the times that your photograph 'looks sad'. But especially I want to write a kind of long elegy to you . . . perhaps not in poetry. Nor perhaps in prose. Almost certainly in a kind of *special prose*.

And, lastly, I want to keep a kind of *minute notebook*, to be published some day. That's all. No novels, no problem stories, nothing that is not simple, open.

*

February 16   I *found The Aloe*[1] this morning. And when I had re-read it I knew that I was not quite 'right' yesterday. No, dearest, it was not just the spirit. *The Aloe* is right. *The Aloe* is lovely. It simply fascinates me, and I know that it is what you would wish me to write. And now I know what the last chapter is. It is your birth – your coming in the autumn. You in Grandmother's arms under the tree, your solemnity, your wonderful beauty. Your hands, your head – your helplessness, lying on the earth, and, above all, your tremendous solemnity. That chapter will end the book. The next book will be yours and mine. And you must mean the world to Linda; and before ever you are born Kezia must play with you – her little Bogey. Oh, Bogey – I must hurry. All of them must have this book. It is good, my treasure! My little brother, it is good, and it is what we really meant.

February 17   I am sad tonight. Perhaps it is the old forlorn wind. And the thought of you *spiritually* is not enough tonight. I want you by me. I must get deep down into my book, for then I shall be happy. Lose myself, lose myself to find you,

1. 'The Aloe' was revised and published under the title 'Prelude'.

dearest. Oh, I want this book to be written. It must be done. It must be bound and wrapped and sent to New Zealand. I feel that with all my soul . . . It will be.

*

[*February 1916*]

J.'s application is a perpetual reminder to me. Why am I not writing too? Why, feeling so rich, with the greater part of this to be written *before* I go back to England, do I not begin? If only I have the courage to press against the stiff swollen gate, all that lies within is mine; why do I linger for a moment? Because I am idle, out of the habit of work and spendthrift beyond belief. Really it is idleness, a kind of immense idleness – hateful and disgraceful.

I was thinking yesterday of my *wasted, wasted* early girlhood. My college life, which is such a vivid and detailed memory in one way, might never have contained a book or a lecture. I lived in the girls, the professor, the big, lovely building, the leaping fires in winter and the abundant flowers in summer. The views out of the windows, all the pattern that was – weaving. Nobody saw it, I felt, as I did. My mind was just like a squirrel. I gathered and gathered and hid away, for that long 'winter' when I should re-discover all this treasure – and if anybody came close I scuttled up the tallest, darkest tree and hid in the branches. And I was so awfully fascinated in watching Hall Griffin and all his tricks – thinking about him as he sat there, his private life, what he was like as a man, etc., etc. (He told us he and his brother once wrote an enormous poem called the Epic of the Hall Griffins.) Then it was only at rare intervals that something flashed through all this busyness, something about Spenser's Faerie Queene or Keats's Isabella or the Pot of Basil, and those flashes were always when I disagreed flatly with H.G. and wrote in my notes – This man is a fool. And Cramb, wonderful Cramb! The figure of Cramb was enough, he was 'history' to me. Ageless and fiery, eating himself up again and again, very fierce at what he had seen, but going a

bit blind because he had looked so long. Cramb striding up
and down, filled me up to the brim. I couldn't write down
Cramb's thunder. I simply wanted to sit and hear him.
Every gesture, every stopping of his walk, all his tones and
looks are as vivid to me as though it were yesterday – but of
all he said I only remember phrases – 'He sat there and his
wig fell off – ' 'Anne Bullen, a lovely *pure* creature stepping
out of her quiet door into the light and clamour,' and looking
back and seeing the familiar door shut upon her, with a little
click as it were, – final.

But what coherent account could I give of the history of
English Literature? And what of English History? None.
When I think in *dates* and *times* the wrong people come in –
the right people are missing. When I read a play of Shakespeare I want to be able to place it in relation to what came
before and what comes after. I want to realize what England
was like then, at least a little, and what the people looked like
(but even as I write I feel I can do this, at least the latter
thing), but when a man is mentioned, even though the man
is real, I don't want to set him on the right hand of Sam
Johnson when he ought to be living under Shakespeare's
shadow. And this I often do.

Since I came here I have been very interested in the Bible.
I have read the Bible for hours on end and I began to do so
with just the same desire. I wanted to know if Lot followed
close on Noah or something like that. But I feel so bitterly I
should have known facts like this: they ought to be part of
my breathing. Is there another grown person as ignorant as
I? But why didn't I listen to the old Principal who lectured
on Bible History twice a week instead of staring at his face
that was very round, a dark red colour with a kind of bloom
on it and covered all over with little red veins with endless
tiny tributaries that ran even up his forehead and were lost
in his bushy white hair. He had tiny hands, too, puffed up,
purplish, shining under the stained flesh. I used to think
looking at his hands – he will have a stroke and die of paraly-

sis ... They told us he was a very learned man, but I could not help seeing him in a double-breasted frock-coat, a large pseudo-clerical pith helmet, a large white handkerchief falling over the back of his neck, standing and pointing out with an umbrella a probable site of a probable encampment of some wandering tribe, to his wife, an elderly lady with a threatening heart who had to go everywhere in a basket-chair arranged on the back of a donkey, and his two daughters, in thread gloves and sand shoes – smelling faintly of some anti-mosquito mixture.

As he lectured I used to sit, building his house, peopling it – filling it with Americans, ebony and heavy furniture – cupboards like tiny domes and tables with elephants' legs presented to him by grateful missionary friends ... I never came into contact with him but once, when he asked any young lady in the room to hold up her hand if she had been chased by a wild bull, and as nobody else did I held up mine (though of course I hadn't). 'Ah,' he said, 'I am afraid you do not count. You are a little savage from New Zealand' – which was a trifle exacting, for it must be the rarest thing to be chased by a wild bull up and down Harley Street, Wimpole Street, Welbeck Street, Queen Anne, round and round Cavendish Square ...

And why didn't I learn French with M. Huguenot? What an opportunity missed! What has it not cost me! He lectured in a big narrow room that was painted all over – the walls, door, and window-frames, a grey shade of mignonette green. The ceiling was white, and just below it there was a frieze of long looped chains of white flowers. On either side of the marble mantelpiece a naked small boy staggered under a big platter of grapes that he held above his head. Below the windows, far below there was a stable court paved in cobble stones, and one could hear the faint clatter of carriages coming out or in, the noise of water gushing out of a pump into a big pail – some youth, clumping about and whistling. The room was never very light, and in summer

M.H. liked the blinds to be drawn half-way down the window . . . He was a little fat man.

*

March Jinnie Moore was awfully good at elocution. Was she better than I? I could make the girls cry when I read Dickens in the sewing class, and she couldn't. But then she never tried to. She didn't care for Dickens; she liked something about horses and tramps and shipwrecks and prairie fires – they were her style, her reckless, red haired, dashing style.

[*March 1916*]

. . . I'm so hungry, simply empty, and seeing in my mind's eye just now a sirloin of beef, well browned with plenty of gravy *and* horseradish sauce and baked potatoes, I nearly sobbed. There's nothing here to eat except omelettes and oranges and onions. It's a cold, sunny, windy day – the kind of day when you want a tremendous feed for lunch and an armchair in front of the fire to boa-constrict in afterwards. I feel sentimental about England now – English food, *decent* English *waste!* How much better than these thrifty French, whose flower gardens are nothing but potential salad bowls. There's not a leaf in France that you can't 'faire une infusion avec', not a blade that isn't 'bon pour la cuisine'. By God, I'd like to buy a pound of the best butter, put it on the window sill and watch it melt to spite 'em. They are a stingy uncomfortable crew for all their lively scrapings . . . For instance, their houses – what appalling furniture – and never one comfortable chair. If you want to talk the only possible thing to do is to go to bed. It's a case of either standing on your feet or lying in comfort under a puffed-up eiderdown. I quite understand the reason for what is called French moral laxity. You're simply forced into bed – no matter with whom. There's no other place for you. Supposing a *young* man comes to see about the electric light and will go on talking and pointing to the ceiling – or a friend drops in to tea and asks you if you believe in Absolute Evil. How can you give your mind to these things when you're sitting on four knobs and a square inch of cane? How much better to lie snug and *give yourself up to it*.

*

Having read the whole of *The Idiot* through again, and fairly carefully, I feel slightly more bewildered than I did before as regards Nastasya Filippovna's character. She is really not well done. She is badly done. And there grows up as one reads on a kind of irritation, a *balked* fascination, which almost succeeds finally in blotting out those first and really marvellous 'impressions' of her. What was Dostoevsky really aiming at?

The Possessed. Shatov and his wife.

There is something awfully significant about the attitude of Shatov to his wife, and it is amazing how, when Dostoevsky at last turns a soft but penetrating and full light upon him, how we have managed to gather a great deal of knowledge of his character from the former vague side-lights and shadowy impressions. He is just what we thought him; he behaves just as we would expect him to do. There is all that crudity and what you might call 'shock-headedness' in his nature – and it is wonderfully tragic that he who is so soon to be destroyed himself should suddenly realize – and through a third person – through a little squealing baby – the miracle just being alive is.

*

Page 545. ' "Surely you must see that I am in the agonies of childbirth," she said, sitting up and gazing at him with a terrible, hysterical vindictiveness that distorted her whole face. "I curse him before he is born, this child!" '

This vindictiveness is *profoundly* true.

How did Dostoevsky know about that extraordinary

vindictive feeling, that relish for little laughter – that comes
over women in pain? It is a very secret thing, but it's profound, profound. They don't want to spare the one whom
they love. If that one loves them with a kind of blind de-
votion as Shatov did Marie, they long to torment him, and
this tormenting gives them real positive relief. Does this
resemble in any way the tormenting that one observes so
often in his affairs of passion? Are his women ever happy
when they torment their lovers? No, they too are in the agony
of labour. They are giving birth to their new selves. And
they never believe in their deliverance.

Poems

Bandol   [*1916*]

Sanary

Her little hot room looked over the bay
Through a stiff palisade of glinting palms,
And there she would lie in the heat of the day,
Her dark head resting upon her arms,
So quiet, so still, she did not seem
To think, to feel, or even to dream.

The shimmering, blinding web of sea
Hung from the sky, and the spider sun
With busy frightening cruelty
Crawled over the sky and spun and spun.
She could see it still when she shut her eyes,
And the little boats caught in the web like flies.

Down below at this idle hour
Nobody walked in the dusty street;
A scent of dying mimosa flower
Lay on the air, but sweet – too sweet.

To L.H.B. (*1894–1915*)

Last night for the first time since you were dead
I walked with you, my brother, in a dream.

We were at home again beside the stream
Fringed with tall berry bushes, white and red.
'Don't touch them: they are poisonous,' I said.
But your hand hovered, and I saw a beam
Of strange, bright laughter flying round your head
And as you stooped I saw the berries gleam.
'Don't you remember? We called them Dead Man's Bread!'
   I woke and heard the wind moan and the roar
Of the dark water tumbling on the shore.
Where – where is the path of my dream for my eager feet?
By the remembered stream my brother stands
Waiting for me with berries in his hands . . .
'These are my body. Sister, take and eat.'

5

Cornwall, Summer 1916; London, 1916-17

D. H. Lawrence, living in North Cornwall, had been writing urging Murry and Katherine Mansfield to come and live next door. He had a cottage in view for them, and in April 1916 they went. Why they had responded to this call was not entirely clear and became less so in retrospect when they were in a position to look back on their stay at the Villa Pauline, Bandol, and compare the felicity of that time with the sourness that overtook all four of them living side by side in Cornwall. K.M. in particular, perhaps, felt disappointed that Murry had been so ready to give up that Bandol villa at a call from Lawrence. She was fond of Lawrence but seems to have found Frieda Lawrence a slightly trying companion.

Lawrence's view of the relationship between the two couples at this time was one of the most important elements that went into the writing of Women in Love *– though Murry claimed afterwards that he recognized little of himself and Katherine in the portraits of Gerald and Gudrun.*

Relations were soon strained. By June Murry and K.M. had found an excuse for moving to a cottage at Mylor in South Cornwall. They continued to see the Lawrences, however, and the old under-lying affection remained on both sides.

To Beatrice Campbell

[May 1916]

I have been wanting to write to you but felt that Ireland wouldn't permit. Now that I've heard from you and seen Mary Clarke (whom I quite understand) I feel free to ask you for that prescription for poor Murry's remaining hair. For though he is about to be taken he must rub something into his roots while he is on sentry-go – send it when you find it . . . I can imagine what you and G. must have felt. This morning there is news that three leaders are shot and it's horrible reading. It's difficult to get any coherent account of anything down here but Garvin in *The Observer* last Sunday very nearly brought one off. There is no accounting for Ireland – The fact that while one street was under hot fire and people falling in all directions the milkmen with their rattling little cans went on delivering milk seemed, as Lawrence would say, 'pretty nearly an absolute symbol.' Tell me more about Mary Clarke and hers when you know.

If I had a box I'd send you flowers; but I've nothing but a Vinolia Soap box and the violets would arrive in a lather. As soon as I have a box you shall have some. This country is very lovely just now with every kind of little growing thing – and the gorse among the grey rocks is, as Mrs Percy H[utchinson] would agree, 'very satisfactory.' There are a great many adders here too. How does one cure oneself of their bite? You either bathe the afflicted part with a saucer of milk *or* you give the saucer of milk to the adder. There is a creek close by our house that rushes down a narrow valley and then falls down a steep cliff into the sea. The banks are covered with primroses and violets and bluebells. I paddle in it and feel like a faint, far-off reflection of the George Meredith Penny Whistle Overture, but awfully faint. Murry spends all his time hunting for his horn-rimmed spectacles for whenever he leaps over a stile or upon a mossy stone they fly from him, incredible distances, and undergo a strange and secret change into caterpillars, dragon flies or bracken uncurling.

Today I can't see a yard, thick mist and rain and a tearing wind with it. Everything is faintly damp. The floor of the tower is studded with Cornish pitchers catching the drops. Except for my little maid (whose *ankles* I can hear stumping about the kitchen) I am alone, for Murry and Lawrence have plunged off to St Ives with rucksacks on their backs and Frieda is in her cottage, looking at the children's photographs, I suppose. It's very quiet in the house except for the wind and the rain and the fire that roars very hoarse and fierce. I feel as though I and the Cornish Pasty[1] had drifted out to sea – and would never be seen again. But I love such days – rare lonely days. I love above all things, my dear, to be alone. Then I lie down and smoke and look at the fire and begin to think out an EXTRAORDINARILY good story about Marseilles. I've re-read my novel today, too and now I can't believe I wrote it. I hope that Gordon reads it one of these days.

I want to talk about the L's, but if I do don't tell Kot or Gertler for then it will get back to Lawrence and I will be literally murdered. He has changed very much. He's quite 'lost'. He has become very fond of sewing, especially hemming, and of making little copies of pictures. When he is doing these things he is quiet and gentle and kind, but once you start talking I cannot describe the frenzy that comes over him. He simply *raves*, roars, beats the table, abuses everybody. But that's not such a great matter. What makes these attacks insupportable is the feeling one has at the back of one's mind that he is completely out of control, swallowed up in an acute *insane*[?] irritation. After one of these attacks he's ill with fever, haggard and broken. It is impossible to be anything to him but a kind of playful acquaintance. Frieda is more or less used to this. She has a passion for washing clothes – and stands with big bowls of blue and white water round her wringing out check tablecloths – and looking very much at home indeed. She says this place suits her. I am sure it does.

They are both too tough for me to enjoy playing with. I hate games where people lose their tempers in this way – it's so witless. In fact they are not my kind at all. I cannot discuss blood affinity to beasts for instance, if I have to keep ducking to avoid the flat-irons and the saucepans. And I *shall never* see sex in trees, sex in the running brooks, sex in stones and sex in everything. The number of things that are

1. The maid.

really phallic, from fountain pen fillers onwards! But I shall
have my revenge one of these days – I suggested to Lawrence
that he should call his cottage 'The Phallus' and Frieda
thought it was a very good idea. It's lunchtime already and
here is the pasty looming through the mist with a glimmering
egg on a tray. Have you read so far? Give my dear love to
Gordon and keep it yourself.

*

[*May 1916*]

It is still awfully difficult to credit what has happened
and what is happening in Ireland. One can't get round it.
This shooting, Beatrice, this incredible shooting of people!
I keep wondering if Ireland really minds. I mean really
won't be pacified and cajoled and content with a few fresh
martyrs and heroes. I can understand how it must fill your
thoughts, for if Ireland were New Zealand and such a thing
had happened there . . . it would mean the same for me. It
would really (as *un*fortunately George-out-of-Wells would
say) Matter Tremendously . . . Dear woman, I am a little
afraid of jarring you by writing about the whole affair, for I
know so little (except what you've told me) and I've heard
no discussion or talk . . .

To S. S. Koteliansky

[*May 1916*]

I am quite alone for all the day so I shall write to you. I
have not written before because everything has been so
'unsettled'; now it is much more definite. I wish I could
come and see you instead of writing; next month I shall come
to London probably for a little time and then we shall be
able to meet and talk.

You may laugh as much as you like at this letter, darling,
all about the COMMUNITY. It *is* rather funny.

Frieda and I do not even speak to each other at present.
Lawrence is about one million miles away, although he

lives next door. He and I still speak but his very voice is faint like a voice coming over a telephone wire. It is all because I cannot stand the situation between those two, for one thing. It is degrading – it offends ones soul beyond words. I don't know which disgusts me worse – when they are very loving and playing with each other or when they are roaring at each other and he is pulling out Frieda's hair and saying 'I'll cut your bloody throat, you bitch' and Frieda is running up and down the road and screaming for 'Jack' to save her!! This is only a half of what literally happened last Friday night. You know, Catalina, Lawrence isn't healthy any more; he has gone a little bit out of his mind. If he is contradicted about *anything* he gets into a frenzy, quite beside himself and it goes on until he is so exhausted that he cannot stand and has to go to bed and stay there until he has recovered. And whatever your disagreement is about he says it is because you have gone wrong in your sex and belong to an obscene spirit. These rages occur whenever I see him for more than a casual moment for if ever I say anything that isn't quite 'safe' off he goes! It is like sitting on a railway station with Lawrence's temper like a big black engine puffing and snorting. I can think of nothing, I am blind to everything, waiting for the moment when, with a final shriek – off it will go! When he is in a rage with Frieda he says it is she who has done this to him and that she is 'a bug who has fed on my life'. I think that is true. I think he is suffering from quite genuine monomania at present, through having endured so much from her. Let me tell you what happened on Friday. I went across to them for tea. Frieda said Shelleys Ode to a Skylark was false. Lawrence said 'You are showing off; you don't know anything about it.' Then she began. '*Now* I have had enough. Out of my house. You little God Almighty you. I've had enough of you. Are you going to keep your mouth shut or aren't you.' Said Lawrence: 'I'll give you a dab on the cheek to quiet you, you dirty hussy'. Etc. Etc. So I left the house. At dinner time Frieda appeared. '**I** have finally done with him. It is all over for ever.' She then

went out of the kitchen and began to walk round and round
the house in the dark. Suddenly Lawrence appeared and
made a kind of horrible blind rush at her and they began to
scream and scuffle. He beat her – he beat her to death – her
head and face and breast and pulled out her hair. All the
while she screamed for Murry to help her. Finally they dashed
into the kitchen and round and round the table. I shall
never forget how L. looked. He was so white – almost green
and he just hit – thumped the big soft woman. Then he fell
into one chair and she into another. No one said a word. A
silence fell except for Frieda's sobs and sniffs. In a way I felt
almost glad that the tension between them was over for ever,
and that they had made an end of their 'intimacy'. L. sat
staring at the floor, biting his nails. Frieda sobbed . . . Suddenly, after a long time – about a quarter of an hour – L.
looked up and asked Murry a question about French literature. Murry replied. Little by little, the three drew up to the
table . . . Then F. poured herself out some coffee. Then she
and L. glided into talk, began to discuss some 'very rich but
very good macaroni cheese'. And next day, whipped himself, and far more thoroughly than he had ever beaten
Frieda, he was running about taking her up her breakfast
to her bed and trimming her a hat.

Am I wrong in not being able to accept these people just
as they are – laughing when they laugh and going away from
them when they fight? *Tell me*. For I cannot. It seems to me so
degraded – so horrible to see I can't stand it. And I feel so
furiously angry: I *hate* them for it. F. is such a liar, too. To
my face she is all sweetness. She used to bring me in flowers,
tell me how 'exquisite' I was – how my clothes suited me –
that I had never been so 'really beautiful'. Ugh! how humiliating! I thank heaven it is over. I must be the real enemy of
such a person. And what is hardest of all to bear is Lawrence's
'hang-doggedness'. He is so completely in her power and yet
I am sure that in his heart he loathes his slavery. She is not
even a good natured person really; she is evil hearted and her
mind is simply riddled with what she calls 'sexual symbols'.

Its an ugly position for Lawrence but I can't be sorry for him just now. The sight of his humiliating dependence makes me too furious.

Except for these two, nothing has happened here. A policeman came to arrest Murry the other day, and though Murry staved him off he will have to go, I think. I am very much alone here. It is not really a nice place. It is so full of huge stones, but now that I am writing I do not care for the time. It is so very temporary. It may all be over next month, in fact it will be. I don't belong to anybody here. In fact I have no being, but I am making preparations for changing everything. Write to me when you can and scold me.

Goodbye for now. Don't forget me.

To Lady Ottoline Morrell

[*June 1916*]

I loved hearing from you this morning, and I had intended to write to you today and tell you that Lawrence has gone home again. We walked with him as far as the ferry and away he sailed in a little open boat pulled by an old, old man. Lawrence wore a broad white linen hat and he carried a rucksack on his back. He looked rather as though the people of Falmouth had cried to him as the Macedonians did to Paul and he was on his way over to help them.

That journey with F. I built myself a bower of newspapers and sat in it until the train reached Paddington but F. talked over and round it and kept pointing to little financial paragraphs ... leaping upon them, you know, with a shout of excitement, with the ardour of a young man discovering mountains and torrents. Fancy *thrilling* to the fact that Pig Iron is nominal and Zinc Sheets are unchanged ...

They returned to London in the early autumn of 1916, Murry to take a job in the War Office. Katherine Mansfield had written little or nothing since completing 'The Aloe' in Bandol, and there are few letters or journal entries from this period. During 1917 she rewrote 'The Aloe' renaming it 'Prelude'.

To J. M. Murry

[1917]

I got up at that moment to re-read your article on Léon Bloy. The memory of it suddenly *rose* in my mind like a scent. I don't like it. I don't see its use at all, even artistically. It's a *Signature* style of writing and its *appeal* is in some obscure way – to me – mind me: I suppose only to me – indecent. I feel that you are going to uncover yourself and quiver. Sometimes when you write you seem to abase yourself like Dostoevsky did. It's *perfectly* natural to you, I know, but oh, my God, don't do it. It's just the same when you say, talking to Fergusson and me: 'If I am not killed – if *they don't kill* me.' I always laugh at you then because I am ashamed that you should speak so.

What is it? Is it your desire to torture yourself or to pity yourself or something far subtler? I only know that it's tremendously important because it's your way of damnation.

I feel (forgive fanciful me!) that when certain winds blow across your soul they bring the smell from that dark pit and the uneasy sound from those hollow caverns, and you long to lean over the dark swinging danger and just not fall in – but letting us all see meanwhile how low you lean.

Even your style of writing changes then – little short sentences – a hand lifted above the waves – the toss of a curly head above the swirling tumble. It's a terrible thing to be alone. Yes, it is – it is. But don't lower your mask until you have another mask prepared beneath – as terrible as you like – but a mask.

*

Forgive me for not telling you frankly when you read it to me what I felt. I was wrong.

Journal

[*May 1917*]

Putting my weakest books to the wall last night I came across a copy of *Howard's End* and had a look into it. But it's not good enough. E. M. Forster never gets any further than warming the teapot. He's a rare fine hand at that. Feel this teapot. Is it not beautifully warm? Yes, but there ain't going to be no tea.

And I can never be perfectly certain whether Helen was got with child by Leonard Bast or by his fatal forgotten umbrella. All things considered, I think it must have been the umbrella.

Love and Mushrooms

If only one could tell true love from false love as one can tell mushrooms from toadstools. With mushrooms it is so simple – you salt them well, put them aside and have patience. But with love, you have no sooner lighted on anything that bears even the remotest resemblance to it than you are perfectly certain it is not only a genuine specimen, but perhaps *the* only genuine mushroom ungathered. It takes a dreadful number of toadstools to make you realize that life is not one long mushroom.

*

Dreams and Rhubarb

My sticks of rhubarb were wrapped up in a copy of the *Star* containing Lloyd George's last, *more* than eloquent speech. As I snipped up the rhubarb my eye fell, was fixed and fastened on that sentence wherein he tells us that we have grasped our niblick and struck out for the open course.

Pray Heaven there is some faithful soul ever present with a basket to catch these tender blossoms as they fall. Ah, God! it is a dreadful thought that these immortal words should go down into the dreamless dust uncherished. I loved to think, as I put the rhubarb into the saucepan, that years hence – P.G. many, *many* years hence – when in the fullness of time, full of ripeness and wisdom, the Almighty sees fit to gather him into His bosom, some gentle stone-cutter living his quiet life in the little village that had known great David as a child would take a piece of fair white marble and engrave upon it two niblicks crossed and underneath:

In the hour of England's most imminent peril he grasped his Niblick and struck out for the Open Course.

But what *does* rather worry me, I thought, turning the gas down to a pinch as the rhubarb began to boil, is how these mighty words are to be translated so that our Allies may taste the full flavour of them. Those crowds of patient Russians, waiting in the snow, perhaps, to have the speech read aloud to them – what dreadful weapon will it present to their imagination? Unless *The Daily News* suggests to Mr Ransome that he walk down the Nevsky Prospekt with a niblick instead of an umbrella for all the world to see. And the French – what *espèce de Niblickisme* will they make of it. Shall we read in the French papers next week of someone *qui manque de niblick*. Or that '*Au milieu de ces évènements si graves ce qu'il nous faut c'est du courage, de l'espoir et du niblick le plus ferme . . .*' I wondered, taking off the rhubarb.

*

May 30 To be alive and to be a 'writer' is enough. Sitting at my table just now I saw one person turning to another, smiling, putting out his hand – speaking. And suddenly I clenched my fist and brought it down on the table and called out – There is *nothing* like it!

To the Hon. Dorothy Brett

[*11 October 1917*]

... It seems to me so extraordinarily right that you should be painting Still Lives just now. What can one do, faced with this wonderful tumble of round bright fruits; but gather them and play with them – and *become them*, as it were. When I pass an apple stall I cannot help stopping and staring until I feel that I, myself, am changing into an apple, too, and that at any moment I can produce an apple, miraculously, out of my own being, like the conjuror produces the egg ... When you paint apples do you feel that your breasts and your knees become apples, too? Or do you think this the greatest nonsense. I don't. I am sure it is not. When I write about ducks I swear that I am a white duck with a round eye, floating on a pond fringed with yellow-blobs and taking an occasional dart at the other duck with the round eye, which floats upside down beneath me ... In fact the whole process of becoming the duck (what Lawrence would perhaps call this consummation with the duck or the apple!) is so thrilling that I can hardly breathe, only to think about it. For although that is as far as most people can get, it is really only the 'prelude'. There follows the moment when you are *more* duck, *more* apple, or *more* Natasha than any of these objects could ever possibly be, and so you *create* them anew.

Brett (switching off the instrument[1]) : 'Katherine I *beg* of you to stop. You must tell us all about it at the Brotherhood Church one Sunday evening.'

K.: 'Forgive me, but that is why I believe in technique, too. (You asked me if I did.) I do just because I don't see how art is going to make that divine *spring* into the bounding outline of things if it hasn't passed through the process of trying to *become* these things before re-creating them.'

I have left your letter unanswered for more days than I could have wished. But don't think it was just because I am so

1. Brett's hearing aid.

careless and faithless. No, really not. I enjoyed keeping silent with the letter just as one enjoys walking about in silence with another until the moment comes when one turns and puts out a hand and speaks.

I threw my darling to the Wolves[1] and they ate it and served me up so much praise in such a golden bowl that I couldn't help feeling gratified. I did not think they would like it at all and I am still astounded that they do.

'What form is it?' you ask. Ah, Brett, it's so difficult to say. As far as I know, it's more or less my own invention. And 'How have I shaped it?' This is about as much as I can say about it. You know, if the truth were known I have a perfect passion for the island where I was born. Well, in the early morning there I always remember feeling that this little island has dipped back into the dark blue sea during the night only to rise again at gleam of day, all hung with bright spangles and glittering drops. (When you ran over the dewy grass you positively felt that your feet tasted salt.) I tried to catch that moment – with something of its sparkle and its flavour. And just as on those mornings white milky mists rise and uncover some beauty, then smother it again and then again disclose it, I tried to lift that mist from my people and let them be seen and then to hide them again ... It's so difficult to describe all this and it sounds perhaps over-ambitious and vain. But I don't feel anything but intensely a longing to serve my subject as well as I can.

But the unpardonable unspeakable thrill of this art business. What is there to compare! And what more can we desire? It's not a case of keeping the home fire burning for me. It's a case of keeping the home fire down to a respectable blaze, and little enough. If you don't come and see me soon there'll be nothing but a little heap of ashes and two crossed pens upon it.

1. Leonard and Virginia Woolf, who were publishing 'Prelude'.

To J. M. Murry

[*4 November 1917*]

... By the way, isn't *Furnished Rooms* a good title for a story
which plays in the Redcliffe Road? I can't resist it. Come and
look over my shoulder. The meeting on the dark stairs –
you know, someone is coming down and someone is coming
up. *Is* someone there? The 'fright', the pause – the unknown
in each other glaring through the dark and then passing
(which is almost too terrifying to be borne). Then the whole
street. And for backcloth, the whole line of the street – and
the dressmakers calling to the cat, the Chinamen, the dark
gentlemen, the babies playing, the coal cart, the line of the
sky above the houses, the little stone figure in one of the
gardens who carries a stone tray on his head, which in
summer is filled with flowers and in winter is heaped with
snow, the lamenting pianos, and all those faces hiding behind
the windows – and the *one* who is always on the watch. I see
the heroine very small, like a child, with high-heeled boots
and a tiny muff of *false* astrachan, and then the restless des-
pairing hero for whom 'all is over'. She cannot understand
what is the matter with him. Does she ever know? And what
happens?

It is the extreme coldness of my room and the brown paper
wagging over the sooty fireplace which gives me such a
veine. Nothing will go up the chimney while this tempest
lasts. And I begin to feel 'the blighted Mongol' stir and
clamour in me.

It was a good thing that you did not step next door with me
last night. Heavens above – a party! M. 'Bourrelet', Mrs
Bustle, Mrs Manfe, Major Jardine, Miss Francis etc. etc.
etc. And 'Thank you so much!' and 'Should we play German music during the war?' and 'Do you ever get anony-
mous letters?' and 'Will it, *can* it last another year?' M.
Bourrelet's voice was true *bourrelet*. Instead of stopping a hole
to keep the wind away it let the wind in. I was very unhappy

and felt a strange, unreasonable desire to pretend to be a
German and cry 'Wunderbar!' after the French songs.
There was a boiled fowl for dinner and such great tumblers of
cold water that I more than once suspected a goldfish of
flicking through mine . . .

[*14 December 1917*]

. . . It's a nice day here. Very quiet and warm. Even the
milkman crying milk sounds to me like a bird trying its
note – a funny sort of big bird, you know – a bird penguinian.
The clock ticks on tiptoe and the yellow curtains wave
gently. I love such a day. It's such a rest – not having been
outside for these days. I love to be out of the streets and buses
– out of the nudging crowds. Oh, I must work. The very
shadows are my friends. Don't forget to weigh yourself again
when the week is up, and if you are not heavier you must
melt a horseshoe in your next glass of milk so as not to dis-
appoint me.

[*23 December 1917*]

Here is the certificate which the doctor has just given me. Is
it alright? He says that left lung of mine that had the *loud
deafening* creak in it is 'no end better' but there is a S P O T in
my right lung which 'confirms him in his opinion that it is
absolutely imperative that I go out of this country and keep
out of it all through the future winters.' It is *evidemment*
rather a bad 'un of its kind – at any rate it would become so if
I did not fly.

*

Although I am still snapping up fishes like a sea-lion,
steaks like a land-lion, milk like a snake (or is that only a
'tale'?) and eggs, honey, creamb, butter and nourishing
trimmings galore, they seem to go to a sort of Dead Letter
Office. However he has given me a Tonic today which will

put that right. Of course, I feel now that I've only to get into the sun and I'll simply burst into leaf and flower again. It is this old place that does it to me, and I keep sweeping out *our* house with a branch of acacia tree, picking a rose to tuck into my bodice, and then hurrying off just in time to catch the train which tumbles you, my treasure, in my arms. And I keep going into that room and putting my arm round you and saying: 'Look! there's that diamond of light in the shutter!'

I know quite well, I appreciate absolutely, that you must be faithful to England. Hell it would be to know you were away and felt its call. But, all the same, you will have to have two homes, and we shall have to have all our babies in pairs so that we possess a complete 'set' in either place.

6

Bandol Again; Paris, January–April 1918

Following the illness referred to in the previous letter Katherine Mansfield was advised to avoid the English winter. She grasped at this advice as a way to get back to the South of France – a journey now more difficult because of the extending effects of the war. Perhaps, having written so little fiction during the previous year, she hoped that Bandol would work its old magic and set her writing again; and since Murry's War Office work would not permit him to travel she determined, despite the dangerous state of her health, to go without him. At first it was intended that Ida Baker ('L.M.') should go too, but permission for her travel to France was refused and K.M. set off alone.

Later Ida Baker, moved by some intuition that she was needed, managed to get the necessary permission to travel and made her way to Bandol. K.M. did not welcome her, but was soon forced by the worsening state of her health and the need of assistance if she was to make the return journey, to accept all that her friend was able to do for her.

Some of the terrors and disillusionments of this trip to Bandol, and the delays and dangers of the return through Paris, are related in the extracts which follow.

To J. M. Murry

[11 January 1918]

My enthusiastic letter from Paris has been in my mind ever since. *And* mocked me. I took it to post; it was dark by then, piercing cold and so wet underfoot that one's feet felt like 2 walking toads. After a great deal of bother I got established in the train (no pillows to be had nowadays) and then the fun began. I liked my fellow-passengers, but God! how stiff one got and my feet hurt and the flat-iron[1] became hot enough to burn the buttoned back against which I leaned. There was no restaurant car on the train— no chance of getting anything hot – a blinding snow-storm until we reached Valence.

I must confess the country was exquisite at sunrise – exquisite – but we did not arrive at Marseilles till *one* o'clock. Good! As I got out a pimp getting *in* to hold a seat for some super-pimp gave me such a blow in the chest that it is blue today. I thought: 'This is Marseilles, *sans doute*.' Feeling very tired and hungry I carried my baggage 3 miles to the consigne, and finding that the train left for Bandol at 3.30 decided to have a snack at the buffet just outside – that place under a glass verandah. It was rather full, so I sat down opposite an elderly lady who eyed me so strangely that I [asked] if 'cette place est prise?' 'Non, Madame,' said she, insolent beyond everything, 'mais il y a des autre tables, n'est-ce pas? Je préfère beaucoup que vous ne venez pas ici. D'abord, j'ai déja fini mon déjeuner, et c'est très dégoûtant de vous voir commencer car j'ai l'estomac délicat, et puis . . .' And then she raised her eyebrows and left it at that. You can judge what I ate after that and what I thought.

At 1.30 I went to get my baggage registered, waited for one hour in a queue for my ticket and then was told I could not have one until my passport was viséd. I had that done, waited again, carried my luggage to the platform finally at 3 o'clock *juste*, and waited there in a crowd until four. Then a train came in at another platform, and the people swarmed in just like apes climbing into bushes, and I had just thrown my rugs into it when it was stated that it was only for *permissionaires* and did not stop before Toulon. Good again! I staggered out and got into *another* train on *another* platform, asked 3 people if it was the right one, who did not know and sat down in the corner, completely dished.

There were 8 Serbian officers in the compartment with me

1. The burning sensation in her lung.

and their 2 dogs. Never shall I say another word against Serbians. They looked like Maiden's Dreams, excessively handsome and well cared for, graceful, young, dashing, with fine teeth and eyes. But that did not matter. What *did* was that after shunting for 2 hours, five yards forward, five back, there was a free fight at the station between a mob of soldiers and the civilians. The soldiers demanded the train – and that *les civils* should evacuate it. Not with good temper, but furious – very ugly – and VILE. They banged on the windows, wrenched open the doors and threw out the people and their luggage after them. They came to our carriage, swarmed in – told the officers they too must go, and one caught hold of me as though I were a sort of packet of rugs. I never said a word for I was far too tired and vague to care about anything except I was determined not to *cry* – but one of the officers then let out – threw out the soldiers – said I was his wife and had been travelling with him five days – and when the *chef militaire de la gare* came, said the same – threw *him* out – banged the door, took off their dogs' leads and held the door shut. The others then pressed against the connecting door between the carriages and there we remained in a state of siege until seven o'clock when the train started. You should have heard the squalling and banging. They pinned the curtains together and I hid behind them until we were under way. By this time it was pitch dark and I knew I should never find the station as a terrific mistral was blowing and you could not hear the stations cried – but as we came to each stop they pulled the window down and shouted in their curious clipped French to know which it was. Ah, but they were very nice chaps – splendid chaps – I'll not forget them. We reached Bandol at 9. I felt that my *grande malle* was gone for ever but I seized the other 2 and dashed across the line. I could not have walked here but happily the boy from the Hotel des Bains was at the station and though he said 'qu'il n'était pas bon avec le patron', he brought me.

When I arrived the hall was rather cold and smoky. A strange woman came out, wiping her mouth with a serviette

... I realized in a flash that the hotel had changed hands. She said she had received *no* letter – but there were plenty of rooms – and proceeded to lead me to them. My own was taken. I chose finally the one next door which had 2 beds on the condition that she removed one. Also it was the cheapest, 12 francs a day! The others have had *de l'eau courante* put into them and cost 13! The big stoves were not lighted in the passages ... I asked for hot water and a hot water bottle, had some soup, wrapped up to the eyes, and simply fell into bed after finishing the brandy in my flask. For I felt that the whole affair wanted thoroughly sleeping over and not thinking about ...

In the morning when I opened the persiennes it was so lovely outside, I stayed in bed till lunch. *Ma grande malle* really did turn up. Then I got up, and after lunch went into the town. The Maynards are gone for the present. The *tabac* woman did not know me and had no tobacco. Nobody remembered me at all. I bought writing things and a few bull's-eyes – about a penny for two, they were – and suddenly I met Ma'am Gamel. She, too, did not recognize me until I had explained who I was. Then she was very kind. 'Ah! Ah! Ah! Vous êtes beaucoup changée. Vous avez été *ben* malade, n'est-ce pas? Vous n'avez plus votre air de p'tite gosse, vous *sa*-avez!' I went with her to the shop which is just the same and saw the old mother who was most tender about you. I bought a tiny pot of cherry jam and came home – to find my room not yet done.

You can see, love, I am depressed. I feel faible still after cet voyage, but I shall get better and I shall arrange things here as soon as I have la force nécessaire. The place is, even to my blind eyes, as lovely as ever, glittering with light, with the deep hyacinth blue sea, the wonderful flashing palms and the mountains, violet in the shadow and jade-green in the sun. The mimosa outside my window is in bud. Don't worry about me. Having got over that journey and that Paris thaw, I shall never fall by the way; and when my room is ready, I shall *work*. That I do feel, and that is what matters,

Bogey. I am not even very sad. It has been a bit of a bang,
though, hasn't it? And I'll tell you exactly what I feel like.
I feel like a fly who has been dropped into the milk-jug and
fished out again, but is still too milky and drowned to start
cleaning up yet. Letters will take a long time – perhaps
6 or 8 days – so do not worry if you do not hear.

And take care of yourself and *love me* as I *love you*. Ah, this
is not the day to start writing about that, for my bosom begins
to ache and my arms fly out to embrace you. I want you. I
am lonely and fainting by the way, but only for now – you
know.

[*13 January 1918*]

I got so cold yesterday that I decided, willy-nilly, to take
a small walk and try and 'warm up' before the evening. So I
made myself into a bundle, and started off. . . The afternoon
was very cold and grey and just going dusky. The sea was
high and made a loud noise. When I passed the vineyard
where the two little boys used to work I realized quite
suddenly that I was suffering – terribly, terribly, and was
quite faint with this emotion. Then came at last the road
with GRAVIER 2K written on the post. And then came our
little home in sight. I went on, though I don't know how,
pushed open the Allègres' singing gate, walked over those
crunching round stones. The outer door of our villa was
open. When I reached the stone verandah, and looked again
upon the almond tree, the little garden, the round stone table,
the seat scooped out of stone, the steps leading down to the
cave, and then looked up at our pink house, with the swags of
shells painted over the windows and the strange blue-grey
shutters, I thought I had never, in my happiest memories,
realized all its beauty. I could not get any answer from the
Allègres', but I felt certain I heard someone moving in our
villa, so finally I knocked on our door. You remember how
hard it was to open. It tugged open, and there stood Ma'am
Allègre in the same little black shawl, lean and grey as ever.

'Vous désirez, Madame?' said she. I just managed to say 'Bonjour, Madame. Vous m'avez oubliée?' And then she cried, 'Ah! Ah! I know your voice. Come in, come in, Madame. I am just airing the villa. Come in to the little salon. Comment ça va? Et votre mari? etc., etc. etc.'

I crossed the hall; she opened one half of the persiennes, and we sat on either side of the table, she in your place, I with my back to the fire in mine, and had a long talk. She remembers us well. Many times her husband and she have talked of us and wished to have us back again. Her husband always wondered what had happened to us. We were like 'deux enfants,' said she, and it was a happiness to them to know that we were there. Her son is wounded, and is on the Swiss frontier in a post office. They went all the way to Paris to see him. I asked her what has happened to the flowers; for there is not a single flower – not a jonquil, not a geranium, not a rose, not an orange – and she promised they would all be here 'plus tar', plus tar'. C'est la faute du mauvais *temps*, vous sa-avez!'

But oh, as we sat there talking and I felt myself answer and smile and stroke my muff and discuss the meat shortage and the horrid bread and the high prices and *cette guerre*, I felt that somewhere, upstairs, you and I lay like the little Babies in the Tower, smothered under pillows, and she and I were keeping watch like any two old crones! I could hardly look at the room. When I saw my photograph, that you had left, on the wall, I nearly broke down, and finally I came away and leaned a long time on the wall at the bottom of our little road, looking at the violet sea that beat up, high and loud, against those strange dark clots of sea-weed. As I came down your beautiful narrow steps, it began to rain. Big soft reluctant drops fell on my hands and face. The light was flashing through the dusk from the lighthouse, and a swarm of black soldiers was kicking something about on the sand among the palm-trees – a dead dog perhaps, or a little tied-up kitten.

. . . I had just got that far when Victorine poked in her head: 'C'est une dame qui vous demande en bas', and suddenly I heard steps, and there was Madame Geoffroi. 'Ma chère amie, j'avais l'idée que vous êtes paralysée'. She took me into her arms and I wept and she wept and I wept all over the collar of her impossible coat and she wept. Then I tried to explain how I had wired, and *she* that your telegram had come the evening before. She had been travelling to get to me since 8 that morning and was worn out. It was a *bit awful*. We both went on explaining and chère amieing each other until I thought I'd simply fall down like Slatkowsky – and finally she understood and she said she would write that I had très bonne mine and was pas plus fatiguée parceque ce pauvre enfant votre mari – doit être a la folie etc. etc. etc. She said her husband *never* practised and at any rate he is the Mayor now. Voilà! And kept saying that I must eat and put on wool and eat – abundantly – and wants me to go to Carpentras in March until I leave for England.

At last the gong went for dinner, and we dined together, and then she came back to my room and sat till 11.30! talking about le Swinburne, Mistral, d'Aubanel, le Keats – le silence qui a pris pour sa maison la maison d'Henri Fabre. Finally, she left me and I simply groaned into bed. At 8.15, my dear – figurez-vous – she was in my room dressed, ready pour aller envoyer la télegramme à ce pauvre M. Bowden. Good! We did that. Afterwards she sat and talked of literature with me until *lunch*. Then I took her to the 1.15 train, which did not arrive until 5 *moins quart*! It poured with rain; it was utterly cold and cheerless; and she poor creature will not be home until tomorrow – Avignon 2 heures du matin. God! what a pilgrimage of love on her side! And how *I* bore the conversations I have no idea. I simply died with them and rose again – died and rose again – and I am sure that there is not a poem unturned in the whole of the Provençal literature after that. She is gone, confident that she will reassure you, and my left lung aches and aches so as I write that I must ask Jeanne if she knows of a doctor here just to tell me *what* this ache can be. It is like an appalling *burn*. Sometimes, if I lift my arm over my head it seems to give it relief. What is it?

The Times and *The Nation* came today. Thank you, my love.

25 to seven. Saturday. I love you so, I love you so. The wind howls and the shutters squeak, and this old deserted hotel seems to be on an island – far, far away. But I love you so, I love you so. I am absolutely all yours for ever.

My precious, please don't ever send me a *penny* of extra money. That is very straight dinkum. Save it. Put it away. We shall want all our pockets full for later. I shall save all I can and *faire des économies* as far as I can. *Trust me*.

[*21 January 1918*]

I am only going to write you a note today just to say that I still feel better. The weather is 1000 times rougher. Never, not even on shipboard or in my own little country or anywhere, have I heard such wind. And in the night when one lay quiet in bed and listened, God knows how many Ancient Mariners cried in it or how many lost souls whirled past. I thought then what an agony it must be to be a wife to a fisherman. How could a poor soul comfort herself and to whom could she pray when such a wind and such a sea fought against her? . . . I thought, too, it must have been just such a storm when Shelley died . . .

[*22 January 1918*]

. . . The wind still blows a hurricane here. In the night the rain joined in but now the sun beats in the air like a kite. It is like living on a ship. The hotel is all bolted and barred up, the big doors closed and a strange twilight in the hall. People go about in shawls and coats. If a window is opened the seas of the air rush in and fill it. The great palm trees have snapped like corks, and many a glittering plume trails in the dust. They say it never has been known before. I have begun to like it . . .

[*28 January 1918*]

. . . have you read *Our Mutual Friend*? Some of it is really *damned good*. The satire in it is first chop – all the Veneering business *par exemple* could not be better. I never read it before and am enjoying it immensely, and Ma Wilfer is after my own heart. I have a huge capacity for seeing 'funny' people, you know, and laughing, and Dickens does fill it at times quite amazingly . . .

[*3 February 1918*]

Sunday Morning . . . I really feel I *ought* to send you some boughs and songs, for never was time or place more suited, but to tell you the truth I am pretty well absorbed in what I am writing[1] and walk the blooming countryside with a 2d. notebook shutting out *les amandiers*. But I don't want to discuss it in case it don't come off . . .

I've two 'kick offs' in the writing game. *One* is joy – real joy – the thing that made me write when we lived at Pauline, and that sort of writing I could only do in just that state of being in some perfectly blissful way *at peace*. Then something delicate and lovely seems to open before my eyes, like a flower without thought of a frost or a cold breath – knowing that all about it is warm and tender and 'ready'. And *that* I try, ever so humbly, to express.

The other 'kick off' is my old original one, and (had I not known love) it would have been my all. Not hate or destruction (both are beneath contempt as real motives) but an *extremely* deep sense of hopelessness, of everything doomed to disaster, almost wilfully, stupidly, like the almond tree and

1. 'Je ne parle pas français.'

'pas de nougat pour le noël'. There! as I took out a cigarette paper I got it exactly – *a cry against corruption* – that is *absolutely* the nail on the head. Not a protest – a *cry*, and I mean corruption in the widest sense of the word, of course.

I am at present fully launched right out in the deep sea, with this second state. I may not be able to 'make my passage,' I may have to put back and have another try: that's why I don't want to talk about it, and have breath for so little more than a hail. But I must say the boat feels to be driving along the deep water as though it smelt port (no, darling, better say 'harbour' or you'll think I am rushing into a public house).

Sunday Night   I don't dare to work any more tonight. I suffer so frightfully from insomnia here and from night terrors. That is why I asked for another Dickens; if I read him in bed he diverts my mind. My work excites me so tremendously that I almost feel *insane* at night, and I have been at it with hardly a break all day. A great deal is copied and carefully addressed to you, in case any misfortune should happen to me. Cheerful! But there is a great black bird flying over me, and I am so frightened he'll settle – so terrified. I don't know exactly what *kind* he is.

If I were not working here, with war and anxiety I should go mad, I think. My night terrors here are rather complicated by packs and packs of growling, roaring, ravening, prowl-and-prowl-around dogs.

God! How tired I am! How I'd love to curl up against you and sleep. Goodnight, my blessed one. Don't forget me in your busy life.

[*6 February 1918*]

. . . I am still in *a state of work* – you know, my precious: dead quiet and spinning away . . .

Have you got your meat card? Of course, I think the meat cards will stop the war. Nothing will be done but *spot-*

counting, and people will go mad and butchers and pork butchers will walk about with bones in their hair, distracted. Talking of hair – do you know those first days I was here I went a bit GREY over both temples. Real grey hair. I know – I felt the very moment it came, but it is a blow to see it . . .

Another thing I hate the French bourgeoisie for is their absorbed interest in evacuation. What is constipating or what not? That is a real *criterion* . . . At the end of this passage there is a W.C. Great Guns! they troop and flock there . . . and not only that . . . they are all victims of the most amazing Flatulence imaginable. Air raids over London don't hold a candle to 'em. This, I suppose, is caused by their violent purges and remedies, but it seems to me very 'unnecessary'. Also the people of the village have a habit of responding to their serious needs (I suppose by night) down on the shore round the palm trees. Perhaps it's the sailors, but my English gorge rises and my English lips curl in contempt. The other day one palm tree had a placard nailed on it *Chiens Seulement*. Was that funny? It provided a haw-haw for the day, here. But on my life, I'd almost rather, like that English lady, not know whether my husband went to the lavatory or not, than be so unbuttoned . . .

[*10 February 1918*]

. . . I *dreamed* a short story last night, even down to its name, which was *Sun and Moon*. It was very light. I dreamed it all – about children. I got up at 6.30 and wrote a note or two because I knew it would fade. I'll send it some time this week. It's so nice. I didn't dream that I read it. No, I was in it, part of it, and it played round invisible me. But the hero is not more than 5. In my dream I saw a supper table with the eyes of 5. It was awfully queer – especially a plate of half-melted ice-cream. . . But I'll send it you . . .

Journal

[*1918*]

February 19   I woke up early this morning and when I opened the shutters the full round sun was just risen. I began to repeat that verse of Shakespeare's: 'Lo, here the gentle lark weary of rest', and bounded back into bed. The bound made me cough – I spat – it tasted strange – it was bright red blood. Since then I've gone on spitting each time I cough a little more. Oh, yes, of course I'm frightened. But for two reasons only. I don't want to be ill, I mean 'seriously', away from Jack. Jack is the first thought. 2nd, I don't want to find this is real consumption, perhaps it's going to gallop – who knows? – and I shan't have my work written. *That's what matters.* How unbearable it would be to die – leave 'scraps', 'bits' . . . nothing real finished.

To J. M. Murry

[*19 February 1918*]

I want to tell you some things which are a bit awful – so hold me *hard*. I have not been so well these last few days. Today I saw a doctor. There happens by an extraordinary chance to be an English doctor here just now, and L.M. got him to come. Look here! I can't leave this place till April. It's no earthly go. I can't and mustn't – see. Can't risk a draught or a chill, and mustn't walk. I've got a bit of a temperature and I'm not so fat as when I came – and, Bogey, this is *not* serious, does *not* keep me in bed, is absolutely easily curable, but I have been spitting a bit of blood. See? Of course, I'll tell you. But if you worry – unless you laugh like Rib does – I can't tell you: you mustn't type it on the typewriter or anything like that, my precious, my own – and after all Lawrence often used to: so did, I think, Belle Trinder. But while it goes on, I've got to be most enormously careful. See? I've got this doctor and I've got the Slave – so I am provided for, and determined to stick it out till April and not come back till the first week of *then*. It's agony to be parted from you, but it would be imbecile to get the March winds, as I am so parky – and everybody would be so madly cross – and I couldn't stick in bed in 47. I'd only be a worry. So here I stay and work – and try to bear it. I've *ample* money for everything and my journey money fastened up with a pin and locked away.

I can do all this and everything as long as I know you are taking care of yourself and that you don't worry about me and do *feed* and don't overwork too dreadfully . . .

[*20 February 1918*]

. . . Since this little attack I've had, a queer thing has happened. I feel that my love and longing for the external world – I mean the world of *nature* – has suddenly increased a million times. When I think of the little flowers that grow in grass, and little streams and places where we can lie and look up at the clouds – Oh, I simply *ache* for them – for them with you. Take you away and the answer to the sum is O. I feel so awfully like a tiny girl whom someone has locked up in the dark cupboard, even though it's daytime. I don't want to bang at the door or make a noise, but I want you to come with a key you've made yourself and let me out, and then we should tiptoe away together into a kinder place where everybody was more of our heart and size.

You mustn't think, as I write this, that I'm dreadfully sad. Yes, I am, but you know, at the back of it is *absolute faith* and *hope* and *love*. I've only, to be frank like we *are*, had a bit of a fright. See? And I'm still 'trembling'. That just describes it.

Tomorrow, my own, I shall write a gayer letter. Oh, just to forget me for a minute, do you remember or have I mentioned how the Fool in *King Lear* says: "'Twas her brother who, in pure kindness, *buttered* his horse's *hay*.' I thought that was a good phrage for nowadays. 'It is hardly the moment to *butter* the horse's *hay*.' Isn't it? Pin it in *The Nation.*

I hate to ask you to spend on me, but now I'm staying, can I have another Dickens some time? *Bleak House* or *Edwin Drood*? If you can get them in a 7d., do. If you feel you cannot afford them, I understand. Mrs Gaskell positively fascinated me. I think she's an extremely good writer. The 2nd story in the *Cranford* book, 'Moorland Cottage', is really a little masterpiece. *We shall read it at home.* Now I am quite cheerful again and can leave you with a smile and a wave instead of almost turning away like I had to on page 3. And, oh my own lover, you just go on looking after yourself for me and I will go on looking after myself for you. Eight more days and this month is over – and then there's only March.

[*24 February 1918*]

. . . Have you read any reviews of Yeats's book? And did you see the pompous ass' remarks on Keats? There was a good story agin him (though he didn't know it) in a quote I saw. He dreamed once 'in meditations' (!?) that his head was circled with a flaming sun. Went to sleep and dreamed of a woman whose hair was afire, woke up, lighted a candle, and by and by discovered 'by the odour' that he'd set his own hair ablaze. This *he* calls sort of prophetic. I think it's wondrous apt. It's just as far as he and his crew can get – to set their hair afire – to set their lank forlorn locks a-frizzle. God knows there's nothing else about them that a cartload of sparks could put a light to . . .

[*27 February 1918*]

. . . I have read *Le P'tit*[1] It's *very* good – very well done. I think it's got one fault, or perhaps I am too ready to be offended by this. I think the physical part of Le P'tit's

1. by P. J. Toulet.

feeling for Lama, is unnecessarily accentuated. I think if I'd
written it I wouldn't have put it in at all – not on his side.
On hers, yes. But never once on his. Am I wrong, do you
think? Yes, of course, I agree it's well done, that part, but I
would have left it more mysterious. Lama must do all she
does, and Le P'tit must say: 'Si tu savais comme je t'aime!'
But 'lorsqu'un spontané baiser dans l'affolement furieuse
de l'instinct chez le jeune homme . . .' that I don't like.

But the 'way' it is done, the 'method', I *do* very much.
Nausicaa[1] has got something very charming too. If he wasn't
a Frenchman, he'd be a most interesting chap. But I do find
the French language, style, attack, point of view, hard to
stomach at present. It's all *tainted*. It all seems to me to lead
to dishonesty – Dishonesty Made Easy – made superbly easy.
All these *half* words – these words which have never really
been born and seen the light – like 'me trouble' – 'tiède' –
'blottant' – 'inexprimable' (these are bad examples, but
you know the kinds I mean and the phrases and whole
paragraphs that go with them) – they won't at the last moment, *do* at all. Some of them are charming and one is loth
to do without them, but they are like certain plants – once
they are in your garden they spread and spread and spread,
and make a show perhaps, but they are *weeds*. No, I get up
hungry from the French language. I have too great an appetite for the real thing to be put off with pretty little kick-
shaws, and I am offended intellectually that 'ces gens'
think they can so take me in.

It's the result of Shakespeare, I think. The English language is damned difficult, but it's also damned rich, and so
clear and bright that you can search out the darkest places
with it. Also it's *heavenly* simple and true. Do you remember
where Paulina says:

> I, an old turtle,
> Will wing me to some withered bough
> And there my mate that's never to be found again
> Lament till I am lost.

1. by P. J. Toulet.

You can't beat that. I *adore* the English language, and that's a fact.

> Your eyes be musical, your dewy feet
> Have freshly trod the lawns for timeless hours,
> O young and lovely dead!

There's a man who can 'use' it!
That is all very bady put. But do you agree? . . .

[*2 March 1918*]

. . . L.M. has made me perfectly *sick* today. She's skittish. 'Dearie, I'm very proud. I remembered the word for candle – *bougie*. That's right, isn't it? I'm not really very stupid, you know. It's only when I am with you, because you are so many million miles ahead of all the rest of mankind –' and so on. I *squirm*, try and hold my tongue, and then – *bang!* and again I shoot her dead, and up she comes again . . .

[*4 March 1918*]

. . . Love, it is very late. The winds are howling, the rain is pouring down, I have just read Wordsworth's poem, *To Duty*, and a description in a N.Z. letter of how to grow that neglected vegetable, the Kohl-rabi. I never heard a wilder, fiercer night: but it can't quench my desire – my burning desire to grow this *angenehme* vegetable, with its fringe of outside leathery leaves, and its heart which is shaped and formed and of the same size as the *heart* of a *turnip*. It is of a reddish purple colour, will grow where there have been carrots or peas. Of course, I can see *our* Kohl-rabi – the most extraordinary looking thing – and Wig and Jag staring at it.

Do you think it ought to look like that?
No. Do you?
No. I think it's done it on purpose.
Shall I show it to somebody and ask?
No. They'll only laugh.

And as they turn away the Kohl-rabi wags and flaps its leathery leaves at them . . .

In March Katherine Mansfield decided to return to England. Ida Baker had managed to reach her in February and was there to help her, but there were difficulties at first getting permission to travel again and then they were held up several weeks in Paris by the German bombardment.

To J. M. Murry

Marseilles   [*18 March 1918*]

Everything seems changed. My whole life is *uprooted*, and living in Bandol, even with the G's and L.M., feels like *calm* compared to this violent battle. I arrived here, very late this evening, too late for the Consul or for Cook's: the train was 2 hours en retard. And so I got a room at the Hotel de Russie, had some food, and here I am. I must bring you up to date with this Battle of the Wig.

Last night after I wrote you I felt desperate and sent L.M. after Doctor Poached Eyes; even though it really was rather late. He was at dinner – fatal time! – but promised to turn up. Whereupon I set to, turned L.M. out of my room, dressed in my new frock, and a black swanny round my neck, *made up*, drew chairs to the fire, and waited for this little toad. If you could have come in, you would have been horribly shocked, I think. I have not felt so cynical for years. I knew my man and I determined to get him by the only weapon I could and that *he* could understand. He came far more than 3 parts on, and I sat down and played the old game with him – listened – looked – smoked his cigarettes – and asked finally for a chit that would satisfy the Consul. He gave me the chit, but whether it will I'll not know till tomorrow. It could not be more urgent in its way. I dictated it *and* had to spell it *and* had to lean over him as he wrote *and* hear him say – what dirty hogs do say. I am sure he is here because he has killed some poor girl with a dirty button-hook. He is a maniac on *venereal* diseases and *passion*. Ah, the filthy little brute! There I sat and smiled and let him talk. I was determined to get him for our purpose – any way that didn't involve letting him touch me. He could say what he liked: I laughed and spelled – and was so sweet and soft and so *obliged*. Even if this chit fails I think he can get me through in other ways. He has, for all his shadiness, a good deal of very useful influence in high quarters in Marseilles and Toulon – and it's all at my disposal. So I'll use it.

Oh dear, oh dear! I feel so strange. An old, dead, sad, wretched self blows about, whirls about in my feverish brain – and I sit here in this café – drinking and looking at the mirrors and smoking and thinking how utterly corrupt life is – how hideous human beings are – how loathsome it was to catch this toad as I did – with *such* a weapon. I keep hearing him say, very thick, 'Any trouble is a pleasure for a lovely woman' and seeing my *soft smile* . . . I am very sick, Bogey.

Marseilles is so hot and loud. They scream the newspapers and all the shops seem full of caged birds, parrots and canaries, shrieking too. And the hags sell nuts and oranges – and I run up and down *on fire*. Anything – anything to get home! It all spins like a feverish dream. I am not *un*happy or happy. I am just as it were in the thick of a bombardment, writing you, here, from a *front* line trench. I do remember that the fruit trees on the way were all in flower and there were such big daisies in the grass and a little baby smiled at me in the train. But nothing matters till I have seen the Consul. I am staying tonight at the Hôtel de Russie. It is clean and good. I have *Elle et Lui* to read. But this is all a dream, you see. I want to come home – to come home. Tomorrow I'll wire you after I've seen the man. Under it – above it – through it I am yours – fighting and tired – but yours for ever.

Paris [*30 March 1918*]

... I suppose the blockade has started, for no post has come today here or at Cook's. It is raining fast, and the bombardment is – frankly – *intensely* severe. The firing takes place every 18 minutes as far as I can make out. I won't try and tell you where the bombs fall. It is a very loud ominous sound, this super-*Kanon*. I am not frightened by it even though I have been extremely near the place where the explosions have taken place, but I *do* feel there is a pretty big risk that one may be killed by it. You see, there is no warning as to where the next shell will fall, neither is it frequent enough to make one stay in the icy cellars. Also, one *must* go about to Consuls etc. and try and get away. If it were not for you I should not care whether I were killed or not. But as you *are* there, I care passionately and will take all the precautions you would have me take, and I you in the same straits. Today, people are frightened – quite otherwise to what they have been before. And the ghastly massacre in the church has added very much to their feeling ...

[*1 April 1918*]

... At that moment a knock came at my door and the maid opened it, pushing in front of her a tiny little boy in a white pinafore and white socks with red shoes. *Very* small, just two years old. He was eating his goûter – a bit of bread – and he staggered in, and when he saw me, turned his back. She said might she leave him a moment, and when she had gone I remembered that I had a little piece of chocolate in my despatch case. When I mentioned it he was so moved that he sort of – waded 100 miles over to me and about 200 more to the cupboard, and there he stood, beating time with his toes as fast as possible while I got the chocolate out. He was so very nice I held him up to the glass, and he gave the other little baby first a crumb of bread and then a taste of the other, and when the maid came for him, being anxious to kiss his hand, he kissed the bread instead and waved it at me. How fine and lovely little children can be! While he sat in my lap I felt a moment of almost *peace*, as though the Sodom and Gomorrah world had stopped just for an instant. But now he's gone again . . .

Every taxi that stops at this hotel, stops at my heart, too. I know how utterly absurd that is. But I feel – by some miracle . . . and I wonder: Would they 'phone me from downstairs, or should I just hear steps along the passage? . . .

[*2 April 1918*]

. . . Since yesterday the 'lutte', as they say, has continued. Gunfire last evening – and at 3.15 this morning one woke to hear the air *screaming*. That is the effect of these sirens; they have a most diabolical sound. I dressed and went down to the *cave*. Everybody else was there – the place was packed with hideous humanity: *so* hideous indeed that one felt a bomb on them wouldn't perhaps be as cruel, after all. I don't think I can go to the *cave* again. The cold and agony of those stone dusty steps and these filthy people *smoking* in that air. I crept back to bed and to sleep and woke to a perfect deafening roar of gunfire. It was followed by the sound of people running in the streets. I got up again and went to look. Very ugly, very horrible. The whole top of a house as it were bitten out – all the windows broken, and the road of course covered with ruin. There were trees on both sides of the street and these had just come into their new green. A great many branches were broken, but on the others strange bits of clothes and paper hung. A nightdress, a chemise, a tie – they looked extraordinarily pitiful, dangling in the sunny light.

One thing which confirms me again in my dreadful feeling that I live wherever I am in another Sodom and Gomorrah . . . this. Two workmen arrived to clear away the débris. One found, under the dust, a woman's silk petticoat. He put it on and danced a step or two for the laughing crowd . . . That filled me with such horror that I'll never never get out of my

mind the fling of his feet and his grin and the broken trees
and the broken house.

*

I am writing to you in the Café Mahieu. It is a divine,
warm day. I keep thinking and thinking only of you, my
darling, and wishing and wishing – you know what. I went
to Cook's this morning. The man seemed to think the boats
would start again at the end of this week. But no, I don't
dare to hope until I have been to the M.P.O. tomorrow.

On my way home I fell in with an accident. A man on the
pavement said he had broken his ankle. A large crowd
collected, but nobody believed him. Two policemen nearly
swore him away, but as he groaned and sweated a great deal
they decided to take off his boot and sock and see. After
pulling off the boot – I said: 'Cut the sock! Don't drag it!' and
really it is just a fluke I wasn't arrested. You should have
heard the 'Taisez-vous!' that was flung at me, *and* the rest.
So they pulled it off, and the ankle was all broken. His whole
foot was at right angles – pale green in colour, with black
nails. 'When did you do it?' they asked him, and the fool
said 'Pas aujourd'hui'. At that the whole crowd began to
laugh – looked at the foot and laughed. He had evidently
been going about for days with this foot, and I should think
it will have to be amputated. But, God, what a joke it was for
these Parisians! . . .

7

Cornwall, May–July 1918

Katherine Mansfield arrived back in London on 11 April 1918. She had at last secured a divorce from George Bowden, and she and Murry were married on 3 May.

Her ordeal in France had left her health considerably worse than it had been when she set off to escape the English winter. She had lost fourteen pounds in weight and she coughed incessantly. She wanted to stay with Murry in his rooms at Redcliffe Road but he insisted she should go to Cornwall until he had found a more suitable place for them. She accepted this and went down to Looe on 16 May, but she seems to have had to fight hard against disappointment and a feeling that Murry found her burdensome. In Cornwall she particularly enjoyed the company of her American-born painter friend, Anne Estelle Rice (1879–1959), and the best of her letters from Looe are happy. But under the gaiety there was continuing anxiety and fear.

To the Hon. Dorothy Brett

[*12 May 1918*]

... Murry is lying down upon the shell shaped 1840 sofa reading a book. He is wearing a mauve shirt and pinkish socks, and above his head on the black marble mantelpiece there is a bowl of dying lilacs.

I saw Virginia[1] on Thursday. She was very nice. She's the only one of them I shall ever see, but she *does* take the writing business seriously and she *is* honest about it and thrilled by it. One can't ask more. My poor dear *Prelude* is still piping away

1. Virginia Woolf, who, with her husband, Leonard, was first publisher of 'Prelude'.

in their little cage and not out yet. I read some pages of it and scarcely knew it again, it all seems so once upon a time. But I am having some notices printed and they say it will be ready by June. And won't the 'Intellectuals' just hate it. They'll think it's a New Primer for Infant Readers. Let 'em . . .

To J. M. Murry

Looe, Cornwall   [*17 May 1918*]

Anne and Drey[1] were at Liskeard. Anne just as I had imagined, *bronze*-coloured with light periwinkle eyes carrying a huge white bag bulging with *her* Thermos flask and a vest of Drey's (I didn't find where *it* came from or how) and a box of paints and a handful of hedge flowers and 'the most beautiful lemon'. Drey was awfully kind: he did everything. We featherstitched off to Looe. It was very hot – all glowing and quiet with loud birds singing and the blue-bells smelled like honey. The approach to Looe is amazing, it's not English, certainly not French or German. I must wait to describe it. The hotel buggy met us driven by a white-haired very independent boy who drove the horse as though it were a terribly fierce ramping white dragon – just to impress us, you know. We drove through lanes like great flowery loops with the sea below and huge gulls sailing over – or preening themselves upon the roof tiles, until we came to this hotel which stands in its garden facing the open sea. It could not be a more enchanting position. The hotel is large, 'utterly first-class' – *dreadfully expensive*. It has a glassed-in winter garden for bad weather with long chairs – a verandah – the garden hung between the sun and the sea. Anne had taken for me a really vast room with three windows all south; the sun comes in first thing in the morning until 3 in the afternoon. It is clean as a pin, gay, with a deep armchair, a bed with two mattresses – just across the corridor is a 1st

1. Anne Estelle Rice and her husband.

class bathroom with constant hot water and a lavatory so superb that it and the salle de bains might be part of a sanatorium . . . It's ten o'clock. I am going to bed. My room has all the sea spread before it. Now with the blinds down there floats in the old, old sound, which really makes me very sad. It makes me feel what a blind, dreadful, losing and finding affair our life has been just lately, with how few golden moments, how little little rest. But I am not across the water, and you are coming down for your holiday – *next month*. It is agony to be away from you, but what must be must be. Forgive me if I have been – what was it? I've forgotten. I·find it *so* hard to be ill. But ah, if you knew how I loved you . . .

[*18 May 1918*]

The old woman who looks after me is about 106, nimble and small, with the loveliest *skin* – pink rubbed over cream – and she has blue eyes and white hair and *one tooth*, a sort of family monument to all the 31 departed ones . . .

[*23 May 1918*]

. . . Friday morning in bed. Drey and Anne came last evening and we sat up late talking of Anne's life. She has had a great deal of rich variety and change in her life – far more than I'd known. You know she is an exceptional woman – so gay, so abundant – in full flower just now and really beautiful to watch. She is so healthy and you know when she is happy and working she has great personal 'allure' – physical 'allure'. I love watching her.

It's such strange weather – not warm – with big sighing puffs of wind and the sea a steely glitter. At four o'clock I got up and looked out of window. It was not dark. Oh, so wonderful. I had forgotten such things . . .

[*26 May 1918*]

. . . It's Sunday. Cornwall in black with black thread gloves promenades on the edge of the sea: little tin bells ring and the Mid-day Joint is in the air. Pas de soleil. Low tide and the sea sounds to have got up very late and not found its voice yet.

Damned queer thing. I have dreamed for two nights in succession of the name of a street *Rue Maidoc*. 'Not Rue Medoc,' says Chummie, 'but Rue Maidoc'. There is an exhibition of pictures there and Chummie is showing 3 – 'two landscapes and a portrait by Leslie H. Beauchamp'. We idled down the street afterwards arm in arm. It was very hot. He fanned himself with the catalogue. And he kept saying, 'Look dear,' and then we stopped, as one person, and looked for about 100 years, and then went on again. I woke and heard the sea sounding in the dark, and my little watch raced round and round, and the watch was like a symbol of imbecile existence . . .

There is a circulating library here. Not quite bare. It's got *In a German Pension* and *Eve's Ransom* by Gissing. I took out the second yesterday. Although, like all poor Gissing's books, it's written with cold wet feet under a wet umbrella, I do feel that if his feet had been dry and the umbrella furled, it would have been extremely good. As it is, the woman of the book is quite a little creation. The whole is badly put together, and there is so much which is entirely irrelevant. He's very clumsy, very stiff, and, alas, poor wretch! almost all his 'richness' is eaten up by fogs, catarrh, Gower Street, landladies with a suspicious eye, wet doorsteps, Euston Station. He must have had an infernal time.

I'll send you back D.W.'s[1] *Journal* in a day or two, just in case you have a moment to glance into them – to refresh yourself with the sight of W. sticking peas and D. lying in the orchard with the linnets fluttering round her. Oh, they *did* have a good life.

1. Dorothy Wordsworth's.

Well, I'm going to walk down till [?] lunch. Goodbye, dearest.

[*5 June 1918*]

Last night (this letter is like kalter Aufschnitt, please forgive it) I read *The Well-Beloved* by Thomas Hardy. It really is *appallingly bad, simply rotten* – withered, bony and pretentious. This is very distressing. I thought it was going to be such a find and hugged it home from the library as though I were a girl of fifteen. Of course, I wouldn't say this about it to another human being except you – c'est entendu. The style is so PREPOSTEROUS, too. I've noticed that before in Hardy occasionally – a pretentious, snobbish, schoolmaster vein (Lawrence echoes it), an 'all about Berkeley Square-ishness,' too. And then to think, as he does, that it is the study of a temperament! I hope to God he's ashamed of it now at any rate. You won't like me writing like this about him. But don't you know the feeling? If a man is 'wonderful' you want to fling up your arms and cry 'Oh, do *go on* being wonderful. Don't be less wonderful.' (Which is unreasonable, of course.)

[*6 June 1918*]

. . . I have just eaten a juicy, meaty orange – an orange that *hasn't* riped among soup squares and blotting paper like the ones down here. And they're not only food for the body, they positively *flash* in my room, a pyramid of them, with on either side attending, a jar of the brightest, biggest, vividest marigolds I've ever seen. (Yesterday on m'a fait un cadeau from Mr Palliser's cliff garden of Spanish irises and mari-golds – a boatload full.)

*

Well, yesterday, Anne and I went to Polperro. It's all my I, you know, to go to places like Étaples and so on while these

spots are here. Polperro is *amazing*, a bit spoilt by 'artists'
who have pitched garden-suburb tents in and out among the
lovely little black and white and grey houses – houses that
might have been built *by* seagulls *for* seagulls. But you must
see this yourself. You'll *not* believe it. I didn't, and can't even
now. It was a divine afternoon, foxgloves out everywhere,
AND we found the most SUPERB fresh strawberries.

Anne was a darling yesterday. You can imagine both of us
at finding these – our excitement. We each bought a basket
and had a basket put by for us to bring home *and* arranged
for the carrier (for 2d.) to bring us fresh berries 3 times a
week.

Wig (feverishly) : Will they last till the 20th of this month ?
Strawberry Woman : 'Why, bless eë, they be just a coming on.'

They are grown there in gardens overhanging the sea.
Anne and I took ours and ate them on the cliffs – ate a basket
each ($\frac{1}{2}$ lb., 8d.) and then each ate and drank our propre thé
and became 'quite hysterical,' as she says. We could hardly
move and stayed much longer than we had meant to. The
whole afternoon in my memory is hung with swags of
strawberries. We carried home our second baskets (just
having 'one more occasionally') and talked about raspberries and cherries and plums, and tried not to say too
often 'When Murry comes'.

Looe is much more beautiful than Polperro. Polperro
smells – like those Italian places do, and the people (families
who have been there since the Armada: that's true) are
dark, swarthy, rather slovenly creatures. Looe is brilliantly
clean. But, dearest, it really is, you know, a place to have in
one's inward eye. I saw Hugh W.'s cottage, but went no
furder.

As I wrote that I have kept up a running fire with Mrs
Honey. *She* says I ought to have children. 'It might maäke
eë a deal stronger, and they do be such taking little souls.'
I agreed and asked her to order me a half-dozen. The other
night her husband 'waited' for her outside, and she asked
me to 'come and look at him on the bal-*coney*'. A fine, neat

old man, walking a bit shaky. She said, 'He don't look his age, do eë? He wur a rare *haändsome* lad.' There is still love between those two: that's what attracts me to Mrs Honey.

Oh, don't forget to bring a bathing-suit. The beach here – the beaches, in fact, are perfect for bathing or you can take Pengelly's boat and bathe from that. At any rate, you've got to bathe. I must ask Pagello if I can, too. Otherwise, I will sit on your cricket shirt under my parachute and wave a lily hand at your darling sleek head.

I wonder if you feel how I love you just *here, now* – I wonder if you feel the *quality* of my love for you. I am carrying you with me wherever I go, especially as I lean over and look at the new boat or read the names of the other boats. (There is one, pray tell Johnnie, which is called *The Right Idea*). But they have such lovely names: *Harvest Home, A Ring of Bells*.

Tomorrow fortnight. It will be a real holiday, won't it?

(Don't tell L.M.) I eat marmalade puddings – all kinds of boiled puddings. They are delicious. And these people give me *plenty* of sugar.

[*7 June 1918*]

All the morning a thin fine mist-rain came spinning down and the only people on the *plage* were the sea-gulls. I saw them (when I got out of bed for my cigarettes) standing on the wet lovely sand in rows waiting for the waves that came in, heavy and reluctant and soft like *cream* waves. I never had had such a bird's-eye view of voluptuousness . . . Then Anne came with some berries for me and sat on the bed and smoked and talked about hospitals in New York, and the helpless feeling of the patient and the triumphant sensation of the nurses being a question of ANGLES. The patient being horizontal etc., etc. *Then* I had a hot bath and dressed and went across to East Looe and bought a shady chapeau (Feltie is too hot). The little hand-glass had an emerald bow on it; it looked exactly like a cat. When I heard myself explaining to the girl – 'the hat must appear to be painted on the head – *one* with the head – an ensemble – not a projection as it were' – and saw her Cornish eyes gazing at me – *horrified*, I walked out, feeling very humbled. Everything smells so good – oh, so good – and two men are lying on their backs painting the belly of *The Good Fairy* – they are wearing green overalls and they are painting her bright red. The ferryman says we're in for another three months' spell of fine weather. You will like him. His boat is called the *Annie*. He is particularly handsome and fine – though he has only one eye – and only one good 'arm' and that one ends in a thumbless hand. (He was blown up in that explosion. 'Oh, *yess!*') All the same he don't look in the least mutilated.

It is very warm, now – 'soft', you know – Cornish weather – and the sea is half green, half violet. I had a very large, commodious, tough old mutton chop for lunch while everybody else had a teeny little bean cutlet. This caused horrible bad blood.

Ladies: 'I wish I had thought to apply for *extra* rations. I could have, quaite easily, with may health.' I pretended of course that it was divinely tender – melted in the mouth – and I tried to waft the choppiness of it in their direction.

No post today – not a sign. Mrs Honey promises there shall be one this afternoon. She has confided in the manageress: 'It's in my heart, and I must out with it. I *dearly love* my little fine leddy' ... Oh, if only she could be at the Heron with her 'little maidy' to help her! She's only got one tooth and she's small with these rose cheeks and big soft blue eyes and white hair, but how fond I am of her!

Now the tide is nearly high. I've just been on the balcony. I heard a boat *hooting*. It's a queer little lugger with one orange sail and a tiny funnel. A man has put off from it in a boat – not rowing – standing up and – sort of deep-sea punting along. The lugger is called the *Eliza Mary* and she comes from FY.

People have such funny names here – there's a man called Mutton and another called Crab. You must please take me

into *The Jolly Sailorman* when you come down. It's so lovely
– I *must* see inside.

*

Suggestions for the Trappings of the Elephant[1]
I think front door, windy frames and gate bright green.
A house must be handsome to support blue – and green seems
more in its period. But not a cooked-spinach green – an
'emerald' green.

Kitchen and garden-room and basement generally
WHITE with all the woodwork and dresser a bright BLUE –
what they call *hyacinth* blue, I think. China and glass and
food and fruit look so lovely with these 2 colours. P'raps its
Wedgwood blue. Do you know what I mean?

All the rest of the woodwork in the house is best WHITE,
don't you feel? One can always paint a fireplace with flat
Ripolin if one wants to, later, but I think coloured woodwork,
unless one is going in for an immensely intensive colour
scheme looks patchy. We'd better, I think then, put as it
were, a *white frame to the house* inside. This applies to the
staircase, too.

For the hall and staircase-walls I suggest a good *grey*.
Yellow ties one in the matter of a carpet, and altogether grey
with a purple carpet and *brass stair rods* which give the grey
the 'gilt' it wants, and drawings with a gilt frame or two. *Or*
one could have a blue stair carpet (lovely with grey). Grey
is so kind to you as you come in, don't you think?

With all our furniture in my eye, I really am inclined to
say *grey* again for the huge big two-in-one studio. I don't
know exactly why, but I am a bit 'off' yellow walls. I feel
yellow wants introducing in curtains etc. but one can use
purples, blues, reds and greens with grey, and especially, as
you are so fond of *chintz* – it's the best background for it.
However, if you incline to yellow for the studio – c'est entendu. Again, books are good against grey, and inclined to go a
bit muddy against yellow. Does that seem nonsense?

1. The Murrys' house at Hampstead – 2 Portland Villas.

I'd like my two rooms to be WHITE – quite white. Both of them.

I suggest for L.M. who, of course, must choose for herself, GREEN – the green of my sponge bag. All her bits of Rhodesian fur and everything would be lovely with green – all *tawny* colours – and the washstand set, par exemple. She ought not to have white, I am *sure*. No – stop it. The room faces North. A really *deep* yellow? It's not a big room. But that's for her to say. I'd *still* say green.

Why not have a little delicate flowery paper for your bedroom? If not, I'd have *pink* with white paint, like we had at Acacia Road. Oh, that would be lovely, wouldn't it? With coloured, much-patterned, 'fruity' curtains – and your workroom I'd have a deep cream (with engravings of the poets against it.)

I hope this don't sound dull. But I have, and so have you, a horror of *patchiness*. People are so *patchy*. And I think we must carefully avoid smacks in the eye. A cushion, or a bowl, or a curtain are pleasant little flips, but a door, skirting board and mantelpiece are positive *blows*. I feel that the body of the house enfin ought to be *spring* – real spring – and we'll put all the other seasons in it, in their time. But this [is] absolutely nothing but suggestions. You tell me, dearest, what you feel, and say if you think me a very dull little puppy.

Don't forget the kitchen range is broken.

[*8 June 1918*]

I have had a divine letter from you this morning writ on Thursday night. No, dear love, God knows, my 'blackness' does not come from anything in your letters. Truthfully, I think it comes from my health: it's a part of my illness – just that. I feel 'ill' and I feel a longing, longing for you: for our home, our life, and for a little baby. A very dark, obscure, frightening thing seems to rise up in my soul and *threaten* these desires... that is all. I know this will recur and when it is there I cannot put it away or even say: This is *temporary*,

this is just because of so and so . . . No, again I am enveloped
and powerless to withstand it. So please try and understand
it when it comes . . .

[*9 June 1918*]

I have just been writing about Gus Bofa. Now I want to
write to you. It all feels so different today; it's been raining
and 'tis loövely air, as Mrs Honey says. No sun – rather
cold – the curtains blowing – very, very desolate and far
away from everybody – 11,500 miles[1] away at least . . . Oh,
dear! I wish I were in London (but you'd be angry). I
wish I could have some tea (but you wouldn't let me go into
the kitchen.) In the middle of last night I decided I couldn't
stand – not another day – not another hour – but I have
decided that so often – in France *and* in Looe, and have stood
it. 'So that proves,' as they would say, 'it was a false alarm'.
It doesn't. Each time I have decided that, I've died again.
Talk about a pussy's nine lives: I must have 900. Nearly
every night at 11 o'clock I begin wishing it were 11 a.m. I
walk up and down, look at the bed, look at the writing table,
look in the glass and am frightened of that girl with burning
eyes, think 'Will my candle last until it's light?' and then sit
for a long time *staring* at the carpet – so long that it's only a
fluke that one ever looks up again. And, oh God, this
terrifying idea that one must *die*, and may be *going* to die . . .
the Clovelly Mansions, S. of F. 'writing a few last words'
business . . . This will sound like exaggeration, but it isn't.
If you knew with what feelings I watch the last gleam of
light fade! . . . If I could just stroll into your room, even if
you were asleep and BE with you a moment, 'all would be
well'. But I really have suffered such AGONIES from loneliness and illness combined that I'll never be quite whole
again . . .

1. The distance to New Zealand.

[*10 June 1918*]

. . . There's another telegram come. Oh, now I wish I had delayed this morning's wire until I had your Monday night letter which won't arrive until tomorrow – might if a cherub was about to be wafted me by the afternoon's post – but *im*probably. I am so afraid that you'll take this – my morning wire – as an answer to your Monday night letter. Will you understand that your Monday night letter can't have travelled so fast. One of your chiefest charms is that one never knows *what* you are going to understand . . .

[*16 June 1918*]

. . . This morning when I woke up Mrs Honey was particularly honeycomb. Dear old soul – in her black Sunday dress. She said 'You've not slept. Thäat's bad. I'll see to it that you haäve your coffee right hot.' And she brought me boiling coffee and 'a fried egg with bacon fried for a relish'. When I had done up all my buttons and was having a small sit down she said, looking at me with her kind old eyes, 'Shall I recite you some verses I learned when I was a girl? Will eë haäve *The Death of Moses* or *A Mother's Memories*?' I said I'd have both. Down she sat. Each had, I should think, about 40 verses to it. She never hesitated for a word. She folded her hands and on and on went her soft old voice, telling of the 'crested waves' – telling of 'the lion the King of Beasts' who sat under the mountain where Moses was buried and 'forgot to roar'.

'Yea, from the monster's golden eyes
The golden tears dropped down . . .'

I listened and suddenly I thought of Wordsworth and his 'faith' in these people – and again, Bogey, in spite of everything, I believed in England. Not only in England – in mankind . . .

Journal

Hotels   [*21 June 1918*]

I seem to spend half of my life arriving at strange hotels. And asking if I may go to bed immediately.

'And would you mind filling my hot water bottle? ... Thank you; that is delicious. No, I shan't require anything more.'

The strange door shuts upon the stranger, and then I slip down in the sheets. Waiting for the shadows to come out of the corners and spin their slow, slow web over the Ugliest Wallpaper of All.

Pulmonary Tuberculosis

The man in the room next to mine has the same complaint as I. When I wake in the night I hear him turning. And then he coughs. And I cough. And after a silence I cough. And he coughs again. This goes on for a long time. Until I feel we are like two roosters calling to each other at false dawn. From far-away hidden farms.

*

Remembrance

Always, when I see foxgloves, I think of the Lawrences.

Again I pass in front of their cottage, and in the window – between the daffodil curtains with the green spots – there are the great, sumptuous blooms.

'And how beautiful they are against whitewash!' cry the Lawrences.

As is their custom, when they love anything, they make a sort of Festa. With foxgloves everywhere. And then they sit in the middle of them, like blissful prisoners, dining in an encampment of Indian Braves.

8

London, July 1918–August 1919

Katherine Mansfield returned to London in July 1918, to Murry's rooms at 47 Redcliffe Road where she stayed until the move to 'The Elephant', their house in Hampstead, at the end of August. Despite the advice of specialists who warned that she would only live three or four years if she did not enter a sanatorium K.M. set her face firmly against such a course, which she said would kill her. Murry ('weakly', one is inclined to feel, but she was a formidable woman) acquiesced.

At the beginning of 1919 Murry was offered the editorship of The Athenaeum. *This meant financial security and a more regular outlet for K.M.'s writing. Some of her stories were published there, and for a period of about eighteen months she wrote regular reviews of fiction.*

Journal

[July 1918]

The Eternal Question

I pose myself, yet once more, *my* Eternal Question. What is it that makes the moment of delivery so difficult for me? If I were to sit down – now – and just to write out, plain, some of the stories – all written, all ready, in my mind 'twould take me days. There are so many of them. I sit and *think* them out, and if I overcome my lassitude and *do* take the pen they ought (they are so word perfect) to write themselves. But it's the activity. I haven't a place to write in or on — the chair isn't comfortable – yet even as I complain *this* seems the place and *this* the chair. And don't I want to write them? Lord! Lord! it's my only desire – my one *happy issue*. And only yesterday I was thinking – even my present state of health is a great gain. It makes things so rich, so important, so longed for ... changes one's focus.

*

The Middle of the Note

Whenever I have a conversation about Art which is more or less interesting I begin to wish to God I could destroy all that I have written and start again: it all seems like so many 'false starts'. Musically speaking, it is not – has not been – in the middle of the note – you know what I mean? When, on a cold morning perhaps, you've been playing and it has sounded all right – until suddenly, you *realise* you are warm – you have only just begun to play. Oh, how badly this is expressed! How confused and even ungrammatical!

*

The Redcliffe Road

On these summer evenings the sound of the steps along the street is quite different. They knock-knock-knock along, but lightly and easily, as if they belonged to people who were walking home at their ease, after a procession or a picnic or a day at the sea.

The sky is pale and clear: the silly piano is overcome and reels out waltzes – old waltzes, spinning, drunk with sentiment – gorged with memory.

This is the hour when the poor underfed dog appears, at a run, nosing the dry gutter. He is so thin that his body is like a cage on four wooden pegs. His lean triangle of a head is down, his long straight tail is out, and up and down, up and down he goes, silent and fearfully eager. The street watches him from its creeper-covered balconies, from its open windows – but the fat lady on the ground floor who is no better than she should be comes out, down the steps to the gate, with a bone. His tail, as he waits for her to give it him, bangs against the gate post, like a broom-handle – and the street says she's a fool to go feeding strange dogs. Now she'll never be rid of him.

(What I'd like to convey is that, at this hour, with this half light and the pianos and the open, empty sounding houses, he is the spirit of the street – running up and down, poor dog, when he ought to have been done away with years ago.)

To the Hon. Dorothy Brett

[*20 July 1918*]

I went to see the Naval Photographs today. They are wonderful. And all the middle of the gallery is occupied by a Naval *Band* which, at the first beat carries you far, far out into the open sea, my dear, so that you positively bob up and down in an open boat upon huge immense waves of sound, gasping, breathless, holding on to ropes and trying to bale out your mind with the catalogue before you are swept on again. When I reached the final room I really *did* give way and was floated down the stairs and into the kind air by two Waacs and a Wren who seemed to despise me very much (but couldn't have as much as I did myself). They asked me, when I had drunk after a glass of the most dispassionate water, whether I had *lost* anybody in the Navy – as though it were nothing but a kind of gigantic salt-water laundry –

To Lady Ottoline Morrell

[*21 July 1918*]

Will you pass through London on your way to the sea? If you do – *please* let me know. I long to see you. I was so glad to hear from you yesterday. I wish I were with you now – not on the lawn but sitting under some tree with all the dazzling, silent brightness just beyoud – where we could talk and be alone.

I heard the *infinitely* sad news yesterday that my darling little mother is dead. She was the most exquisite, perfect little being – something between a star and a flower – I simply cannot *bear* the thought that I shall not see her again –

We move to Hampstead on the 25th.

To the Hon. Dorothy Brett

[*14 August 1918*]

I was so glad of your letter today. Yes, it is an *immense* blow. She was the most precious, lovely little being, even so far away, you know, and writing me such long, long letters about the garden and the house and her conversations in bed with Father, and of how she loved sudden, unexpected cups of tea 'out of the air, brought by faithful ravens in aprons' – and letters beginning 'Darling child, it is the most exquisite day' – She *lived* every moment of life more fully and completely than anyone I've ever known – and her gaiety wasn't any less real for being *high courage* – courage to meet anything with.

Ever since I heard of her death my memories of her come flying back into my heart – and there are moments when it's unbearable to receive them. But it has made me realise more fully than ever before that I love *courage* – spirit – poise (do you know what I mean? all these words are too little) more than anything. And I feel inclined to say (not to anybody in particular) 'Let us love each other. Let us be *kind* and rejoice in one another and leave all squabbles and ugliness to the dull dogs who only become articulate when they bark and growl. The world is so dreadful in many ways. Do let us be tender with each other.'

To Lady Ottoline Morrell

[*22 August 1918*]

... *Isn't* David Copperfield adorable? I like even the Dora part, and that friend of Dora's – Julia – somebody, who was 'blighted.' She is such a joy to me. Yes – doesn't Charley D. make our little men smaller than ever – and such *pencil sharpeners* –

Journal

[*1918*]

September 20 My fits of temper are really terrifying. I had one this (Sunday) morning and tore up a page of the book I was reading – and absolutely lost my head. Very significant. When it was over J. came in and stared. 'What is the matter? What have you done?'

'Why?'

'You look *all dark*.' He drew back the curtains and called it an effect of light, but when I came into my studio to dress I saw it was not that. I was a deep earthy colour, *with pinched eyes*. I was *green*. Strangely enough these fits are Lawrence and Frieda over again. I am more like L. than anybody. We are *unthinkably* alike, in fact.

It is a dark, reluctant day. The fire makes a noise like a flag – and there is the familiar sound from below of someone filling buckets. I am very stiff, very unused to writing now, and yet, as I sit here, it's as though my dear one, my ONLY one, came and sat down opposite me and gazed at me across the table. And I think suddenly of the verses which seemed so awfully good in my girlhood.

Others leave me – all things leave me,
You remain.

L.M. in her turban with her one big eye and one little one. Do I love her? Not really. And then, just now, I mounted to J.'s room and opened the door. He was sitting at the table, working. All was in indescribable disorder, and the air was thick with smoke. He held out his hand to me, but it was not my place. Oh no! I came away.

I came away back to my room which really had for me a

touch of fairy. Is there anything better than my room? Anything outside? The kitten says not – but then it's such a hunting ground for the kitten; the sun throws the shape of the window on to the carpet, and in these four little square fields the silly flies wander, ever so spied upon by the little lion under the *sommier* frill . . .

Oh dear – Oh dear – *where* are my people? With whom have I been happiest? With nobody in particular. It has all been much of a mushness.

To Lady Ottoline Morrell

[*October 1918*]

I am lying in my basket with a spiritual flannel round my chaps. Occasionally the Mountain[1] (8000 feet high) swoops over me and says: 'Shall I *steam* it and put the custard *round* or –' and occasionally Murry drops an *Evening News* on to me, as a sort of sign from the great world beyond – I have read *War and Peace* again – and then *War and Peace* again – and then I feel inclined to positively sing to it:

'If You were the Only Book in the World!'

To the Hon. Dorothy Brett

[*27 October 1918*]

Lawrence and Frieda have been in town. Frieda was ill and in bed but I saw a very great deal of Lawrence – For me, at least, the dove brooded over him, too. I loved him. He was just his old, merry, rich self, laughing, describing things, giving you pictures, full of enthusiasm and joy in a future where we become all 'vagabonds' – we simply did not talk about people. We kept to things like nuts and cowslips and fires in woods and his black self *was* not. Oh, there is something so loveable about him and his eagerness, his passionate

1. 'The Mountain' was the name Lady Ottoline gave to Ida Baker.

eagerness for life – that is what one loves so. Now he is gone back to the country.

To Lady Ottoline Morrell

[*4 November 1918*]

I have felt so cut off from the world without a pen. I lay and read *The Egoist*. It seemed to me marvellously good in its way – and I had quite forgotten how much Meredith enjoyed writing. It's delightful how this enjoyment comes through – he shares your laugh, catches your eye, sees the point just as you do. But really a very difficult book for Englishmen to read without *twinging*.

But when I read *Rhoda Fleming*, and that seemed to me so *false*, so preposterous – one could only groan for it – and it's so odious. All this lingering over the idea of a lily white, white as snow jeune fille in the embrace of an ugly, vicious, little old man made me want to cry like Lawrence that 'His sex was all wrong' – But he is a big man, and he *can* write wonders.

These strange, wild evenings shaken with wind and rain have something of Spring in them. One can't help feeling that tomorrow the first green will be there, and perhaps you will meet a little child with a fist of wan daffodils – It does not matter dreadfully that it is not true. If Peace comes I really do feel that the winter will not be real winter, it can't be cold and dark and malignant. A miracle will happen.

But I wish the horrible old knitting women at Versailles would *hurry, hurry* – Do you see that President Wilson is coming to attend the Conference in Person – Already – I fondly dream of – Oh, such a meeting! A sort of glorified Christina Pontifex interview between us. I am afraid I am staying in bed too long!

Lawrence has sent me today a new play of his – very long, just written. I must read it. I have glanced inside and it looks *black* with miners.

Oh, what *shall* I do to celebrate the end of the war?

[*13 November 1918*]

My thoughts *flew* to you immediately the guns sounded.
I opened the window and it really *did* seem – just in those
first few moments that a wonderful change happened – not
in human creatures hearts – no – but in the *air*, there seemed
just for a breath of time – a silence, like the silence that
comes after the last drop of rain has fallen – you know?

It was so wonderful – and I saw that in our garden a
lilac bush had believed in the South wind and was covered in
buds –

Oh, why is the world so ugly – so corrupt and *stupid*? When
I heard the drunks passing the house on Monday night,
singing the good old pre-war drunken rubbish, I felt cold
with horror. *They* are not changed – and then the loathsome
press about Germany's cry for food.

My baby longing for people to 'kiss and be friends' –

How horrid they are *not* to – Why don't they fly at each
other, kiss and cry and share everything. One feels that
about nations – but alas! about individuals, too. Why do
people hide and withdraw and suspect – as they do? I
don't think it is just shyness . . . I used to. I think it is *lack of
heart*: a sort of blight on them which will not let them ever
come to full flower.

And the worst of it is I can't just accept that, calmly,
like M., for instance, and say – 'Very well – Let them go
then.' No *still* I feel full of love – still I desire lovely friends –
and it will always be so, I think. But Life is so short I want
them *here now at once* before Next Christmas – radiant beings
– bursting open my door –

I suppose it's great nonsense.

I have been translating Maxim Gorki's Journal of the
Revolution all last week. I find Gorki wonderfully sympathetic — This journal is dreadful. It makes you feel, *anything
anything* rather than revolution . . .

[*November 1918*]

... These preparations for Festivity are too odious. In addition to my money complex I have a food complex. When I read of the preparations that are being made in all the workhouses throughout the land – when I think of all those toothless old jaws guzzling for the day – and then of all that beautiful youth feeding the fields of France – Life is almost too ignoble to be borne. Truly one must hate human-kind in the mass, hate them as passionately as one loves the few, the very few. Ticklers, squirts, portraits eight times as large as life of Lloyd George and Beatty blazing against the sky – and drunkenness and brawling and destruction. I keep seeing all these horrors, bathing in them again and again (God knows I don't want to) and then my mind fills with the wretched little picture I have of my brother's grave. What is the meaning of it all? ...

[*February 1919*]

... This is a grey, grim, pavement of a day, with slow dropping rain. When the Mountain brought me my early-morning tea this morning she whispered, tenderly: 'Do you think it would be a good idea to change one ton of coal for two of large anthracite? I don't think we require a special permit and even if we do I think it is worth it.' My bed turned into a railway truck, shuffled off to the pit head, and two tons of large anthracite were tumbled on it ... a very lourd paquet to begin the day with ...

To S. S. Koteliansky

[*7 April 1919*]

... I wish you would come in now, this moment, and let us have tea and talk. There is no one here except my cough. It is like a big wild dog who followed me home one day and has taken a most unpleasant fancy to me. If only he would be tame! But he has been this last week wilder than ever. It is raining but it's not winter rain ...

To Virginia Woolf

[*April 1919*]

I have burned to write to you ever since you were here last. The East Wind made my journey in the train an impossibility; it set up ponds and pools in my left lung wherein the Germs and the Toxins – two families I detest – bathed and refreshed themselves and flourished and multiplied. But since then so many miracles have happened that I don't see how one will be able to bear real, full Spring. One is almost tired already – one wants to swoon, like Charles Lamb, before the curtain rises –

*

On April 5th our one daffodil came into flower and our cat, Charlie Chaplin, had a kitten.

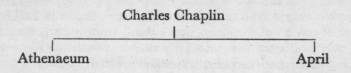

Athenaeum is like a prehistoric lizard, in very little. He emerged very strangely – as though hurtling through space flung by the indignant Lord. I attended the birth. Charles implored me. He behaved so strangely: he became a beautiful, tragic figure with blue-green eyes, terrified and wild. He would only lie still when I stroked his belly and said, 'It's all right, old chap. It's bound to happen to a man sooner or later.' And, in the middle of his pangs, his betrayer, a wretch of a cat with a face like a penny bun and the cat-equivalent of a brown bowler hat, rather rakish over one ear, began to *howl* from outside. 'Fool that I have been!' said Charles, grinding his claws against my sleeve. The second kitten, April, was born during the night, a snug, compact little girl. When she sucks she looks like a small infant saying its prayers and *knowing* that Jesus loves her. They are both loves; their paws inside are very soft, very pink, just like unripe raspberries . . .

Virginia, I have read your article on Modern Novels. You write so *damned* well, so *devilish* well.

But I positively must see you soon. I want to talk over so much – Your room with the too deep windows – I should love to be there now. Last time the rambler roses were nearly over and there was a sound of someone sawing wood.

Journal

[*1919*]

June 10   I have discovered that I cannot burn the candle at one end and write a book with the other.

June 21   Bateson[1] and his love of the louse for its own sake. Pedigree lice. £100 a year from the Royal Institute; a large family – desperately poor: but he never notices. The lives he saved in the Balkan war with shaving and Thymol. Cases reduced from 7000 to 700. No reward, not even an O.B.E. He dissects them, finds their *glands* and so on, keeps them in tiny boxes; they feed on his arm. The louse and the bed-bug.

Hydatids: the Australian who got them: handfuls of immature grapes. They attack the liver. In the human body they reproduce *in*definitely. When they are passed and a sheep is attacked by them, they develop *hooks* and become long worms.

The Egyptian disease: a parasite which attacks the veins and arteries and causes fluxion – constant bleeding. It is another

1. Possibly William Bateson, Professor of Biology at Cambridge.

egg drunk in water. After it has been in man the only thing it can affect is a water-snail. It goes through an entirely new cycle of *being* until it can attack man again.

Dysentery: another parasite.

Hydrophobia: the virus from the dog is taken and a rabbit is infected. That rabbit is used to infect another rabbit: the 2nd a 3rd, and so on, until you get a rabbit who is practically *pure* virus.

The spinal cords are then taken from these rabbits and dried by a vacuum. The result is pounded up fine into an emulsion: 1st rabbit, 2nd rabbit, 3rd rabbit, etc., and the patient is injected progressively till at last he receives a dose which, if he had not been prepared to resist it, would kill him outright. The disease develops very slowly; the treatment is very expensive. Symptoms are a profuse shiny bubbling saliva, and gasping and groaning as in gas-poisoning. No barking, no going on all fours.

In lockjaw the jaw does not lock.

Pasteur was a very dreamer of dreamers. Human beings are a *side-line* to science.

All this I talked over with Sorapure,[1] June 21. His point of view about medicine seems to me *just completely right*. I'd willingly let him take off my head, look inside, and pop it on again, if he thought it might assist future generations. Quite the right man to have at one's dying bedside. He'd get me at any rate so interested in the process – gradual loss of sensitiveness, coldness in the joints, etc. – I'd lie there thinking: this is very valuable to know; I *must* make a note of this.

As he stood at the door talking: 'Nothing is incurable; it's all a question of *time*. What seems so useless today may just be that link which will make all plain to a future generation . . .' I had a sense of the *larger breath*, of the mysterious lives within lives, and the Egyptian parasite beginning its new cycle of being in a watersnail affected me like a *great* work of art. No, that's not what I mean. It made me feel how *perfect* the world is, with its worms and hooks and ova, how

1. K. M.'s favourite doctor.

incredibly perfect. There is the sky and the sea and the shape of a lily, and there is all this other as well. The *balance* how perfect! (*Salut,* Tchehov!) I would not have the one without the other.

*

When the coffee is cold L.M. says: These things have to happen sometimes. And she looks mysterious and important, as if, as a matter of fact, she had known all along that this was cold coffee day.

'The feeling roused by the cause is more important than the cause itself . . .' That is the kind of thing I like to say to myself as I get into the train. And then, as one settles into the corner – 'For example' – or 'Take – for instance . . .' It's a good game for *one.*

To Lady Ottoline Morrell

[*28 June 1919*]

. . . The Brontës – Last night in bed I was reading Emily's poems. There is one:

> I know not how it falls on me
> This summer evening, hushed and lone,
> Yet the faint wind comes soothingly
> With something of an olden tone.
>
> Forgive me if I've shunned so long
> Your gentle greeting, earth and air!
> Yet sorrow withers e'en the strong
> And who can fight against despair!

The first line – why it is so moving? And then the exquisite simplicity of 'Forgive me' . . . I think the Beauty of it is contained in one's certainty that it is not Emily disguised – who writes – it is Emily. Nowadays one of the chief reasons for one's dissatisfaction with modern poetry is one can't be sure that it really does belong to the man who writes it. It *is* so tiring, isn't it, never to leave the Masked Ball – never – never.

The house is full of women, today. The peevish[1] old lying cook in the kitchen who says it is *I* who make all the work. L. M. bringing my lunch with a 'Take, eat, this is my body' air, an old 'un sweeping the stairs away and down in the studio a little dwarf sewing buttons and strings on to M.'s clothes and making immense pale darns in his Hebridean socks...

[July 1919]

... Why these young men should lean and lean over the decomposing vapours of poor Jules Laforgue is inexplicable ... It only makes one feel how one adores English prose, how to be a writer – is *everything*. I *do* believe that the time has come for a 'new word' but I imagine the new word will not be spoken easily. People have never explored the lovely medium of prose. It is a hidden country still – I feel that so profoundly.

To the Hon. Dorothy Brett

[29 July 1919]

... The wind set up such a song in my bones that my dear doctor is once more sticking longer, stronger needles into my behind. Although I walk like the only child of a crab and an Indian colonel I feel it is going to do the trick ...

To Anne Estelle Rice

[13 August 1919]

... My Pa arrives tomorrow and my plans are still rather en

1. It looks as if she has T. S. Eliot's 'Gerontion' in mind in making this comparison with Emily Brontë: 'The woman keeps the kitchen, makes tea, Sneezes at evening, poking the peevish gutter.'

l'air until I have seen him. Why, I don't know. But he seems to me a kind of vast symbolic chapeau out of which I shall draw the little piece of paper that will decide my Fate. But that is absurd. For my plans are to go abroad in about three weeks' time and there to remain. We are on the track of several different places, and not decided yet, but c'est tout...

To Virginia Woolf

[August 1919]

This is the first day I am up again and able to write letters. I have been rather badly ill, and it has left me for the moment without an idea ... except that I must go abroad into a Sanatorium until next April. I can't take a villa or manage anything for the next six months. I must just lie in the air and try and turn into a decent creature. Do not think I am forgetful of you. You would not believe me if you knew how often you are in my *heart* and *mind*. I love thinking of you. I expect Asheham is a glory these days.

I will write again very soon. This is just really a wave. I would I were a crocodile. According to your Sir Thomas Browne it is the only creature who does not *cough*: 'Although we read much of their Tears we find nothing of that motion.' Thrice happy oviparous quadruped!

To S. S. Koteliansky

[21 August 1919]

I have re-read *The Steppe*. What can one say? It is simply one of *the* great stories of the world – a kind of Iliad or Odyssey. I think I will learn this journey by heart. One says of things: they are immortal. One feels about this story not that it *becomes* immortal – it always was. It has no beginning or end. T[chehov] just touched one point with his pen (.———.) and then another point: *enclosed* something which had, as it were, been there for ever.

9
Ospedaletti (Italian Riviera), October 1919–January 1920

Katherine Mansfield's health did not improve and her doctors advised against another English winter. It was decided that she should find somewhere to live on the Mediterranean during the winter months. It seemed essential that Murry should retain his editorship of The Athenaeum, *so the ever-faithful Ida Baker was invited to accompany her, and agreed. They left London on 14 September. Murry travelled with the two women and saw them established at the Casetta Deerholm, a small villa overlooking the sea at Ospedaletti (near San Remo and not far from the French–Italian border) before returning to England. Despite her initial attempts to love the place K.M. was soon suffering from loneliness, fear, depression, and an irritation with her companion that blew up at times into blind hatred.*

The full texts of K.M.'s letters and journals of this period have persuaded some critics to see her as neurotic and self-indulgent. Both her husband and Ida Baker, on the other hand, have excused the violence of her outbursts on the grounds that they were simply a manifestation of her disease.

No doubt her disease contributed; but to 'excuse' her seems unnecessary. To appreciate the extent of her suffering at this time it is necessary first to compare the free active life she had led up to the age of thirty – full of intellectual companionship, gaiety, hard work, emotional entanglements, physical pursuits – with the restricted life of the invalid who could now take only short slow walks with the aid of a stick, who was in a foreign country without any friends but one, on whom she was forced to depend absolutely but with whom she could not share more than a small part of her thoughts and feelings. She lacked books, literary talk, companionship; she felt insecure, uncertain whether her husband still really loved her, and, above all, terrified of death.

This serious deprivation of intellectual and emotional life led naturally enough to dreams, fantasies, depressions, to the enlargement of fears which were in any case valid, preventing her from concentrating on her writing. It was all this and not her disease alone which produced her moments of hysteria; and it seems juster to admire the prodigious efforts she made to be positive than to deplore the times when she failed.

To J. M. Murry

[*8 October 1919*]

. . . It is awfully hot here – as hot as when we came. The insects are *simply awful*. It's a good thing you left before they got really bad. My leg is so swollen I can only hop today. It is maddening because otherwise I feel so well and strong. Curse these confounded countries!! We have double nets, powder, bathe in verbena, oatmeal, milk, salt water, fresh – but nothing cures them. I think they make the idea of a life in this country absolutely insupportable. Enough of them.

I took the revolver into the garden today and practised with it: how to load and unload and fire. It terrifies me, but I feel 'like a new being' now that I really can handle it and understand it. I'll never give it back. They are fascinating things; one is childishly fascinated. I almost understand old Brontë *père*. No more coffee to be had in San Remo. The Government has taken it over as it has the rice. Dear knows when we shall get any more. It doesn't matter really.

Please send me some books to review. I have none for next week.

[*12 October 1919*]

I am sitting in the Bastick chair covered with the Jaeger rug, as although the sun is hot the air is chilly (it's about 4.45 p.m.). It has been a marvellous day here; I've not moved except for meals. I've been reading and writing, and after lunch I fell asleep from the general *shipboard* atmosphere. Speaking of ships, such a small jewel of a sailing ship passed the house today, riding close enough in to see the men on board. She had two small sails at the bows, one big one at the stern, and a medium *very* movable one amidships. The sea is my favourite sea, bright, bright blue, but showing a glint of white as far as one can see. That lift of white seen far away, as far as the horizon, moves me terribly. In fact it is *the very thing* I would like to express in writing: it has *the very quality*. Here comes another most interesting little steamboat – a very small trader, she looks, painted black and red, with a most ridiculous amount of smoke coming out of the funnel. [A drawing of the steamer.] No. I can't draw her.

From where I sit, I cannot see any ground below the balustrade. That is threaded through with sea. One would think it was a sheer drop from there into deep water. What a place, eh, Bogey?

I had a nasty jar last night. As there was no water last week, the laundry was put 'out' and it came home exquisite, covered with a white net with a rose on top, carried by the nicest old body on her head, who seemed to take the greatest fancy to me, as I did to her. *Long* conversation. 'Comme vous êtes bien ici,' etc., etc., etc., etc. And under all this a bill for 37.85!! This, of course, after the old 'un had gone and the rose had been smelled admired and Wig had thought how *much* better, after all, they order these things in Italy. L.M. did not really 'think it very heavy. I don't think you could have expected it to be less, Katie'. This with her over-all 4.50 and an immense white petticoat 3.75! As to serviettes at 1 lira apiece, 'Oh well, my dear, that's not quite sixpence if the exchange is still at 41 for £1. It's about . . . let me see. . . hardly fivepence,' and so on and so on and so on. How I should beat her if I were married to her! It's an awful thought. She thinks I'm made of money. That's the worst of it! On her last but one journey to San Remo she bought *one* hecto of coffee for 4.50 from '*such* a funny little shop' and when I protested she thought 'the parcel was small for the money, but the beans felt very tightly packed'. Could you believe it? However – let her go. And I shall never shoot her because the body would be so difficult to dispose of after. One couldn't make it into a neat parcel or put it under a hearth stone, and she would *never* burn.

Every day I love this house more for some new grace, and every day I hold a minute review of the garden, and there is always something fresh and wonderful. Then there is the wild hill, never the same, *satisfying* one's deep love for what is living and ancient in literature. I look at the hill, dearest Bogey, and because I have not had a classical education, it seems to me full of the spirit of those old boys – the wild fig and olive, the low-growing berries and the tufts of sweet roots . . .

This is a place for lovers. (Hullo! there goes a swallow.) Yes, it is made for lovers. You know, don't you, how even now I am preparing it for you. I look at it and think: I shall put net curtains here – and the baskets under the verandah shall be flower-baskets and –. It's enough to keep me busy until May, my very own. Another Sunday. That's two gone – now there are only 26.

[*15 October 1919*]

. . . It is my illness which has made me so bad-tempered at times. Alas! one can't fight without getting battle-stained, and, alas! there have been so many occasions when I've never had time to wash away the stains or renew myself, but have come to you just as I was. You must forget these *melancholy, melancholy things,* my own precious darling.

A year ago I thought I was going to die, and I think I *was.* And now I know we are going to live. Don't let's forget how Sorapure has helped. I really think I should have just died in that room upstairs if he had not taken me by the hand, like you take a little girl who is frightened of a dog, and led me up to my pain and showed it to me and proved that it wasn't going to eat me. That's what he did.

*

Oh dear, on the wild hill today I found thyme and rose-mary – it reminded me of Bandol in the early morning. Very large astonished daisies are beginning to flower everywhere, even in the gravel. The cotton-pods are huge. Exquisite pale yellow butterflies flutter by. The Marygolds unclosed are.

Goodbye for now. I love you more than ever now I am 31,

[19 October 1919]

The Gardener is here; he arrived at Aurora's heels. thumping his tail. I think he has done wonders but oh – I feel inclined to cry to the garden like I do to you when you've been to the barber: 'Why did you let him take off *so much*? When will it grow again?' My cotton plant has lost its curls – a ruthless chopping of them; the roses that had all started what I thought were the most exquisite promising shoots are cut down to the bone and told to try again. I must plant sweet peas immediately. And he is so *delighted* with his work; his good face beams; he shows me all the stones he has taken out (it sounds like an operation) and there on the path lie the pink geraniums. *O Weh! O Weh!* I feel there's an awful moral to be drawn out of all this – Except ye can bear this to be done unto ye, ye shall not bring forth. At any rate some old Gardener or other has been doing it to us for years, and God knows we've had our naked shivering moments. So now I shall *fill* this garden with flowers. I shall make it to blaze and shine and smell ravishing and look celestially beautiful by the time you come, just to point the moral further.

The wind with light, faint footfalls walks over the sea: the water rings against the shore, like a bell, striking softly.

[20 October 1919]

Oh, Bogey, why are people swindlers? My heart *bleeds* when they swindle me, doesn't yours? This gardener – he promised to come and put the garden in order for 10 francs and bring me some little plants too. It was to be 10 francs a day *with* the plants, and now his wife has come and explained the plants are *10 francs more*. And he only came for half a day yesterday, but she says he spent the other half of the day looking for the plants. So they between them charged me 30 francs. It isn't the money that matters, though I felt ashamed as I gave it to them and could not look at their eyes, – it is that *they are dishonest*. That hurts so! Yes, put the wall round the house. Why will people do such things? I'd rather they turned and beat me.

The sun streams through the folded clouds on to the sea in long beams of light, such beams as you see in picture-books when the Lord appears. It is a silent day except for the sound of his *false* pick as he digs up the little beds. L.M. is in San Remo. I have to hide from this old man now. I wish he'd go. His wife was all in grey, with big black hollow places where her teeth had been and she said *firmly*, 'C'est moi qui viens tous les soirs arroser votre jardin pour vous.' When I said 'No,' her 'C'est bien' was like *steel spittle*.

*

Shall I send this letter? Or write another one – a gay one?

No, you'll understand. There is a little boat, far out, moving along, *inevitable* it looks and *dead silent* – a little black spot, like the spot on a lung.

Don't mind me. I am very foolish and ought to be punished. Even as I wrote that the little boat is far away, there have come out of the sea great gold streamers of light such as I never before saw.

[*28 October 1919*]

About the paper[1] for the 24th. Can I go over it a bit with you? All I say I do say as you know dead sincerely and with all respeck to you who know the difficulties as I cannot and the ins and the outs. I wish the printers would not be so scrimpy, cutting the noses off the words, don't you? Bren, for instance, and Lyn.

1. *The Athenaeum.*

Santy[1] is full of the eyebrow this week. But it's good stuff to publish – awfully.

Your Butler, whatever you may think, is extremely good. The writing of the 1st column is first-chop; it is so free. True, I don't feel you spread your wings as you might have, but then you'd said all you had to say before. I always want you to *go on*, as children say, I always want to say: 'Take your time – please, please don't pull me past the doors. *You* know what's inside and you're the only person who has the key.' But that's this cursed Life which puts those horrible demands on you and makes it impossible. Who wrote What is Bolshevism? It's one of those reviews which begins with a bouquet and then goes on to take the flowers back again – at the very least he hands back a stalk or two – but it's a bad *style* of reviewing I think.

'Our Welsh King' *must* have been by a B.A. My Aunts! 'Henry VII turns out the more we study him to be . . .' I smell a B.A. there. *And* 'traits which *smack* of the Celt'. Take 3d. off *her* cheque for that. (It's a lady?)

I don't think Eliot has in the least justified your generosity in his review of Pound. I quite understand that you *had* to give him the chance, but it's lamentable, all the same, for there is no doubt that Pound is a cheat and a charlatan. It makes Eliot look very silly, too, to be carrying cannonballs for the prestidigitateur.

K.M. is tame, I think, and there is not enough shape in her review. She's not looking at it from above as well as all round it. 1/– off her cheque.

As to the Notes from Ireland – Oh! oh! oh! They begin like Fashion Notes *exactly*. And what about 'Much may be said as to the value of *wide culture* but if the *reading of modern literature* etc.' Back to the taypot, Mrs H.T.S., je vous prie. Also 'when the curtain falls and we come to earth again' – oh!

Sullivan is all right, don't you think, but undistinguished. I always feel he's on the point of choosing *The Idylls of the King*

1. George Santayana.

as his great poem. But it's serious and interesting and the wires are quite well laid, – which is, I think, his part of the job in literature.

Dent gets better and better. Really, the Busoni is *famös*. It's excellent. It is indeed like a fine piece of pianoforte playing by Busoni.

The drama is, of course, nobody's child and it feels it. 'The Tempest' is just like a review of *The Tempest*. 'We left with the firm intention' is rather an awkward ending, isn't it? I *did* smile to find our song in your review. Oh Boge, *do* you think it necessary to put the names of actors in brackets? Good God! it's maddening. (Here I am, exaggerating again!) But I'm sure it's not a good plan – what can Mr Percy Parsons mean in the criticism? I don't think *The Net* ought to have *been* reviewed. After all, *The Athenaeum* goes to the theatre to say what *The Athenaeum* has to say – to look at it very specially *from its own angle*. The critiques – 'The Tempest', for instance, is so like any review of *The Tempest*. You'd never let a book-reviewer say such things as: 'She seemed to have but an imperfect control of her instrument of expression,' for that's been *cliché* for years and years. And the *way* in which *The Net* is seen . . . No, I think the theatre wants a New Broom in it – not necessarily a Hard Broom, but a new one, who *speaks out* with wit and sympathy and gives the impression of a man of some learning who finds himself in the theatre for the first time. (I know what it means to find such a man, tho'.)

If you knew how I have this paper at heart! Turn down anything of mine you don't care for – but I am whacking in this week. I am sending 3 novels under one cover and a review of Stella Benson for you to use when you want to, and the little essay. It's a wonderful paper – wonderful, but too big to be carried by one pair of shoulders. I should be there to share the dog's work and make your personal life very easy and look after you. I shall be there after May. Can you stick it as long as that? In May I shall be well again and on the spot. Save yourself all you can till then but *keep it in mind,*

darling. Won't Bertie[1] write some articles? Or some fabulous
tales – an account of his journey to China and his discussions
with the philosophers he met there? Am I mad?

[*3 November 1919*]

. . . I think your poem is extremely beautiful. So awfully like
you to have him *dead* first. But Hardy beautifully understood,
you say. Please do send me the letter you speak of.

*

Later.   L.M. has just returned with your Thursday letter
with Hardy's letter in it: I am more than glad you sent it me.
It is a treasure. What a strange 'situation': how strange to
acknowledge a poem on one's own death! How great the
character that can so do: how different to us impatient
creatures *craving* for life's fitful fever! Life, life! we cry. And
Hardy writes so quietly as though he were already entering
the quiet harbour, the sails furled, drifting in on a silent
tide. You did very well to send them to him, unaltered. He is
a man who, I am sure, would understand you very deeply.
But after all, he is old, he has lived. He is a very old man.
Perhaps with age, with long years, desire dies.

I can imagine you writing this very letter to a jeune homme
of the next generation, in all its particulars, except your wife
won't have a tomb. She'll have at most a butterfly fanning its
wings on her grave, and then off.

[*8 November 1919*]

. . . As usual I thought I was going to have it all my own way
– get well, be happy, the horror of my disease (it *is* a horror)
over, peace with L.M. and ease to work in. What a fathead
I am! Out of those – I'll get well – and that's all and enough.
Let the others wait. *Work* of course. Work is second breath.
When you spoke of planting a tree of hope, I felt – oh, it was
you to speak so. Plant it – plant it, darling – I will not shake

1. Bertrand Russell.

it. Let me sit under it and look up at it – spread it over me and meet me there often and let us hold each other close and look up into the boughs for buds and flowers. No, there's no God. That is queer. This morning I wanted to say 'God keep you!' or 'Heaven guard us!' Then I thought of *The Gods*, but they are marble statues with broken noses. There is no God or Heaven or help of any kind but Love. Perhaps Love can do everything. 'Lo! I have made of love all my religion.' Who said that? It's marvellous . . .

[*10 November 1919*]

. . . Will you please say if my Dosty[1] is all right? I sent it rather in fear and trembling, but I meant it. I am doing Virginia for this week's novel.[2] I don't like it, Boge. My private opinion is that it is a lie in the soul. The war never has been: that is what its message is. I don't want (G. forbid!) mobilization and the violation of Belgium, but the novel can't just leave the war out. There *must* have been a change of heart. It is really fearful to see the 'settling down' of human beings. I feel in the *profoundest* sense that nothing can ever be the same – that, as artists, we are traitors if we feel otherwise: we have to take it into account and find new expressions, new moulds for our new thoughts and feelings. Is this exaggeration? What *has* been, stands, but Jane Austen could not write *Northanger Abbey* now – or if she did, I'd have none of her.

There is a trifling scene in Virginia's book where a charming young creature in a light fantastic attitude plays the flute: it positively frightens me – to realize this *utter coldness* and indifference. But I will be very careful and do my best to be dignified and sober. Inwardly I despise them all for a set of *cowards*. We have to face our war. They won't. I believe, Bogey, our whole strength depends upon our facing things. I mean facing them without any reservation or restraints.

1. A review by K. M. for *The Athenaeum* of Dostoyevsky's *An Honest Thief: and Other Stories*.
2. *Night and Day* by Virginia Woolf.

I fail because I don't face things. I feel almost that I have been ill so long for that reason: we *fear* for that reason: I mean fear can get through our defences for that reason. We've got to stand by our opinions and risk falling by them.

*

Do you want to know how I am? Yesterday, upstairs in my room I suddenly wanted to give a small jump – I have not given a small jump for two years – you know the kind, a jump-for-joy. I was frightened. I went over to the window and held on to the sill to be safer. Then I went into the middle of the room and *did* jump. And this seemed such a miracle I felt I must tell somebody. There was nobody to tell. So I went over to the mirror – and when I saw my excited face I had to laugh. It was a marvellous experience.

[*12 November 1919*]

... Strange, strange day! My party has just gone – Connie, Jinnie (admirable person) and Papa. They arrived at about 10.30 (I expected them two hours later). But it didn't matter. The Casetta seemed to turn into a doll's house. Pa couldn't even find room for his glasses. The womens' furs and coats and silk wraps and bags were scattered everywhere.

Father suggested a run into San Remo, which we took. I was, I am, just a little corrupted, Bogey darling. That big soft purring motor, the rugs and cushions, the warmth, the delicacy, all the uglies so far away. We 'ran' long past San Remo: it was *thrilling* for me. I didn't dare to speak hardly because it was so wonderful, and people laughing and silly Pa talking Maori down the whistle to the chauffeur. Very silly – but very nice somehow. It carried me away. Then we got out and bought a cake and were, as they say, the cynosure of all eyes, and it was nice, too. I was glad the chemist saw me (see what a snob you married!) and then while Connie and Jinnie were at Morandi's, Pa and I talked and the sun streamed into the car and he said we were like a couple of hot-house plants ripening.

They have just gone. Jinnie left me a pair of *horn* speggle-chiks of her grandfather's (the kind on a long black ribbon which suit me admirably). She took photos of the Casetta, too, and said, 'They'll do to send your husband'. I don't know what happened. They seemed to me so many. Father at the last was wonderfully dear to me. I mean, to be held and kissed and called my precious child was almost too much – to feel someone's arms round me and someone saying, 'Get better, you little wonder. You're your mother over again'. It's not being called a wonder, it's having *love* present, close, warm, to be felt and returned. And then both these women had been desperately homesick for their dogs, so they understood Wing.[1] That was nice too.

Pa did not like this place, neither did they. They were horrified by the cold. Pa said at Menton they have had *none* of this bitter wind, that it has never been cold like today. He seemed to think I had made a great mistake to be in such a thin house and so exposed. So, alas, did they. They said Menton was warm, still, with really exquisite walks, sheltered. I said I'd consider going there in the spring. But I won't. When the bad weather is over, here will be warm too, and I don't want a town. I don't want to uproot. At the same time I was a bit sorry it was so much warmer. I *fed* them and Pa left me five 3 Castles cigarettes!!! He made the running, talking French, telling stories, producing spectacles. (He had four pairs of them. Connie had three, and Jinnie had three.) At one moment they were all trying each other's on – in this little room. It was like a dream. [A drawing of many pairs of spectacles.] And here on the table are five daisies and an orchid that Pa picked for me and tied with a bit of grass and handed me. If I had much to forgive him, I would forgive him much for this little bunch of flowers. What have they to do with it all?

[*13 November 1919*]

. . . I am reviewing Virginia to send tomorrow. It's devilish

1. Wingley – one of the Murrys' cats.

hard. Talk about intellectual snobbery – her book *reeks* of it. (But I can't say so.) You would dislike it. You'd never read it. It's so long and so tāhsōme . . .

[*14 November 1919*]

. . . I am glad you have seen Brett. I feel about Lawrence – that I don't in the least know whether I want to see him or not. I do, and then there sweeps over me an *inscrutable* knowledge of his feeling about *you* – about you and me. He doesn't understand *us* or believe in *us* – and there you are. I can't do with people who don't . . .

[*16 November 1919*]

Such a night! Immense wind and sea and cold. This is certainly no 'pensive citadel'. This morning the storm still rages. It's a blow. I long to go out and have a walk, but I daren't face the wind.

What is this about the novel? Tell me, thou little eye among the blind. (It's easy to see who my bedfellow has been.) But seriously, Bogey, the more I read the more I feel all these novels will not do. After them I'm a swollen sheep looking up who is not fed. And yet I feel one can lay down no rules. It's not in the least a question of material or style or plot. I can only think in terms like 'a change of heart'. I can't imagine how after the war these men can pick up the old threads as though it had never been. Speaking to *you* I'd say we have died and live again. How can that be the same life? It doesn't mean that life is the less precious or that 'the common things of light and day' are gone. They are not gone, they are intensified, they are illumined. Now we know ourselves for what we are. In a way it's a tragic know- ledge: it's as though, even while we live again, we face death. But *through Life*: that's the point. We see death in life as we see death in a flower that is fresh unfolded. Our hymn is to the flower's beauty: we would make that beauty immortal because we *know*. Do you feel like this – or otherwise – or how?

But, of course, you don't imagine I mean by this know-ledge let-us-eat-and-drink-ism. No, I mean 'deserts of vast eternity'. But the difference between you and me is (perhaps I'm wrong) I couldn't tell anybody *bang out* about those deserts: they are my secret. I might write about a boy eating strawberries or a woman combing her hair on a windy morning, and that is the only way I can ever mention them. But they *must* be there. Nothing less will do. They can advance and retreat, curtsey, caper to the most delicate airs they like, but I am bored to Hell by it all. Virginia, *par exemple*.

[*17 November 1919*]

... My review of Virginia haunts me. I *must* improve you know ... But I do wish it were not so cold. Cold frightens me. It is ominous. I breathe it and deep down it's as though a knife softly softly pressed in my bosom and said 'Don't be too sure'. That is the fearful part of having been near death. One knows how easy it is to die. The barriers that are up for everybody else are down for you and you've only to slip through.

But this is depressing. Don't mind it.

[*18 November 1919*]

... Your Friday letter frightens me about my Virginia review. I missed it. Did I? Didn't walk round enough? I hope to God you *won't* publish it if you feel that is true. I'd rather write another, gladly, willingly, than that. What a cursed little creature I am! Beat me! ...

[*20 November 1919*]

It's a very dull day here with wild ragged clouds and a cold halting miserable wind. My black fit is on me – not caused by the day altogether. Christ! to *hate* like I do. It's upon me today. You don't know what hatred is because I know you have never hated anyone – not as you have loved – equally. That's what I do. My deadly deadly enemy has got me today and I'm simply a blind force of hatred. Hate is the *other* passion. It has all the opposite effects of Love. It fills you with death and corruption, it makes you feel hideous, degraded and old, it makes you long to DESTROY. Just as the other is light, so this is darkness. I hate like that – a million times multiplied. It's like being under a curse. When L.M. goes I don't know what I shall do. I can only think of breathing – lying quite still and breathing. Her great fat arms, her tiny blind breasts, her baby mouth, the underlip always wet and a crumb or two or a chocolate stain at the corners – her eyes fixed on me – fixed – waiting for what I may do that she may copy it. Think what you would feel if you had consumption and lived with a deadly enemy! That's one thing I shall grudge Virginia all her days – that she and Leonard were together. We can't be: we've got to wait our six months, but when they are up, I WILL not have L.M. near. I shall rather commit suicide. That is dead earnest. In fact, I have made up my mind that I shall commit suicide if I don't tear her up by the roots then. It would be kinder for us both – for you and for me, of course I mean. We'd have no love otherwise. You'd only slowly grow to think I was first wicked and then mad. You'd be quite right. I'm both with her – mad, really mad, like Lawrence was, only worse. I leaned over the gate today and dreamed she'd died of heart-failure and I heard myself cry out 'Oh, what heaven! what heaven!'

Should I *not* send this? I must. I want you to know so that when the time comes for her to go, you will remember. The worst thing about hate is that it never spends itself – is never exhausted and in this case isn't even shared. So you come up against something which says: 'Hit me, hit me, hate me, hate – feel *strongly* about me – one way or the other, it doesn't matter which way as long as I make you FEEL.' The man who murders from sheer hate is right to murder; he does it in self-defence. Worst of all is that I can't write a book while I live with her – I tried now for two months. It won't go. It's no good.

Does this seem to you just absurd? Can you imagine in the least what it is like? I feel I must let you know even though you wave the knowledge aside or think it is just 'Tig's tearing off at a tangent'. It's not. It is a curse, like the curses in old tales.

[*21 November 1919*]

It happened rather luckily yesterday that L.M. and I reached a crise at tea-time and after that the frightful urgency of our feelings died down a bit. So I'll not say more about it. It ruined yesterday and made me so tired that I felt I could have slept days and nights away.

Here is your letter from Oare about the Waterlows' house. They are lucky, aren't they? Shall we really have such a house? It's not too late? We don't just make up dreams – precious dreams? It's not 'all over'? I get overwhelmed at times that it *is* all over, that we've seen each other for the last time (imagine it!) (No, don't imagine it!) and that these letters will one day be published and people will read something in them, in their queer finality, that 'ought to have told us'. This feeling runs exactly parallel with the other – the feeling of hope. They are two roads, I can't keep to either. Now I find myself on one, now on the other. Even when you tell me about the table I think How perfect! but at the very same moment I think 'Will he sell it? Of course not. He must have a table after all.' It's all part of what I've said before, haven't I? I say it so many thousand times over in my mind that I forget whether I've written it. Once the defences are fallen between you and Death they are not built up again. It needs such a little push, hardly that, just a false step, just not looking, and you are over. Mother, of course, lived in this state for years. Ah, but she lived *surrounded*. She had her husband, her children, her home, her friends, physical presences, darling treasures to be cherished – and I've not one of these things. I have only my work. That might be enough for you in like case – for the fine intelligence capable of detachment. But God! God! I'm *rooted* in life. Even if I hate life, I can't deny it. I spring from it and feed on it. What an egoist the woman is!

And now, love, just supposing by a miracle the blissful thing should happen . . . I don't remember where it was I stayed with the Waterlows. It was near Marlboro' and the country was beautiful. There were forest glades – a beautiful forest. They took me for a walk that was miles too long: I remember that. I remember standing in a rank-smelling field and seeing them far ahead and waving very gaily when they looked round . . .

But the country does not really matter a great deal, does it? As long as it *is* country and one can grow things. (Oh, MAKE it happen!) But the money question is pretty dreadful. As to furniture, that we can always accumulate Eric-or-little-by-little, but I should think an anthracite range costs at least £30 or more – and alterations – we know what they run one into. I think we might do it by not paying down. We overdo the paying down, I believe. Other people never have their money in bags. But first we ought to find the house, take it and then consider. That is my idea. The house (like the Jew) first. (I never understood that text.)

Oh God! When you say we'll have to get a builder in, I suddenly dimly see a hall, a staircase with shavings, a man with a rule and a flat pencil measuring for a cupboard. I hear a saw and the piece of sawn wood creaks and tumbles (such a *final* sound). I hear the squee-quee of a plane, and the back door of the house is open and the smell of the uncared garden – so different to the smell of the cared one – floats through, and I put my hand on your sleeve and rest a little against you, and you say Do you agree? and I nod Yes.

But these dreams are so dear that they feel unearthly – they are dreams of heaven. How could they become reality?

This is reality – bed, medicine bottle, medicine glass marked with tea and table spoons, guiacol tablets, balimanate of zinc. Come, tell me, tell me *exactly* what I am to do to recover my faith. I was always the one who had a kind of overplus of it; you hated it in me; it seemed to deny you so many of your more subtle emotions. You made me feel it was so crude a thing – my belief that couldn't be shaken.

Take this all *coolly*: it's all – what? Just add to my diseases a touch of melancholia, let us say, and REMEMBER how I adore you for so long as I live.

[*24 November 1919*]

I had 8 pages from Father at Toulon, written just before he left. You know how in the old days you used to *wring* my heart in letters – *all* the ghastly things that happened just to you. Father does it! If he manages to secure one egg on a journey, it's a bad egg. He loses things, people cheat him, he goes to an hotel where they won't give him a fire – he 'feeling very shaky' – he peels the bad egg, letting the shells fall into the crown of his hat so as not to make a litter, and the 'juice' spirts out all over the lining that he showed me with such pride the other day when he was here – and so on. Of course, he *has money*, but it makes no difference to him. He falls into absolute *pits* of depression and loneliness and 'wanting Mother'.

Talking about Mother, he told me such a typical little story about her in his letter. It was when they first took The Grange. He was at a board meeting and was called away 'in the thick of it' to the telephone. A voice said: 'It's Mrs Beauchamp of The Grange speaking.' He couldn't make out what was happening and thought she had wanted to ring up the *office* to give 'a wholesale order'. But when she heard his voice, Father said, 'All she said was "Hal dear! I'm at home. I love this house. I simply love it. That's all" and rang off.' Can't you hear that? I can.

[*25 November 1919*]

I don't think S.W. brought it off with George Eliot. He never gets under way. The cart wheels want oiling. I think, too, he is ungenerous. She was a deal more than that. Her English warm ruddy quality is hardly mentioned. She *was* big, even though she was 'heavy' too. But think of some of her pictures of country life – the breadth, the sense of sun lying on warm barns, great warm kitchens at twilight when the men came home from the fields, the feeling of *beasts*, horses and cows, the peculiar passion she has for horses. (When Maggie Tulliver's lover walks with her up and down the lane and asks her to marry, he leads his great red horse, and the beast is foaming – it has been hard ridden and there are dark streaks of sweat on its flanks – the *beast is the man*, one feels *she* feels in some queer inarticulate way.) Oh, I think he ought really to have been more generous. And why drag Hardy in? Just because he (S.W.) was living with you and is, I am sure, like certain females powerfully influenced by the climate of the moment. Perhaps that's unjust. But I feel I must stand up for my SEX.

*

It's raining, a heavy, misty rain – most beautiful. I went out to post in it and, after so long, it was thrilling to hear the fine rain sting the stretched silk of my umbrella, the sudden heavy drops drum on it from the gum trees. All the coast is soft, soft colour: the roses hang heavy: the spiders' webs are hung with family jewels. Aged men in pale blue trousers are sweeping up the dead leaves, and there is a succession of bonfires – puffs of white, fine smoke, with the old figures moving in it, sweeping and bending. The sea is still very full – faint to see – with dreamy lines upon it, and my two little royal birds are back in the garden.

[*26 November 1919*]

... The sea sounds like a big old rake. I was awake more than half the night. At one o'clock I called L.M. and she went down and made some tea. Bogey, in my *home* I shall always have the things for tea in my room, so that in the middle of the night I can brew a cup. Mr Salteena's thrill for tea in bed I feel for tea in the middle of the night. Ten years ago I used to have tea and brown bread and butter every morning at half past two. I don't know why it should be such a gay little feast then. I long for somebody to *laugh* with. I think of such funny little jokes – minute little jokes. Wing would perhaps be the perfect companion of such revels: he *shall* be. I see him stuffing his paw into his mouth or the end of his tail so as not to laugh out loud and wake you ...

[*29 November 1919*]

... I couldn't get to sleep last night. When I shut my eyes *gardens* drifted by – the most incredible sort of tropical gardens with glimpses of palaces through the rich green. Trees I've never seen or imagined – trees like feathers and silver trees and others quite white with huge transparent leaves passed and passed. My heart just fluttered: I scarcely had to breathe at all. It was like a vision brought about by drugs. I couldn't stop it and yet it frightened me; but it was too beautiful to stop. One is almost in a state of coma – very strange. I've often got *near* this condition before, but never like last night. Perhaps if one gives way to it and gives way to it one may even be able to get there ... Oh, I don't know, but it *was* a vision, not a memory. I am going to San Remo today to try to get some tea plates for you. Those two items *don't* hang together ...

[*30 November 1919*]

... You know it's madness to love and live apart. That's
what we do. Last time I came back to France do you remember how we *swore* never again. Then I went to Looe –
and after that we *swore*: never again. Then I came here.
Shall we go on doing this? It isn't a married life at all – not
what I mean by a married life. How I envy Virginia; no
wonder she can write. There is always in her writing a calm
freedom of expression as though she were at peace – her roof
over her, her possessions round her, and her man somewhere
within call. Boge, what have I done that I should have *all*
the handicaps – plus a disease and an enemy – and *why*
should we believe this won't happen again? ...

[*4 December 1919*]

The New Husband

Someone came to me and said
Forget, forget that you've been wed.
Who's your man to leave you be
Ill and cold in a far country?
Who's the husband – who's the stone
Could leave a child like you alone?

[*5 December 1919*]

... Now about your talk at Delamare's on poetry. No, you're
NOT too serious. I think you are a trifle over-anxious to
assure people how serious you are. You antagonize them
sometimes or set them doubting because of your emphasis on
your sincerity. In reviewing again you cry sometimes, in
your sincerity: these are the things which have been done,
which have happened, to *me* or to *us*. I think as a critic that *me*
or *us* is superfluous. If they must be there, then you must
write a poem or a story. People are not *simple* enough –
Life is not simple enough – to bear it otherwise. It fills me

with a queer kind of shame; one hears oneself whispering in
one's soul to you: 'Cover yourself – cover yourself quickly.
Don't let them see!' That they think you are asking for alms,
for pity, doesn't matter. That, of course, is just their corruption – their falsity. Nevertheless, though they are wrong, I do
not think you are right. If you speak for your generation,
speak, but don't say 'I speak for my generation,' for the force
is then gone from your cry. When you know you are a voice
crying in the wilderness, *cry*, but don't say 'I am a voice
crying in the wilderness'. To my thinking (and I am as you
know so infinitely, incomparably nearer the public than you)
the force of either the blow you strike or the praise you want
to sing is *broken* by this – what is it? Is it the most infernal
modesty? Innocence?

[*9 December 1919*]

. . . Swinnerton is very good and L'Hôte excellent. So is
Dent. I must, though, say the Christmas Supplement is bad,
Boge, to my thinking: what do you think? It's simply *rotten*
for trade. You can't make an ad. out of a single review, and
then they are so sloppy. Turner makes me burn in not
mentioning a single book. But the women are simply
squashed flies, though I say it as shouldn't. After all in a
Supplement you're out to *sell* – I don't mean vulgarly –
but you're out to let's say make a point . . . And apart from
that, Rebecca West 2½ columns on a 1/9 book that she dis-
misses – whew! I shuddered at the look of the publisher
turning it over . . . Sylvia Lynd on Crusoe is not only so
wrong in idea that the spirit faints – she writes as though she
were baking a cake. Next year we'll do a Korker. We'll have
an article on what children like and *should have*, and list of
books and poetry books and reprints. The copy all in advance
– a dummy ready to be taken round for the ads . . .

[*13 December 1919*]

... G.B.S[haw] on Butler is very fine indeed. He has such a grip of his subject. I admire his tenacity as a reviewer and the way in which his mind follows Butler with a steady light – does not waver over him, find him, lose him, travel over him. At the same time it's queer he should be (G.B.S.) so uninspired. There is not the faintest hint of inspiration in that man. This chills me. You know the feeling that a great writer gives you: 'My spirit has been fed and refreshed: it has partaken of something new.' One could not possibly feel that about Shaw. It's the clang of the gate that remains with you when all's over. What it amounts to is that Shaw is anything you like, but he's not an artist. Don't you get when you read his plays a sense of extraordinary *flatness*? They may be extremely amusing at moments, but you are always laughing *at* and never *with*. Just the same in his prose: You may agree as much as you like, but he is writing *at* not *with*. There's no getting over it: he's a kind of concierge in the house of literature – sits in a glass case, sees everything, knows everything, examines the letters, *cleans the stairs*, but has no part, no part in the life that is going on. But as I wrote that, I thought: Yes, but who *is* living there, living there as we mean life? Dostoevsky, Tchehov and Tolstoy. I can't think of *anybody else*.

Oh God! What wouldn't I give for a TALK. Well, it can't happen.

Journal

[*15 December 1919*]

All these two years I have been obsessed by the fear of death. This grew and grew and grew *gigantic*, and this it was that made me cling so, I think. Ten days ago it went, I care no more. It leaves me perfectly cold.

*

I must put down here a dream. The first night I was in bed here, i.e. after my first day in bed, I went to sleep. And suddenly I felt my whole body *breaking up*. It broke up with a violent shock – an earthquake – and it broke like glass. A long terrible shiver, you understand – and the spinal cord and the bones and every bit and particle quaking. It sounded in my ears – a low, confused din, and there was a sense of flashing greenish brilliance, like broken glass. When I woke up I thought there had been a violent earthquake. But all was still. It slowly dawned upon me – the conviction that in that dream I died. I shall go on living now – it may be for months, or for weeks or days or hours. Time is not. In that dream I died. The *spirit* that is the enemy of death and quakes so and is so tenacious was shaken out of me. I am (December 15, 1919) a dead woman, and *I don't care*. It might comfort others to know that one gives up caring; but they'd not believe any more than I did until it happened. And, oh, how strong was its hold upon me! How I *adored* life and *dreaded* death!

I'd like to write my books and spend some happy time with Jack (not very much faith withal) and see Lawrence in a sunny place and pick violets – all kinds of flowers. Oh, I'd like to do heaps of things, really. But I don't mind if I do not do them.

*

December It often happens to me now that when I lie down to sleep at night, instead of getting drowsy, I get wakeful and, lying here in bed, I begin to *live* over either scenes from real life or imaginary scenes. It's not too much to say they are almost hallucinations: they are marvellously vivid. I lie on my right side and put my left hand up to my forehead as though I were praying. This seems to *induce* the state. Then, for instance, it is 10.30 p.m. on a big liner in mid-ocean ... People are beginning to leave the Ladies' Cabin. Father puts his head in and asks if 'one of you women care for a walk before you turn in. It's glorious up on deck.' That begins it. I am *there*. Details: Father rubbing his gloves, the cold air – the *night* air rather – he brings to the door, the patterns of everything, the feel of the brass stair-rail and the rubber stairs. Then the deck – the pause while the cigar is lighted, the look of all in the moonlight, the *steadying* hum of the ship, the first officer on the deck, so far aloft the bells, the steward going into the smoking-room with a tray, stepping over the high, brass-bound step . . . All these things are far realer, more in detail, *richer* than life. And I believe I could go on until . . . There's *no end* to it.

I can do this about everything. Only there are no personalities. Neither am I there personally. People are only part of the silence, *not* of the pattern – vastly different from that – part of the *scheme*. I could always do this to a certain extent; but it's only since I was really ill that this – shall we call it? – 'consolation prize' has been given to me. My God! it's a marvellous thing.

*

'Any children?' he asked, taking out his stethoscope, as I struggled with my nightgown.
'No – no children.'
But what would he have said if I had told him that until a few days ago I had had a little child, aged five and three-quarters – of undetermined sex. Some days it was a boy. For two years now it had very often been a little girl.

In December Murry, shocked by some verses K.M. had written (see 4 December above), came to visit her at Ospedaletti. He stayed for three weeks, leaving early in January.

Journal

[*1919–20*]

December 29 Catherine brought maid. Jack returned exhausted from San Remo. Bathed his head. In the afternoon played demon. Jack was furious at my lack of sympathy. He was dying, Egypt, dying. But he could laugh heartily at the Smallwood family. 'That's first chop!'

December 30 Calm day. In garden. Read early poems in Oxford Book. Discussed our future library. In the evening read Dostoevsky. In the morning discussed the importance of 'eternal life'. Played our famous Stone Game (Cape Sixpence and Cornwall).[1] But something is wrong.

December 31 Long talk over house. Foster said I could walk. Sea sounded like an island sea. Happy. Lovely fire in my bedroom. Succès éclatant avec demon before dinner. Listened to Wingley's fiddle. The wooden bed.

January 1 Jack prepares to go. Drying figs on the stove, and white socks drying from the mantelpiece. A dish of oranges and rain-wet leaves – a pack of cards on the table. It rains but it is warm. The jonquil is in bud. We linger at the door. L.M. sings.

January 2 Jack left for London. The house very empty and quiet. I was ill all day – exhausted. In the afternoon fell asleep over my work and missed the post. My heart won't lie down. No post. During the night the cat picture became terrifying.

January 3 A load of wood. Sent review. Cold day. Miss K.S. called – deadly dull. Her yawn and recovery. Storm of wind and rain. I had nightmare about Jack. He and I 'separated'. Miss K.S. talked about tulips, but she makes all sound so *fussy*: the threads of her soul all ravelled.

January 4 Cold, wet, windy, terrible weather. Fought it all day. Horribly depressed. Dickinson came to tea; but it was no good. Worked. Two wires from J. According to promise. I cannot write. The jonquils are out, weak and pale. Black clouds pull over.

1. A stone was placed at the edge of a cliff and smaller stones thrown at it. The one who knocked it off received sixpence from the other. Hence the name 'Cape Sixpence', which they had given to the cliff near Bandol where they first played the game.

Immediately the sun goes in I am overcome – again the black fit takes me. I *hate* the sea. There is naught to do but WORK. But how can I work when this awful weakness makes even the pen like a walking-stick?

January 5 Henry IV. Nuit blanche. Decided at 3 a.m. that D. was a homicidal maniac. *Certain* of this. Started my story, *Late Spring*. A cold bitter day. Worked on Tchechov all day and then at my story till 11 p.m. Anna came. We talked about her to her face in English. No letters. Post office strike. Anna's bow and velvet blouse.

January 6 Winter's Tale. Black day. Dark, no sky to be seen; a livid sea; a noise of boiling in the air. Dreamed the cats died of *anti-pneumonia*. Heart attack 8 a.m. Awful day. No relief for a moment. Couldn't work. At night changed the position of my bed, but it was no good: I did not sleep. At five o'clock I thought I was at sea tossing – for ever. N.B.

January 7 On the verandah. I don't want a God to praise or to entreat, but to *share* my vision with. This afternoon looking at the primula after the rain. I want no one to 'dance and wave their arms'. I only want to *feel* they see, too. But Jack won't. Sitting out there in the sun – where is my *mate*? *He* wants neither external life *nor* depression?!!!

January 8 BLACK. A day spent in Hell. Unable to do anything. Took brandy. Determined not to weep – wept. Sense of isolation frightful. I shall die if I don't escape. Nauseated, faint, cold with misery. Oh, I *must* survive it somehow. Wrote to Jinnie.

January 9 BLACK. Another of them. In the afternoon Foster came and agreed that I must leave here. I somehow or other wrote a column. Broke my watch glass. In the evening L.M. and I were more nearly friendly than we have been for years. I couldn't rest or sleep. The roaring of the sea was insufferable. Posted to Jinnie.

January 10   Father's marriage: news from Marie. Spent the evening writing another column. Help me, God! And then L.M. came in to say I was half-an-hour slow. Just did it in time. Had talk with L.M. Our friendship is returning – in the old fashion. Thought out *The Exile*.[1] Appalling night of misery, deciding that J. had no more need of our love.

January 11   Worked from 9.30 a.m. till a quarter after midnight only stopping to eat. Finished the story. Lay awake then until 5.30 too excited to sleep. In the sea drowned souls sang all night. I thought of everything in my life, and it all came back so vividly – all is connected with this feeling that J. and I are no longer as we were. I love him but he rejects my *living* love. This is anguish. These are the worst days of my whole life.

January 12   Posted the story and a telegram. Very tired. The sea howled and boomed and roared away. When will this cup pass from me? Oh, misery! I cannot sleep. I lie *retracing* my steps – going over all the old life before . . . The baby of Garnet Trowell.[2]

January 13   Bad day. A curious smoky effect over the coast. I crawled and crept about the garden in the afternoon. I feel terribly weak and all the time on the verge of breaking down. Tried to work; could not work. At six o'clock went back to bed. Had a dreadful nightmare. Wrote Jack and Marie.

January 14   Foster came: says my lung is remarkably better, but must rest absolutely for two months and not attempt to walk at all. I have got a 'bigger chance'. Bell rang at night. My eye pains me. *Cannot* get a move on.

1. Later called 'The Man Without a Temperament'.
2. Garnet Trowell was the young New Zealand musician by whom she had become pregnant in 1909. The pregnancy miscarried while she was living in Bavaria.

Dreamed about Banks. She gave me her baby to look after.
Heard from Jinnie.

January 15   Sat in my room watching the day change to
evening. The fire like a golden stag. *Thinking of the past*
always; dreaming it over. The cotton plant has turned
yellow. Tonight the sea is *douce*. P.O. strike. No, no letters.

10

Menton (French Riviera), January–April
1920; Hampstead, May–July

*On 21 January, 1920 Katherine Mansfield 'escaped' (as she put it)
from Ospedaletti to Menton on the French side of the border. There
she lived until the spring, cared for by her father's cousin, Miss
Connie Beauchamp, and Connie's friend Miss Jinnie Fullerton,
whose villa (the Villa Flora) she moved in to on 15 February.
Murry has recorded that the letters she wrote during this period seem
to him 'less spontaneous, more "artificial"' than any of her others – and
I find my own selection bears him out. Few of the letters from this
first stay in Menton can be considered among her best. Murry's
explanation for this artificial quality is that K.M. was in a false
position at the Villa Flora, living a life of luxury which she enjoyed
but which warred with her artistic desire for simplicity, and under
some pressure from the ladies, both of whom were devout Catholics,
to become a Catholic herself.*

*Murry's explanation, it seems to me, is inadequate. Neither he,
nor K.M.'s biographer, Anthony Alpers, has sufficiently understood
the extent of her suffering at Ospedaletti. It was from this suffering
that she must have hoped Murry would rescue her – either by giving
up his editorship and staying with her (as he did later), or simply by
taking command and insisting that she come home with him. Instead, Murry made her feel that the weight of her problems added
to those of his work as an editor was more than he could cope with – as
no doubt it was. It was nothing less than the spectre of death she was
facing, and with Murry's departure in January she was left facing
it alone. From the horror of that confrontation she fled into the com-
forting arms of Connie and Jinnie, exercising, as a protective
device, her considerable chameleon powers to take on the colour of
the establishment she was entering.*

This accounts for the falseness that enters her letters once the pressure of standing virtually alone was lifted. In Menton during these months she subsides. The experience at Ospedaletti had been too extreme – it had been destructive – and it is not surprising that her personality took some months to recover.

To J. M. Murry

[*21 January 1920*]

. . . I have escaped. Do you know what that means? There has been a postal strike in Italy. No letters, no wires. Nothing came through it for me – a strike of the railways, and now from today a strike of automobiles. We just got through by taking a roundabout route and escaping the police . . .

I have got away from that hell of isolation, from the awful singing at night, from the loneliness and fright. To tell you the truth, I think I have been *mad*, but really, medically mad. A great awful cloud has been on me . . . It's nearly killed me. Yes. When Jinnie took me in her arms today she cried as well as I. I felt as though I'd been through some awful deathly strain, and just survived – been rescued from drowning or something like that. You can't understand, it's not possible you should, what that isolation was when you left again and I again was ill . . .

If I don't get well here, I'll never get well. Here – after the journey – was this room waiting for me – exquisite, large, with four windows, overlooking great gardens and mountains, wonderful flowers – tea with *toast* and honey and butter – a charming maid – and these two dear sweet women to welcome me with papers, books, etc. This is really a superb place in every way. Two doctors live here . . . The cleanliness is almost supernatural. One feels like a butterfly. One only wants to fan one's wings, on the couch, the chairs. I have a big writing table with a cut-glass inkstand, a waste-paper basket, a great bowl of violets and *your* own anemones and wall-flowers in it. The directress is a very nice Frenchwoman only too anxious to look after me and see that there is no change in anything . . . There is also a sort of Swiss nurse in white who has just been in and says she answers the bell at night. She is so good to look at that I shall have to ring.

I've got away from under that ghastly cloud. All is absolutely changed. I'm here with people, with care. I feel a different creature *really* – different eyes, different hair. The garden is gorgeous. There is a big shelter, chauffèd. What do you think of that?

[*9 February 1920*]

. . . I want to mention something else. Lawrence sent me a letter today. He spat in my face and threw filth at me and said: 'I loathe you. You revolt me stewing in your consumption . . . The Italians were quite right to have nothing to do with you' and a great deal more. Now I do beseech you, if you are my man, to stop defending him after that and never to crack him up in the paper. *Be proud!* In the same letter he said his final opinion of you was that you were 'a dirty little worm'. Well, *be proud*. Don't forgive him for that please . . .

Journal

[*February 1920*]

'But how could you say that about the Blessed Virgin!' said she. 'It must have hurt Our Lady so terribly.'

And I saw the B.V. throwing away her copy of *Je ne parle pas Français* and saying: 'Really, this K.M. is all that her friends say of her to me.'

*

And yet one has these 'glimpses', before which all that one ever has written (what has one written?) – all (yes, all) that one ever has read, pales . . . The waves, as I drove home this afternoon, and the high foam, how it was suspended in the air before it fell . . . What is it that happens in that moment of suspension? It is timeless. In that moment (what *do* I mean?) the whole life of the soul is contained. One is flung up – out of life – one is 'held', and then – down, bright, broken, glittering on to the rocks, tossed back, part of the ebb and flow.

I don't want to be sentimental. But while one hangs, suspended in the air, held, – while I watched the spray, I was conscious *for* life of the white sky with a web of torn grey over it; of the slipping, sliding, slithering sea; of the dark woods blotted against the cape; of the flowers on the tree I was passing; and more – of a huge cavern where my selves (who were like ancient sea-weed gatherers) mumbled, indifferent and intimate . . . and this other self apart in the carriage, grasping the cold knob of her umbrella, thinking of a ship, of ropes stiffened with white paint and the wet, flapping oilskins of sailors . . . Shall one ever be at peace with oneself? Ever quiet and uninterrupted – without pain – with the one whom one loves under the same roof? Is it too much to ask?

February 29 Oh, to be a *writer*, a real writer given up to it and to it alone! Oh, I failed today; I turned back, looked over my shoulder, and immediately it happened, I felt as though I too were struck down. The day turned cold and dark on the instant. It seemed to belong to summer twilight in London, to the clang of the gates as they close the garden, to the deep light painting the high houses, to the smell of leaves and dust, to the lamp-light, to that stirring of the senses, to the langour of twilight, the breath of it on one's cheek, to all those things which (I feel today) are gone from me for ever . . . I feel today that I shall die soon and suddenly: but not of my lungs.

There are moments when Dickens is possessed by this power of writing: he is carried away. That is bliss. It certainly is not shared by writers today. For instance, the death of Cheedle: dawn falling upon the edge of night. One realizes exactly the mood of the writer and how he wrote, as it were for himself, but it was not his will. He *was* the falling dawn, and he *was* the physician going to Bar. And again when . . .

To J. M. Murry

[7 April 1920]

. . . I have [been] steeped in Shakespeare these last days with a note book – looking up every word, finding what are inkles and caddises – and I have felt that we must read more – you and I – read together. I nearly know the sheep shearing scene from *A Winter's Tale* by heart. It's the more *bewitching* scene – but that's one of my favourite plays. If I am strictly truthful I know nearly all of it *almost* by heart. And I began reading the songs in *Twelfth Night* in bed this morning early –

> Mark it Cesario, it is old and plain;
> The spinsters and the knitters in the sun
> And the free maids that weave their thread with bones
> Do use to chant it: it is silly sooth,
> And dallies with the innocence of love,
> Like the old age . . .

Clo: Are you ready, sir?
Duke: Ay, prithee, sing.   (*Music*)
Clo: Come away, come away, death, etc.

Oh, how that does all ravish me.

To Richard Murry

[April 1920]

. . . I am all for feathery-topped carrots – don't you love pulling up carrots, shaking them clean and tossing them on to a heap! And feeling the cauliflowers to see which one is ready to cut. Then OUT comes your knife. When I was about the height of a garden spade I spent weeks – months – watching a man do all these things and wandering through canes of yellow butter beans and smelling the spotted speckled broad bean flowers and helping to plant Giant Edwards and White Elephants. Oh, dear, I do love gardens! Think of little lettuces and washing radishes under the garden tap. I'd better stop. I just saw you climb into a cherry tree, and leaning against the trunk of the tree I saw and smelt the sweet sticky gum . . .

To J. M. Murry

[15 April 1920]

. . . I envy you 'madly' going to see *Cymbeline*. If you knew how full my mind is of Shakespeare! It's a perfect world – his pastoral world. I roam through the Forest of Arden and sit on the spiced Indian sands laughing with Titania. When we *do* get a small quiet moment – *what* talks! But you are going to Stratford-on-Avon. Lucky, lucky boy! And you won't remember for a moment that was the first English country your wife saw, and she used to walk about there with her hair down her back, wearing a pinky-grey hat and even in those days carrying one of those small green Shakespeares (but of course, it was Amleto, then.) . . .

[24 April 1920]

. . . Oh, how I agree about Shylock! I think *The Taming of the Shrew* is so *deadly* too. I am certain Bill never wrote it: he bolstered up certain speeches, but that is all. It's a hateful, silly play, so badly constructed and arranged. I'd never go to see it. I think we shall have a Shakespeare festival one year at Broomies – get actors there to study their parts – act out of doors – a small festa – a real one. I'll be stage director. *I am dead serious about this* . . .

Really, it's grilling hot today! I feel inclined to make a noise like a cicada . . .

Journal

[*April 1920*]

When autograph albums were the fashion – sumptuous volumes bound in soft leather, and pages so delicately tinted that each tender sentiment had its own sunset sky to faint, to die upon – the popularity of that most sly, ambiguous, difficult piece of advice: 'To thine own self be true' was the despair of collectors. How dull it was, how boring, to have the same thing written six times over! And then, even if it was Shakespeare, that didn't prevent it – oh, *l'âge d'innocence!* – from being dreadfully obvious. Of course, it followed as the night the day that if one was true to oneself ... True to oneself! which self? Which of my many – well really, that's what it looks like coming to – hundreds of selves? For what with complexes and repressions and reactions and vibrations and reflections, there are moments when I feel I am nothing but the small clerk of some hotel without a proprietor, who has all his work cut out to enter the names and hand the keys to the wilful guests.

Nevertheless, there are signs that we are intent as never before on trying to puzzle out, to live by, our own particular self. *Der Mensch muss frei sein* – free, disentangled, single. Is it not possible that the rage for confession, autobiography, especially for memories of earliest childhood, is explained by our persistent yet mysterious belief in a self which is continuous and permanent; which, untouched by all we acquire and all we shed, pushes a green spear through the dead leaves and through the mould, thrusts a scaled bud through years of darkness until, one day, the light discovers it and shakes the flower free and – we are alive – we are flowering for our moment upon the earth? This is the moment which, after all, we live for – the moment of direct feeling when we are most ourselves and least personal.

*

At the end of April K.M. returned to London to the Murrys' house in Hampstead.

To the Hon. Dorothy Brett

[*20 May 1920*]

The STOVE is come, installed, burning, giving out the most blessed beneficent heat imaginable! I *cannot* tell you how good it is to be in this room – in a whole warm room with no smoke, no making up fires, just a silent, discreet, never-failing heat. If I were a savage I should pray to it and offer it the bodies of infants. Thank you a billion times for your dear thought. And now a belated thank you for the yellow roses – which are perfection. Now stop being generous, or I'll have to lead a baby elephant washed in rose soap, hung with lily buds and marigolds, carrying a flamingo in a cage made of mutton-fat jade on its back, to your doorstep as a return for past favours.

To Sydney and Violet Schiff

[*May 1920*]

Yesterday I drove down to the city to my Bank. It is almost terrifying to see such blank strained faces – moving in the fog. I drove to the office of the Athenaeum and thought there at least there would be men I knew who responded who . . . were alive and cared about life and the paper and work and – the untidiness of John's desk (laugh, Violet dear!) was my first crushing blow. There was over all the office a smell of stone and dust. Unthinkable disorder and ugliness. Old Massingham like a cat dipped in dough slinking in the doorway and asking whether the French were furious with 'George'[1] – Huxley[2] wavering like a candle who expected to go out with the next open door, poor silly old men with pins

1. Lloyd George.
2. Aldous Huxley.

in their coat lapels, Tomlinson harking back to the mud in
Flanders, Sullivan and E. M. Forster very vague, very
frightened. I heard myself speaking of lemon trees and then
I said that in one valley I knew there was a torrent.[1] Nobody
cared, nobody wanted to know. I ran downstairs back into the
car with Murry (we were going to buy a coffee pot because it
was the anniversary of our wedding). He was sure the shop
would be shut because I'd talked instead of coming away so he
looked out of his window and I looked out of mine and I
listened to that lovely swift rushing sound and remembered
how blue the lavender was the day we sat in that part of the
garden.

[*May 1920*]

. . . Last week here I hadn't time to write a word; this week is
already covered, covered under manuscripts to read,
poems, essays to choose 'finally'; novels to review, schemes to
draft, an article to write on '*why we intend to publish short
stories*', and then there's a special smashing review to be
written for the *Nation* . . . I shall get these things into order
presently; I'll find their each his separate place. Last week –
really – it was like having Murry a wistful shepherd leading
his troup of sheep into the room and I was ill and in dreadful
pain, physical and mental pain, that could not be spoken of.

*

Here's a small letter I had from [T.S.] Eliot. He and
Murry meet very often. I have asked the Eliots here for
Thursday or Friday evening. What will they be like I
wonder? The grey door of my room keeps on opening and
opening in my mind and Mrs Eliot and Eliot enter. I can't
see her at all.

1. She is evidently referring to places around Menton and Roquebrune
(where the Schiffs' villa was).

[*July 1920*]

I have had your note; I have had your postcard and am wondering every day if you are home. The Eliots have dined with us tonight. They are just gone. John has gone downstairs to see them off.

I am so fond of Eliot and as he talked of you both tonight I felt a deep sympathy with him.

11

Menton with Ida Baker,
September–December 1920

Katherine Mansfield's health did not improve, and with the approach of autumn she had to think once again about travelling south to avoid the English winter. She arranged to take the Villa Isola Bella in Menton, and set out, once more accompanied by Ida Baker, in mid-September 1920.

Isola Bella was a small two-storeyed villa at Garavan between Menton and the French–Italian border, with upper balconies and lower terrace looking south over the sea, and the grey-orange rock-faces of the Alpes Maritimes rising behind it. There was a pleasant garden, and under the terrace, opening on to lower ground, an extra room which the town of Menton has since acquired as a Mansfield memorial.

By October K.M. was established and writing, keeping up her reviews of fiction for The Athenaeum, *and writing new stories – among them 'The Young Girl', 'Poison', 'Miss Brill', 'The Life of Ma Parker', and, most notably, 'The Daughters of the Late Colonel'.*

Journal

[*September 1920*]

Isola Bella: How shall I buy it?

Southward Bound

Lying facing the window I woke early. The blind was half pulled down. A deep pink light flew in the sky, and the shapes of the trees, ancient barns, towers, walls were all black. The pools and rivers were quicksilver. Nearing Avignon, the orchard in the first rays of sunlight shone with gold fruit: apples flashed like stars.

L.M.'s legs dangled. She dropped down, slowly waving her big grey legs, as though something pulled her, dragged her – the tangle of rich blue weeds on the red carpet.

'A-vig . . . Avig . . . Avig-non,' she said.

'One of the loveliest names in the world done to death,' said I. 'A name that spans the ancient town like a delicate bridge.'

She was very impressed. But then George Moore *would* impress her.

*

Breakfast Time

It grew hot. Everywhere the light quivered green-gold. The white soft road unrolled, with plane-trees casting a trembling shade. There were piles of pumpkins and gourds: outside the house the tomatoes were spread in the sun. Blue flowers and red flowers and tufts of deep purple flared in the road-side hedges. A young boy, carrying a branch, stumbled across a yellow field, followed by a brown high-stepping little goat. We bought figs for breakfast, immense thin-skinned ones. They broke in one's fingers and tasted of wine and honey. Why is the northern fig such a chaste fair-haired virgin, such a *soprano*? The melting contraltos sing through the ages.

England and France

The great difference: England so rich, with the green bowers of the hops and gay women and children with their arms lifted, pausing to watch the train. A flock of yellow hens, led by a red rooster, streamed across the edge of the field. But France: an old man in a white blouse was cutting a field of small clover with an old-fashioned half-wooden scythe. The tops of the flowers were burnt; the stooks (are they stooks?) were like small heaps of half-burned tobacco.

En Voyage

Four little boys, one minute, three larking. When the three

ran on to the lines and tried to dash themselves to death, the
little one obviously suffered tortures and did his best to drag
them back again. I realized this would have been just the
same if it had been deep water.

An old man, an old woman, and a tiny boy in a cape. When
the old woman disappeared, the ancient took the little boy
with such tender care. He had a little pipe in his beard. It
looked as though his beard were curling.

Poplars springing in green water – red willows.

To J. M. Murry

[*15 September 1920*]

. . . I think I've got a maid, too, Mme. Reveilly, 5bis. Rue
des Poilus. She's a police inspector's *sister* and she looks
indeed as though she had sprung out of a nest of comic
policemen. Fat, dark, sitting on the sofa edge, grasping,
strangling indeed a small black bead bag. 'Si vous cherchez
une personne de confiance Madame et *pas une imbécile* . . .' she
began. I felt that was a poor compliment to my appearance.
Did I look like a person who wantonly cherched imbeciles to
do the house work? But of course all the time she recounted
her virtues I saw the most charming imbecile with woolly
shoes like rabbits and a great broad beaming smile . . . which
I couldn't help dismissing rather regretfully.

*

I've begun my journal book. I want to offer it to Methuen
– to be ready this Xmas. Do you think that's too long to
wait? It ought to be rather special. *Dead* true – and by dead
true I mean like one takes a sounding – (yet gay withal). Oh,
it's hard to describe. What do you advise? . . .

[*18 September 1920*]

I'm longing to see your 'Wilde-Harris'. I am sure O.W.

was negligible but he *is* an astonishing figure. His letters, his mockeries and thefts – he's a Judas who betrays himself.

... Which is the more tragic figure – the master without a disciple or the disciple without a master? ... That's by the way. Can I have the *Times Lit. Sup.*? I freeze, I burn for the printed word.

[*19 September 1920*]

As to the weather it is really heavenly weather. It is too hot for any exertion, but a breeze lifts at night, and I can't tell you what scents it brings, the smell of a full summer sea and the bay tree in the garden and the smell of lemons. After lunch today we had a sudden tremendous thunderstorm, the drops of rain were as big as marguerite daisies – the sky was all glittering with broken light – the sun a huge splash of silver. The drops were like silver *fishes* hanging from the trees. I drank the rain from the peach leaves and then pulled a shower bath over my head. Every violet leaf was full. I thought of you – these are the things I want you to have. Already one is conscious of the whole sky again and the light on the water. Already one listens for the grasshopper's fiddle, one looks for the tiny frogs on the path – one watches the lizards ... I feel so strangely as though I were the one who is home and you are away. I long for you here.

[*25 September 1920*]

... I heard again from Methuen today. They now say they'd like 2 books for next spring. I think there must have been some trunk work, some back stair work in this on [your part.] But I'll see what I can do without promising in my fatal way what I can't perform. I wish I could begin real creative work. I haven't yet. It's the atmosphere, the ... tone which is hard to get. And without it nothing is worth doing. I have such a horror of *triviality* ... a great part of my Constable book[1] is

1. *Bliss and Other Stories* (1920).

trivial. It's not good enough. You see it's too late to beat about
the bush any longer. They are cutting down the cherry
trees; the orchard is sold – that is really the atmosphere I
want. Yes, the dancing and the dawn and the Englishman
in the train who said 'jump!' – all these, with the background.
I feel – this is jet sincere – that you and I are the only 2
persons who realise this really. That's our likeness and that's
what makes us, too, the creatures of our time.

Speaking of something else, which is nevertheless connected – it is an awful temptation, in face of all these novels to
cry 'Woe – woe!' I cannot conceive how writers who have
lived through our times can *drop* these last ten years and re-
vert to why Edward didn't understand, Vi's reluctance to be
seduced or (see Bennett) why a dinner of twelve covers needs
remodelling. If I did not review novels I'd never read them.
The writers (practically all of them) seem to have no idea of
what one means by continuity. It is a difficult thing to
explain. Take the old Tartar waiter in *Anna* who serves Levin
and Stepan – Now, Tolstoy only has to touch him and he
gives out a note and this note is somehow important, persists,
is a part of the whole book. But all these other men – they
introduce their cooks, aunts, strange gentlemen, and so on,
and once the pen is off them they are *gone* – dropped down a
hole. Can one explain this by what you might call – a
covering atmosphere – Isn't that a bit too vague? Come down
O Youth from yonder Mountain height and give your Worm
a staff of reason to assist her. What it *boils down to* is . . .
'either the man can make his people live and keep 'em alive
or he can't.' But criticks better that . . .

[*27 September 1920*]

The lizards here *abound.* There is one big fellow, a perfect
miniature crocodile, who lurks under the leaves that climb
over a corner of the terrace. I watched him come forth today
– *very* slithy – and eat an ant. You should have seen the little
jaws, the flick flick of the tongue, the great rippling pulse

just below the shoulder. His eyes, too. He listened with them
– and when he couldn't find another ant, he stamped his
front paw – and then, seeing that I was watching, *deliberately*
winked, and slithered away.

There is also a wasps' nest in the garden. Two infant wasps
came out this morning and each caught hold of a side
of a *leaf* and began to tug. It was a brown leaf the size of
three tea leaves. They became furious. They whimpered,
whiney-pined – snatched at each other – wouldn't give way
and finally one *rolled* over and couldn't roll back again –
just lay there kicking. I never saw such a thing. His twin then
couldn't move the leaf at all. I pointed out the hideous moral
to my invisible playmate.

[*4 October 1920*]

... *Whatever* my feelings are, I am *not* justified in giving way
to them before you or in letting you see even the shadow of the
border of that shadowy country that we exiles from health
inhabit. It is not fair. So I'm resolute that you shan't be
plagued again, my dearest darling, and determined to keep
my resolution. Help me to.

I'm sending you and Milne a dozen kāhki (I don't know
how to spell it: that's phonetic) to eat for your breakfasts.
They are very good and very healthy. I send them unripe.
You must wait until they are soft, then cut off the top,
squeeze a *lot* of lemon-juice inside and eat with a teaspoon.
Perhaps they won't be a treat, after all. I always long to
send you things. Please give my love to Milne. He sounds
so nice in the house. I wonder what Wing thinks of the
clarinet.

Walpole's novel which I mean to do for next week (1 col)
ought to be a very good prop to hang those very ideas on
that I tried to communicate to you. I want to take it seriously
and really say why it fails – for, of course, it does fail. But his
'intention' was serious. I hope I'll be able to say what I do
mean. I am *no* critic of the homely kind. 'If you would only

explain quietly in simple language,' as L.M. said to me yesterday. Good Heavens, that *is* out of my power.

The garden menagerie includes snakes – a big chap as thick as my wrist, as long as my arm, slithered along the path this morning and melted into the bushes. It wasn't horrid or fearful, however. As to the mice – Marie's piège seems to snap in the most revolting way. A fat one was offered to a marauding cat at the back door yesterday, but it *refused* it. 'Polisson! Tu veux un morceau de sucre avec?' I heard Marie scold. She is very down on the cats here; she says they are malgracieux.

*

I feel this letter is cold and poor; the fruit is not good to eat. It's rather like that withered fig tree. Do you know there is a kind of fig tree which is supposed to be of the family of that unfortunate one – it is dark stemmed and its leaves are black, they flap on the blackened boughs, they are like leaves that a flame has passed over. *Terrible.* I saw one once in a valley, a beautiful valley with a river flowing through it. There was linen drying on the banks and the women were beating the water and calling to one another – gaily – and there was this *sad* tree. L.M. who was with me said 'Of course the *explanation* is that one must never cease from giving'. The fig tree has no figs – so Christ cursed it. *Did you ever!* There's such a story buried under the whole thing – isn't there – if only one could dig it out . . .

[*5 October 1920*]

. . . The Journal – I have absolutely given up. I dare not keep a journal. I should always be trying to tell the truth. As a matter of fact I dare not tell the truth. I feel I *must* not. The only way to exist is to go on and try and lose oneself – to get as far as possible away from *this* moment. Once I can do that all will be well. So it's stories or nothing. I expect I shall kick off soon – perhaps today. Who knows? In the meantime I peg away too, darling, in my fashion . . .

[*10 October 1920*]

Just as I folded that, I had *callers*. A.M. and Madame showed on to the terrace – very gracious, but *Oh dear*! what a ghastly idea it is. What can one say? I can't play 'ladies' unless I know the children I am playing with.

Now there's an asp come out of a hole – a slender creature, red, about 12 inches long. It lies moving its quick head. It is very evil looking, but how much nicer than a caller! I was warned yesterday against attempting to kill them. (Do you see me trying to kill them, Boge?) But they *spring* at you, if you do. However, darling, I'll catch this one for you at the risk of my life and put it in your Shakespeare for a marker at the scene where the old man carries in the basket of figs. You will have to hold your Shakespeare *very firmly* to prevent it from wriggling, Anthony darling.

Lovingly yours,
Egypt

[*11 October 1920*]

I send the story.[1] As usual I am in a foolish panic about it. But I know I can trust you. You know how I *choose* my words; they can't be changed. And if you don't like it or think it is wrong *just as it is* I'd rather you didn't print it. I'll try and do another.

Will you tell me – if you've time – what you think of it? Again (as usual) I burn to know and you see there's NO ONE here.

It was one of my queer hallucinations; I wrote it straight off. And I've no copy.

*

I hope you like my little boy. His name is HENNIE.

1. 'The Young Girl'.

Journal

[*October 1920*]

'What about a cauliflower?' I said. 'A cauliflower with white sauce.'

'But they are so dear, Madame,' wailed Marie. 'So dear. One little cauliflower for 2 fr. 50. It's robbery, it's . . .'

Suddenly through the kitchen window I saw the moon. It was so marvellously beautiful that I walked out of the kitchen door, through the garden and leaned over the gate before I knew what I was doing. The cold bars of the gate stopped me. The moon was full, transparent, glittering. It hung over the sighing sea. I looked at it for a long time. Then I turned round, and the little house faced me – a little white house quivering with light, a house like a candle shining behind a feather of mimosa-tree. I had utterly forgotten these things when I was ordering the dinner. I went back to the kitchen.

'Let us have a cauliflower at any price,' I said firmly.

And Marie muttered, bending over a pot – *could* she have understood? – '*En effet*, the times are dangerous!'

*

The Doll

October 18, 1920   'Well, look!' muttered Miss Sparrow. 'I've nothing to be ashamed of. Look as much as you like. I defy you. It's what I've wanted all my life,' she cried brokenly, 'and now I've got it. I defy you. I defy the world!' And she drew herself up in front of the window, proudly, proudly; her eyes flashed, her lips gleamed. She pressed the doll to her flat bosom. She was the Unmarried Mother.

Of course, I *can't* write that. I'm surprised to have made such a crude note. That's the raw idea, as they say. What I ought to do, though, is to write it, *somehow*, immediately, even if it's not good enough to print. My chief fault, my overwhelming fault is *not writing* it out. Well, now that I know it (and the disease is of very long standing) why don't I begin, at least, to follow a definite treatment? It is my experience that when an 'evil' is recognized, *any* delay in attempting to eradicate it is fatally weakening. And I, who love order, with my mania for the 'clean sweep', for every single thing being ship-shape – I to know there's such an ugly spot in my mind! Weeds flourish in neglect. I must keep my garden open to the light and in order. I must at all costs plant these bulbs and not leave them (oh, shameful!) to rot on the garden paths. Today (October 18, 1920) is Monday. I have raised my right hand and sworn. Am I ever happy except when overcoming difficulties? Never. Am I ever free from the sense of guilt, even? Never. After I had finished that slight sketch, *The Young Girl*, wasn't there a moment which surpasses all other moments? Oh, yes. Then – why do you hesitate? How can you? I take my oath. Not one day shall pass without I write something – original.

Coleridge's Table Talk

'It is intolerable when men, who have no other knowledge, have not even a competent understanding of that world in which they are always living, and to which they refer everything.'

Hear! Hear!

'Although contemporary events obscure past events in a living man's life, yet, so soon as he is dead, and his whole life is a matter of history, one action stands out as conspicuously as another.'

Totally wrong!

'Intense study of the Bible will keep any writer from being *vulgar* in point of style.'

In point of *language*.

'I, for one, do not call the sod under my feet my country. But language, religion, laws, government, blood – identity in these makes men of one country.'

The sod under my feet makes *mine*.

' "Most women have no character at all," said Pope, and meant it for satire. Shakespeare, who knew man and woman much better, saw that it, in fact, was the perfection of woman to be characterless. Everyone wishes a Desdemona or Ophelia for a wife – creatures who, though they may not always understand you, do always feel you and feel with you.'

Now you are being silly.

To J. M. Murry

[*18 October 1920*]

I return de la Mare's letter. I long to hear of your time with him. It's very queer; he haunts me here – not a persistent or substantial ghost but as one who shares $\begin{cases} \text{our} \\ \text{my} \end{cases}$ joy in the silent world – joy is not the word, I only used it because it conveys a stillness, a remoteness, because there is a far-away sound in it.

You know, darling, I have felt very often lately as though the silence had some meaning beyond these signs, these intimations. Isn't it possible that if one yielded there is a whole world into which one is received? It is so near and yet I am conscious that I hold back from giving myself up to it. What is this something mysterious that waits – that beckons?

And then suffering, bodily suffering such as I've known for three years. It has changed for ever everything – even the *appearance* of the world is not the same – there is something added. *Everything has its shadow.* Is it right to resist such suffering? Do you know I feel it has been an immense privilege. Yes, in spite of all. How blind we little creatures are! Darling, it's only the fairy tales we *really* live by. If we set out upon a journey, the more wonderful the treasure, the greater the temptations and perils to be overcome. And if someone rebels and says, Life isn't good enough on those terms, one can only say: 'It *is*!' Don't misunderstand me. I don't mean a 'thorn in the flesh, my dear' – it's a million times more mysterious. It has taken me three years to understand this – to come to see this. We resist, we are terribly frightened. The little boat enters the dark fearful gulf and our only cry is to escape – 'put me on land again'. But it's useless. Nobody listens. The shadowy figure rows on. One ought to sit still and uncover one's eyes.

I believe the greatest failing of all is *to be frightened*. Perfect Love casteth out Fear. When I look back on my life all my mistakes have been because I was afraid . . . Was that why I had to look on death? Would nothing less cure me? You know, one can't help wondering, sometimes . . . No, not a personal God or any such nonsense. Much more likely – the soul's desperate choice . . .

Am I right in thinking that you too have been ridden by Fear (of quite a different kind). And now it's gone from you and you are whole. I feel that only now you have *all* your strength – a kind of *release*.

We are as different as can be, but I do believe we have the same devils as well as the same gods.

Here are your letters back again, love. They interested me deeply. Your Stendhal article . . . seemed to fetch the French ducks off the water . . . didn't it? I'm sorry about Knopf and the Yazpegs[1] – but can't be helped.

Take care of yourself, my beloved child, with all these wild men about throwing stones and striking. Make yourself small – fold yourself up. I'm (privately – doesn't do to tell you these things) terrified that in your lunch hour you'll take your bisticks into the street and get caught in a crowd and march away. *Eat* – don't catch cold whatever you do. I want to put my hands on you – to touch you – anxiously and longingly. I *miss* you. Do you miss me? I miss your voice and your presence and all your darling ways.

1. Murry's book *Aspects of Literature*, which Knopf had declined.

To Hugh Walpole

[27 October 1920

I must answer your letter immediately. It has dropped into the most heavenly fair morning. I wish instead of writing you were here on the terrace and you'd let me talk of your book which I *far* from detested. What an impression to convey! My trouble is I never have enough space to get going – to say what I mean to say – fully. That's no excuse, really. But to be called very unfair – that hurts, awfully, and I feel that by saying so you mean I'm not as honest as I might be. I'm prejudiced. Well, I think we're all of us more or less prejudiced, but cross my heart I don't take reviewing lightly and if I appear to it's the fault of my unfortunate manner.

Now I shall be *dead frank*. And please don't answer. As one writer to another (tho' I'm only a little beginner, and *fully realise* it).

The Captives impressed me as more like a first novel than any genuine first novel I've come across. Of course, there were signs enough that it wasn't one – but the movement of it was the movement of one trying his wings, finding out how they would bear him, how far he could afford to trust them, that you were continually risking yourself, that you had, for the first time, really committed yourself in a book. I wonder if this will seem to you extravagant impertinence. I honoured you for it. You seemed to me determined to shirk nothing. You know that strange sense of insecurity *at the last*, the feeling 'I know all this. I know more. I know down to the minutest detail and *perhaps more still*, but shall I dare to trust myself to tell all?' It is really why we write, as I see it, that we may arrive at this moment and yet – it is stepping into the air to yield to it – a kind of anguish and rapture. I felt that you appreciated this, and that, seen in this light, your *Captives* was almost a spiritual exercise in this kind of courage. But in fact your peculiar persistent consciousness of what you wanted to do was what seemed to me to prevent your book from being a creation. That is what I meant when I used the clumsy word 'task'; perhaps 'experiment' was nearer my meaning. You seemed to lose in passion what you gained in sincerity and therefore 'the miracle' didn't happen. I mean the moment when the act of creation takes place – the mysterious change – when you are no longer writing the book, *it* is writing, *it* possesses you. Does that sound hopelessly vague?

But there it is. After reading *The Captives* I laid it down thinking: Having 'broken with his past' as he has in this book, having 'declared himself,' I feel that Hugh Walpole's next novel will be the one to look for. Yes, curse me. I should have said it!

I sympathise more than I can say with your desire to escape from autobiography. Don't you feel that what English writers lack today is experience of Life. I don't mean that superficially. But they are self-imprisoned. I think there is a very profound distinction between any kind of *confession* and creative work – not that that rules out the first by any means.

About the parson and his sister. Yes, they *are* truly observed, but they wouldn't come into my review because I didn't think they really came into the book! What was Maggie to them – or they to Maggie? What did they *matter* to Maggie – what was their true relation? I can't see it. I can't see the reason for those two. I can imagine Maggie forgetting them utterly the moment she set foot in London. That their religion was more foreign to her than the other one doesn't need to be told. The point is Maggie never was in Skeaton; she was somewhere else. As to her holiday in that place where everything was green – I never knew what happened on that holiday? The parson's sister – what a story you might have made of her and Paul! (I don't think that Paul's passion for Maggie would have lasted, either. He would have become frightened of her, physically – and terribly ashamed). Yes, I feel Skeaton could have had a book to itself with Paul's sister – getting old you know, her descent into old age, her fears increasing, and then something like the Uncle Matthew affair breaking into her life . . .

And I stick to what I said about Caroline. Yes, you might have trusted Caroline, but a young female wouldn't. If Caroline had come to her father's door Maggie would have *stiffened*, have been on her guard immediately. As to trusting her with a letter to Martin – never!

Some of their love making was very beautiful – it has that tragic, youthful quality.

But enough. Forgive this long letter. I'll try to see more round the books. I've no doubt at all I'm a bad reviewer. Your letter made me want to shake hands with you across the vast.

I hope this isn't too illegible. But I'm rather a feeble creature in a chaise longue.

To J. M. Murry

[*28 October 1920*]

. . . I would have enjoyed Goodyear pa-man. I remember giving F.G. my photo and he telling me his father had said it was a *fine head*. I remember how he laughed and so did I – and I said 'I shall have to grow a pair of horns and have it stuffed to hang on Murry's door'. When I recall Goodyear I can't believe he is – nowhere – just as when I think about Chummie he comes before me, *warm*, laughing, saying 'Oh abso*lu*tely.' What a darling boy he was! You were always so beautifully generous in your thoughts of him. One – just one, my precious, of the things I love in you is the way you speak of him sometimes. Because, after all, you saw him so little.

I love this place more and more. One is conscious of it as I used to be conscious of New Zealand. I mean if I went for a walk there and lay down under a pine tree and looked up at the wispy clouds through the branches I came home plus the pine tree – don't you know? Here it's just the same. I go for a walk and I watch the butterflies in the heliotrope and the young bees and some old bumble ones and all these things are added unto me. Why I don't feel like this in England Heaven knows. But my light goes out in England, or it's a very small and miserable shiner . . .

[*30 October 1920*]

Your Tuesday letter came, telling me you intended to visit Achner (wise boy!) and that you were reading Mrs Asquith.[1] I read certain parts of her book and felt – just that – there *was* something decent. At the same time the whole book seems to me *in*-decent. Perhaps I feel more than anything that she's one of those people who have no past and no future. She's capable of her girlish pranks and follies today – in fact, she's at the mercy of herself now and for ever as she was then. *And that's bad.* We only live by somehow absorbing the past – changing it. I mean really examining it and dividing what is important from what is not (for there IS waste) and transforming it so that it becomes part of the life of the spirit and we are *free of it*. It's no longer our personal past, it's just in the highest possible sense, our servant. I mean that it is no longer our master. That is the wrong image. I used to think this process was fairly unconscious. Now I feel just the contrary. With Mrs A. this process (by which the artist and the 'living being' lives) never takes place. She is for ever driven. She is of the school of Ottoline isn't she?

'I am the Cup that thirsteth for the Wine' –

These half people are very queer – very tragic, really. They are neither simple – nor are they artists. They are between the two and yet they have the desires (no, appetites) of both. I believe their *secret whisper* is: 'If only I had found THE MAN I might have been anything . . .' But the man isn't born and so they turn to life and parade and preen and confess and dare – and lavish themselves on what they call *Life*. 'Come woo me – woo me.' How often I've *seen* that in Ottoline as her restless distracted glance swept the whole green countryside . . .

1. The autobiography of Margot Asquith.

[*31 October 1920*]

... You say just what I had meant to convey in my letter and I, too, feel that I don't *want* a God to appeal to – that I only appeal to the spirit that is within me.

You say you would 'dearly [love] to know exactly what I feel' – I thought I had told you. But my writing is so bad, my expression so vague that I expect I didn't make myself clear. I'll try to.

	'Between the acting of a dreadful thing
What a	And the first motion, all the interim is
book is	Like a phantasma or a dreadful dream;
hidden	The genius and the mortal instruments
here!	Are then in council; and the state of man
	Like to a little Kingdom suffers then
	The nature of an insurrection.'

The 'thing' was not always 'dreadful' neither was the 'dream', and you must substitute 'spirit' for genius – otherwise there you have my life as I see it up till now – complete with all the alarms, enthusiasms, terrors, excitements – in fact the nature of an insurrection.

I've been dimly aware of it many times – I've had moments when it has seemed to me that this wasn't what my little Kingdom ought to be like – yes, and longings and regrets. But only since I came away this time have I *fully realised* it – confronted myself as it were, looked squarely at the extra-ordinary 'conditions' of my existence.

... It wasn't flattering or pleasant or easy. I expect your sins are of the subconscious; they are easier to forgive than mine. You are, I *know*, a far nobler and stronger nature. I've *acted* my sins, and then excused them or put them away with 'it doesn't do to think about these things' or (more often) 'it was all experience'. But it hasn't ALL been experience. There IS waste – destruction, too. So, Bogey, – and my inspiration was our love: I never should have done it other-wise – I confronted myself. As I write I falsify slightly. I can't help it; it's all so difficult. The whole thing was so much *deeper* and more *difficult* than I've described it – *subtler* – less conscious and more conscious if you know what I mean. I didn't walk up and down the room and groan, you know, darling. As I am talking to you I'll dare say it all took place on another plane, because then we can smile at the description and yet mean something by it.

But as I say my inspiration was Love. It was the final realisation that Life for me was intimacy with you. Other things attend this. But this *is* my life on this earth. I see the Fairy Tale as our history really. It's a tremendous symbol. The Prince and Princess do wed in the end and do live happy ever after as King and Queen in their own kingdom. That's about as profound a truth as any. But I want to talk to you rather than write to you. I feel – only *now* can we talk.

And I don't want to imply that the Battle is over and here I am victorious. I've escaped from my enemies – emerged – that is as far as I've got. But it is a different state of being to any I've known before and if I were to 'sin' now – it would be mortal.

There. Forgive this rambling involved statement. But, my treasure, my life is ours. You know it . . .

[*1 November 1920*]

It's simply heavenly here today – warm, still, with wisps of cloud just here and there and le ciel deep blue. Everything is expanding and growing after the rain; the buds on the tea roses are so exquisite that one feels quite faint regarding them. A pink rose – 'chinky pink' in my mind – is out – there are multitudes of flowers and buds. And the freezias are up and the tangerines are turning. A painter whose ladder I see against the house across the valley has been singing ancient church music – awfully complicated stuff. But what a choice! How much more suited to the day and the hour than – and, now, I'm dished. For every song I wanted to find ridiculous seems somehow charming and appropriate and quite equally lovable.

> I put more whitewash on the old woman's face
> Than I did on the gar-den wall!

– for instance. That seems to me a thoroughly good song. You know the first two lines are:

> Up an' down, up an' down, in an' out the window,
> I did no good at all.

Sam Mayo used to sing it. Things weren't so bad in those days. I really believe everything was better. The tide of barbarism wasn't flowing in.

Oh, Bogey, I wanted to ask you: Did you care about the Mayor of Cork? It was a most terrible shock to me. I'd been reading about his appalling suffering in the *Eclaireur* and you know I never thought he *could* die. I thought he simply couldn't. It was a ghastly tragedy. Again, I feel the people ought to have rushed out of the prison and made Lloyd George or whoever it was free him. My plan (this sounds heartless; yes, but I would have done it; I'm not laughing at the Lord Mayor – God forbid!) was to kidnap Megan Lloyd George and inform the père that so long as the Lord Mayor was imprisoned she went unfed. Why don't the Sinn Feiners do things like this? Murder Carson, for instance, instead of hunger strike.

After lunch. I've read your Baudelaire. I think it's extremely fine – really *masterly*. It made me thirst after a book of such critical portraits. You've made a most extraordinary leap forward in your *power of interpreting*. One used to feel with you a certainty that the knowledge was there but a kind of difficulty prevented you from sharing it. There was in spite of your desire to express yourself *almost an involuntary* withholding of something. That's very difficult to explain. I felt it until recently – quite recently. And now that it's gone not only have I the reader's deep 'relief' but I seem (am I fantastic?) almost to rejoice in your consciousness of your liberation as well.

*

I was all wrong about the house painter!! He's just come back from lunch – in a grey flannel suit – put on his white overall and started singing in English! Elizabethan airs. He must be some sensible fellow who's taken the little house and is doing the job himself. He makes me think of you – but his singing is different – more difficult, darling.

'What is milk a metre now?' L.M.

Dream I

I was living at home again in the room with the fire escape. It was night: Father and Mother in bed. Vile people came into my room. They were drunk. Beatrice Hastings led them. 'You don't take me in, old dear' said she. 'You've played the lady once too often, Miss – coming it over me.' And she shouted, screamed *Femme marquée* and banged the table. I rushed away. I was going away next morning so I decided to spend the night in the dark streets and went to a theatre in Piccadilly Circus. The play, a costume play of the Restoration, had just begun. The theatre was small and packed. Suddenly the people began to speak too slowly, to mumble: they looked at each other stupidly. One by one they *drifted* off the stage and very slowly a black iron curtain was lowered. The people in the audience *looked* at one another. Very slowly, silently, they got up and moved towards the doors – stole away.

An enormous crowd filled the Circus: it was black with people. They were not speaking – a low murmur came from it – that was all. They were still. A white-faced man looked over his shoulder and *trying to smile* he said: 'The Heavens are changed already; there are six moons!'

Then I realized that *our* earth had come to an end. I looked up. The sky was ashy-green; six livid quarters swam in it. A very fine soft ash began to fall. The crowd parted. A cart drawn by two small black horses appeared. Inside there were Salvation Army women doling tracts out of huge marked boxes. They gave me one! 'Are you corrupted?'

It got very dark and quiet and the ash fell faster. Nobody moved.

Dream II

In a café Gertler[1] met me. 'Katherine, you must come to my table. I've got Oscar Wilde there. He's the most marvellous man I ever met. He's splendid!' Gertler was flushed. When he spoke of Wilde he began to cry – tears hung on his lashes, but he smiled.

Oscar Wilde was very shabby. He wore a green overcoat. He kept tossing and tossing back his long greasy hair with the whitest hand. When he met me he said: 'Oh *Katherine*!' – very affected.

But I did find him a fascinating talker. So much so that I asked him to come to my home. He said would 12.30 tonight do? When I arrived home it seemed madness to have asked him. Father and Mother were in bed. What if Father came down and found that chap Wilde in one of the chintz armchairs? Too late now. I waited by the door. He came with Lady Ottoline. I saw he was disgustingly pleased to have brought her. 'Dear *Lady* Ottoline!' and Ottoline in a red hat on her rust hair houynhyming along. He said, 'Katherine's hand – the same gentle hand!' as he took mine. But again when we sat down – I couldn't help it. He *was* attractive – as a curiosity. He was fatuous *and* brilliant!

'You know, Katherine, when I was *in that dreadful place* I was haunted by the memory of a *cake*. It used to float in the air before me – a little delicate thing *stuffed* with cream and with the cream there was something *scarlet*. It was made of pastry and I used to call it my little Arabian Nights cake. But I couldn't remember the name. Oh, Katherine, it was *torture*. It used to *hang* in the air and *smile* at me. And every time I resolved that next time *they let someone* come and see

1. Mark Gertler, the painter.

me I would ask them to tell me what it was but every time, Katherine, I was *ashamed*. Even now . . .'

I said, 'Mille feuilles à la crême?'

At that he turned round in the armchair and began to sob, and Ottoline who carried a parasol, opened it and put it over him . . .

[*2 November 1920*]

. . . I'm not up to much today. Yesterday was dark and stormy; today is too. And in spite of my feelings the weather affects me physically. I fly so high that when I go down – it's a drop, Boge. Nothing serious, just a touch of cold, but with it to 'bear it company' a black mood. Don't pay any attention to it. I expect it will have lifted utterly by the time this reaches you. And it's really caused by a queer kind of *pressure* – which is work to be done. *I am writing* – do you know the feeling and until this story is finished I am engulfed. It's not a tragic story either – but there you are. It seizes me – swallows me completely. I am Jonah in the whale and only you could charm that old whale to disgorge me. Your letters did for a minute but now I'm in again and we're thrashing through deep water. I fully realize it. It's the price we have to pay – we writers. I'm lost – gone – possessed and everybody who comes near is my enemy.

The very queer thing is tho' that I feel if you were here this wouldn't happen. Work wouldn't be then the *abnormal* but the normal. Just the knowledge that you knew would be enough. Here's egoism!! But it's to excuse a very faded old letter . . .

[*3 November 1920*]

Here it is under my hand – finished – another story about as long as *The Man Without a Temperament* – p'raps longer. It's called *The Stranger*, a 'New Zealand' story. My depression has gone, Boge; so it was just this. And now it's here, thank

God – and the fire burns and it's warm and tho' the wind is howling – it can howl. What a QUEER business writing is! I don't know. I don't believe other people are ever as foolishly excited as I am while I'm working. How could they be? Writers would have to live in trees. I've *been* this man, *been* this woman. I've stood for hours on the Auckland Wharf. I've been out in the stream waiting to be berthed – I've been a seagull hovering at the stern and a hotel porter whistling through his teeth. It isn't as though one sits and watches the spectacle. That would be thrilling enough, God knows. But one IS the spectacle for the time. If one remained oneself all the time like some writers can it would be a bit less exhausting. It's a lightning change affair, tho'. But what does it matter! I'll keep this story for you to read at Xmas. I only want to give it to you now. Accept my new story, my own love. Give it your blessing. It's the best I can do and therefore it is yours. If it pleases you nobody else counts – not one.

Thursday ... I told poor old L.M. yesterday that after I died to *prove* there was no immortality I would send her a coffin worm in a match box. She was gravely puzzled.

[*5 November 1920*]

... Oh, by the way, I had my photo taken yesterday – for a surprise for you. I'll only get des épreuves on Monday tho'. I should think it ought to be extraordinary. The photographer took off my head and then balanced it on my shoulders again at all kinds of angles as tho' it were what Violet would call an art pot. 'Ne bougez PAS en souriant leggerreMENT – Bouche CLOSE.' A kind of drill. Those funny studios fascinate me. I must put a story in one one day. They are the most *temporary shelters* on earth. Why is there always a dead bicycle behind a velvet curtain? Why does one always sit on a faded piano stool? And then, the plaster pillar, the basket of paper flowers, the storm background – and the smell. I love such endroits.

[*7 November 1920*]

All that you said about *Elizabeth* is extremely interesting.
And the queer thing is that she only wants a *male appearance*.
There's her essential falsity. Forgive my frankness: she has
no use for a physical lover. I mean to go to bed with. Anything
but that. That she can't stand – she'd be frightened of. Her
very life, her very being, her gift, her vitality, all that makes
her depends upon her *not surrendering*. I sometimes wonder
whether the act of surrender is not the greatest of all – the
highest. It is one of the [most] difficult of all. Can it be ac-
complished or even apprehended except by the *aristocrats*
of this world? You see it's so immensely complicated. It
'needs' real humility and at the same time an absolute
belief in one's own essential freedom. It is an act of faith.
At the last moments like all great acts it is *pure risk*. This is
true for me as a human being and as a writer. Dear Heaven!
how hard it is to let go – to step into the blue. And yet one's
creative life depends on it and one *desires* to do nothing else.

*

Kissing is a queer thing. I was standing under a tree just
now – a tree that is shedding exquisite golden yellow leaves
all over my garden path. And suddenly one leaf made the
most ethereal advances to me and in another moment we
were kissing each other. Through the silvery branches one
can see the deep blue sky . . . lapis lazuli.

I think the time has come, it really has come for us to do a
little courting. Have we ever had time to stand under trees
and tell our love? Or to sit down by the sea and make fragrant
zones for each other? The tea-roses are in flower. Do you
know the peculiar exquisite scent of a tea-rose? Do you know
how the bud opens – so unlike other roses and how deep red
the thorns are and almost purple the leaves?

I think it must be the orange flower which Marie has
brought home from market. I have been arranging branches
of it in jars and little slips of it in shallow glass bowls. And the

house has a perfume as though the Sultan were expecting the première visite of his youngest bride. Marie, standing over me, chanted the while – almost sang a hymn to the cyclamen sauvage qu'on trouve dans les montagnes and the little violettes de mon pays which grow so thick that one trempe ses pieds dedans.

If I live much longer, I shall become a bush of daphne, or you'll find no one to welcome you but a jasmine. Perhaps, too, it's the effect of receiving the sun every morning – très intime – the lady clad only in a black paper fan. But you must come here; you must live here in the South and forget greyness. It is *divine* here – no less . . .

[*17 November 1920*]

. . . But I must tell you something else. I have been ill for nearly four years – and I'm changed, changed – not the same. You gave twice to your work (which I couldn't see) to what you gave my story. I don't want dismissing as a masterpiece. Who is going to mention 'the first snow'?[1] I haven't anything like as long to live as you have. *I've scarcely any time, I feel*. Arthur will draw posters 100 years. Praise him when I'm dead. Talk to ME. I'm lonely. I haven't ONE single soul.

[*November 1920*]

. . . And about *Poison*. I could write about that for pages. But I'll try and condense what I've got to say. The story is told by (evidently) a worldly, rather cynical (not wholly cynical) man *against* himself (but not altogether) when he was so absurdly young. You know how young by his idea of what woman is. She has been up to now, only the *vision*, only she who passes. You realize that? And here he has put *all* his passion into this Beatrice. It's *promiscuous love*, not understood

1. A reference to her story 'The Stranger': 'But her words, so light, so soft, so chill, seemed to hover in the air, to rain into his breast, like snow.'

as such by him; perfectly understood as such by her. But you realize the vie de luxe they are living – the very table – sweets, liqueurs, lilies, pearls. And you realize? she expects a letter from someone calling her away? *Fully* expects it? Which accounts for her farewell AND her declaration. And when it doesn't come even her *commonness* peeps out – the newspaper touch of such a woman. She can't disguise her chagrin. She gives herself away . . . He, of course, laughs at it now, and laughs at her. Take what he says about her 'sense of order' and the crocodile. But he also regrets the self who dead privately would have been young enough to have actually wanted to *marry* such a woman. But I meant it to be light – tossed off – and yet through it – oh, subtly – the lament for youthful belief. These are the rapid confessions one receives sometimes from a glove or a cigarette or a hat.

I suppose I haven't brought it off in *Poison*. It wanted a light, light hand – and then with that newspaper a sudden . . . let me see, *lowering* of it all – just what happens in promiscuous love after passion. A glimpse of staleness. And the story is told by the man who gives himself away and hides his traces at the same moment.

I realize it's quite a different kind to *Miss Brill* or *The Young Girl*. (She's not 'little', Bogey; in fact, I saw her big, slender, like a colt.) . . .

[*1 December 1920*]

. . . I had a letter from Schiff today, telling me *Miss Brill* was *quite* good, quite *nice* and full of *feeling* and happy phrase – But didn't I think that it was a mistake to rate the Russians above de Maupassant? And that Proust is not only the greatest living writer but perhaps (I like the perhaps) the greatest novelist that ever has been!!!!! And what a dastardly shame to have dismissed Ludovici's novel (one of the 'freshest' voices of our day) in a short notice. And – but that's enough. And to spare. If he comes to Roquebrune I'll never be able to see them. I will reply I would give every single word de Maupassant and Tumpany ever wrote for one short story by Anton Tchekhov. As to Proust with his Morceaux de Salon (who cares if the salon is 'literary') let him tinkle away.

To Sydney Schiff

[*1 December 1920*]

About the Russians. I agree that translations are perfectly terrible. The peculiar *flatness* of them is so strange and it's just that flatness which the story or whatever it is mustn't have – One feels it's superimposed. And yet – and yet – though I hate to agree with so many silly critics I confess that Tchehov does seem to me a marvellous writer. I do think a story like *In Exile* or *Missing* is frankly incomparable. (It's years since I read de Maupassant: I must read him again) – And then Tolstoi – well, you know, Anna's journey in the train when she finds Vronsky is travelling to St Petersburg too and the whole whole figure of Anna – when I think how real, how vital, how vivid she is to me – I feel I can't be grateful enough to Tolstoi – by grateful – I mean full of praise to him for his works.

To J. M. Murry

[*5 December 1920*]

. . . The whole paper needs a stricter form – or could do with one, I feel, a more [sic] form that is scrupulously adhered to. But I realise the difficulty of this with writers like K.M. and Co. who never can learn the length of a page. Still they ought to be hauled over the coals. A big nasty cut now and again would larn 'em.

*

If the paper is shorter, it wants to be more *defined, braced up, tighter*.

In my reckless way I would suggest all reviews were signed
and all were put into the first person. I think that would give
the whole paper an amazing lift-up. A paper that length
must be *definite, personal,* or die. It can't afford the 'we' –
'in our opinion'. To sign reviews, to put them in the 1st
person stimulates curiosity, *makes for correspondence,* gives it
(to be 19-eleventyish) GUTS. You see it's a case of leaning
out of the window with a board and a nail, *or* a bouquet, *or*
a flag – administering whichever it is and retiring *sharp.*
This seems to me essential. Signed reviews are tonic: the
time has gone by for any others. I do wish you could work
this. I am sure it would attract the public. And there's rather
a 'trop de livres, trop de livres' faint cry in it. I read the
first par. of about 4 reviews and I begin to whimper faintly.

You're all right, but the others are not. A letter ought to be
drafted to your regular contributors asking them, now that
the reviews are to be signed (supposing that were to happen)
– asking them to pull themselves together and make their
attack stronger. Do you know what I mean? I feel inclined to
say to them, as if I were taking their photographs: '*Look
Fearless*'. They are huddled up.

I think the shorter paper might be all to the good. But it
must be swifter, too. If all those cobwebs are gone, we must
show the bare boards . . .

[*6 December 1920*]

. . . Just while I'm on the subject I suppose you will think I
am an egocentric to mind the way Constable has advertised
my book and the paragraph that is on the paper cover. I'd
like to say I mind so much so terribly that there are no words
for me. No – I'm DUMB!! I think it so insulting and disgusting
and undignified that – well – there you are! It's no good
suffering all over again. But the bit about 'Women will
learn by heart and not repeat'. Gods! why didn't they have a
photograph of me looking through a garter. But I was
helpless here – too late to stop it – so now I *must* prove – no,

convince people ce n'est pas moi. At least, if I'd known they
were going to say that, no power on earth would have made
me cut a word. I wish I hadn't. I was wrong – very wrong . . .

[*December 1920*]

I have now read your book, and though we can't really
discuss it until you come, I should feel ungracious were I not
to write you quelques mots.

Well, Bogey, I'm your admirer. Accept my admiration.
It's from my heart and head! There is real achievement in
that book. While I read you on Tchekhov, Butler, the first
essay, Shakespeare criticism, I liked to pretend you were a
stranger. I imagined what I'd feel like if this book had fallen
out of the sky – and that really gave me your measure.
(There's a female standard!) At your best no one can touch
you. You simply are first chop. For the first time *je me trouve*
underlining your sentences – putting marks in the margin –
as one so *very* seldom does, Boge. You re-create – no less –
Tchekhov, for instance. I want to make you feel what a
great little fellow you are for this book! And how it makes me
believe in you – stand by you in my thoughts and respect you.
There! Shake hands with me. And of course I want 'to
criticise' – to tell you all I feel. But not before you realise how
firm and unyielding are the foundations of my praise. Here
goes.

Your Hardy doesn't quite come off to my thinking. You
seem to be hinting at a special understanding between yourself and the author. That's not fair: it puts me off. You (in
the name of your age, true, but not quite, not wholly)
intrude your age, your experience of suffering . . . This
destroys the balance.

Your Keats is performance, right enough, but it's more
promise. Makes me feel you ought to write a book on Keats.
It's deeply interesting. The last paragraph is a pity – when
you praise Sir Sidney. Here again I seem to catch a faint
breath of *pride*.

I think Edward Thomas is seen out of proportion. It's not in his poems; he's not *all that*. Your emotions are too apparent. I feel one ought to replace Thomas with another and say it all about *him*. There was the beginning of all that in Thomas but you've filled it out yourself – to suit what you wanted him to be. It's not wholly sincere, either, for that reason.

Let me make my meaning clearer. Take your Tchekhov. Now you make Tchekhov greater than one sees him but NOT greater than he was. This is an *important dangerous* distinction. A critic must see a man as great as his potentialities but NOT greater. Falsity creeps in immediately then.

You ought to guard against this. Its another 'aspect' of your special pleading danger – as in your essay on Hardy. In your tremendously just desire to prove him a major poet, you mustn't make yourself Counsel for the Prisoner! I mean that in all its implications.

You might have borne this trick of yours in mind when you are so down on S.T.C. for his idolatry. Remember how Shakespeare *was* regarded at that time – the extraordinary ignorance, stupidity and meanness of the point of view. I don't think you take that into account enough. It's too easy to talk of laudanum and soft brainedness. The reason for his *überfluss* is more psychological. (I don't defend S.T.C. but I think he and you are both wrong in 'considering' far too specially a 'special' audience). On the other hand you are splendidly just to his amazing *Venus and Adonis* criticism. (I must say that chapter on *V. and A.* is a gem of the first water).

Ronsard is interesting because you have conveyed the chap's quality so well, tho' I deeply disagree with one of the 'charming' quotations – the complexion one is perfect.

Now, I'll be franker still. There are still traces of what I call your sham personality in this book and they mar it – the personality that expressed itself in the opening paragraphs of your Santayana review in *The Nation*. Can't you see what a *farce* it makes of your preaching the good life? The good life indeed, – rowing about in your little boat with the worm-eaten ship and chaos! Look here! How *can* you! How can

you lay up your sweat in a phial for future generations! I
don't ask for false courage from anyone but I do think that
even if you are shivering it is your duty as an artist and a
man *not* to shiver. The devil and the angel in you both fight
in that review. I must speak out plainly because your friends
flatter you. They are not really taken in by your 'sham
personality', but they are too uncertain of themselves not to
pretend that they are, and you are deceived by their pretence
because you want to be. It is this which mars you and it is for
this reason you will not be popular. It's the BAD in you
people can't stomach – not the good. But tho' they don't
understand it, they sense it as treachery – as something that
is not done. Don't be proud of your unpopularity, Bogey. It is
right you should be unpopular for this.

Now let me point to your remark in the preface that you
can 'do no less than afford your readers . . . a similar enjoyment in your case'. My dear Bogey! How could a person
say such a thing. It's so naive as to be silly, or so arrogant as
to be fantastique. Suppose I wrote: 'I have dated my stories
as I venture to hope my readers may enjoy tracing my
development – the ripening of my powers . . .' What *would*
you think! You'd faint? It is indecent, no less, to say such
things. And one doesn't think them!

It always seems to me you let yourself go in *The Nation*
especially; you count on Massingham's weakness. The worst
of it is that whenever one is less than true to oneself in work,
even what is true becomes tainted. I feel whenever I *am* true
my good angel wipes out one bad mark – doesn't give me a
good one – but, at any rate, next time, there is one bad mark
the less to get over. Now you only get half-marks, and they
are no marks at all, because you cannot resist this awful
insidious temptation to show your wounds. Until you do, you
are a great writer marred. Lynd called it 'high-browism'.
It's much more subtle.

There you are. If you were to send me back my 1/9 wedding
ring for this letter, I should send the letter just the same and
keep the ring in a match-box and be very sorry.

I must risk being wrong. In my efforts to be clear I am crude. I must risk that. For as long as I live I never will be other than dead honest and dead sincere with you, as I would have you with me. Do not think I imagine I know all about you. Ah, my darling, I never shall. Forgive me if I hurt you – please forgive me!

But I love you and believe in you.

[*December 1920*]

I made these notes. Read them, will you?

The Lost Girl

It's important. It ought not to be allowed to pass.

The Times gave no inkling of what it was – never even hinted at its dark secret.

Lawrence denies his humanity. He denies the powers of the Imagination. He denies Life – I mean *human* life. His hero and heroine are non-human. They are animals on the prowl. They do not feel: they scarcely speak. There is not one memorable *word*. They submit to the physical response and for the rest go veiled – blind – *faceless* – *mindless*. This is the doctrine of mindlessness.

He says his heroine is extraordinary, and rails against the ordinary. Isn't that significant? But look at her. Take her youth – her thriving on the horse-play with the doctors. They might be beasts butting each other – no more. Take the scene where the hero throws her in the kitchen, possesses her, and she returns singing to the washing-up. It's a *disgrace*. Take the rotten rubbishy scene of the woman in labour asking the Italian into her bedroom. All false. All a pack of lies!

Take the nature-study at the end. It's no more than the grazing-place for Alvina and her sire. What was the 'green hellebore' to her? Of course, there is a great deal of racy, bright, competent writing in the early part – the 'shop' part. But it doesn't take a writer to tell all that.

The whole is false – *ashes*. The preposterous Indian troupe of four young men is – a fake. But how on earth he can keep it up is the problem. No, it's not. He has 'given way'. Why stop then? Oh, don't forget where Alvina feels *'a trill in her bowels'* and discovers herself with child. A TRILL – what does that mean? And why is it so peculiarly offensive from a man? Because it is *not on this plane* that the emotions of others are conveyed to our imagination. It's a kind of sinning against art.

Earth closets, too. Do they exist *quâ* earth closets? No. I might describe the queer noises coming from one when old Grandpa X was there – very strange cries and moans – and how the women who were washing stopped and shook their heads and pitied him and even the children didn't laugh. Yes, I can imagine that. But that's not the same as to build an earth-closet because the former one was so exposed. NO.

Am I prejudiced? Be careful. I feel privately as though Lawrence had possessed an animal and fallen under a curse. But I can't say that. All I know is, this is bad and ought not be allowed. I feel a horror of it – a shrinking. But that's not criticism. But here is life where one has blasphemed against the spirit of reverence.

Journal

[*December 1920*]

Oh Life! accept me – make me worthy – teach me.

I write that. I look up. The leaves move in the garden, the sky is pale, and I catch myself weeping. It is hard – it is hard to make a good death ...

*

The Change

For a long time she said she did not want to change anything in him, and she meant it. Yet she hated things in him, and wished they were otherwise. Then she said she did not want to change anything in him and she meant it. And the

dark things that she had hated she now regarded with indifference. Then she said she did not want to change anything in him. But now she loved him so that even the dark
things she loved, too. She wished them there; she was not
indifferent. Still they were dark and strange, but she loved
them. And it was for this they had been waiting. They
changed. They shed their darkness – the curse was lifted
and they shone forth as Royal Princes once more, as creatures
of light.

At the Bay

At last the milk-white harbour catches the glitter and the
gulls floating on the trembling water gleam like the shadows
within a pearl.

The house-dog comes out of his kennel dragging the heavy
chain and kalop-kalops at the water standing cold in the iron
pan. The house cat emerges from nowhere and bounds on to
the kitchen window sill waiting for her spill of warm morning
milk.

12

Menton with Murry,
December 1920–May 1921

This period is one of some confusion, with a good deal of coming and going on Murry's part. Katherine Mansfield was ill again, having overworked during the previous months. She was also deeply hurt by a misunderstanding that arose between them over Murry's friendship with another woman. K.M. urged him to act freely but not tell her about it; Murry remained faithful to her but clumsily contrived to give the impression he was not; while the 'other woman' (Princess Bibesco, daughter of the Earl of Oxford and wife of a Rumanian aristocrat) wrote a letter chastising K.M. for binding Murry to an invalid wife.

In December Murry came to Menton and found her seriously ill. He had already been thinking of resigning from The Athenaeum, which was not flourishing, and he now decided that that was what he should do. He left for London on 11 January to wind up his affairs, returned to Menton on 19 January when K.M.'s health took a turn for the worse, went again to London during February, and at last returned to settle down with her at Isola Bella.

To Anne Estelle Rice

[*26 December 1920*]

The parcel arrived on Xmas morning but it was a separate fête by itself, just your letter and the two enchanting sketches. I love them, Anne. They remind me of our spring together and the laburnum seems hung with little laughs. If you knew how often I think of that time at Looe, our picnic, the white-eyed kaffir, the midget infant hurling large pieces of Cornwall into the sea on the beach that afternoon! It's all as clear as today.

But you know, don't you? that all the times we have ever spent together are clear like that. And here – I am always sending you greetings, always sharing things with you. I salute you in tangerines and the curved petals of *roses-thé* and the crocus colour of the sea and in the moonlight on the *poire sauvage*. Many, many other things. It will *always* be so with me, however seldom I see you. I shall just go on rejoicing in the fact of you. And loving you and feeling in that family where Monsieur Le Beau Soleil est notre père nous sommes des sœurs.

I am still hard at the story-writing and still feeling that only now do I begin to see what I want to do. I am sending you my book. It is not a good one. I promise the next will be better but I just wanted you to have a copy . . .

Journal

[*27 December 1920*]

'Oh dear,' she said, 'I do wish I hadn't married. I wish I'd been an explorer.' And then she said dreamily, 'The Rivers of China, for instance.'

'But what do you know about the rivers of China, darling,' I said. For Mother knew no geography whatever; she knew less than a child of ten.

'Nothing,' she agreed. 'But I can *feel* the kind of hat I should wear.'

[*1921*]

January 8   I would like to hear J. saying 'We'll have the north meadow mowed tomorrow', on a late evening in summer, when our shadows were like a pair of scissors, and we could just see the rabbits in the dark.

To Richard Murry

[*17 January 1921*]

... It's a very queer thing how *craft* comes into writing. I mean down to details. Par exemple. In *Miss Brill* I choose not only the length of every sentence, but even the sound of every sentence. I choose the rise and fall of every paragraph to fit her, and to fit her on that day at that very moment. After I'd written it I read it aloud – numbers of times – just as one would *play over* a musical composition – trying to get it nearer and nearer to the expression of Miss Brill – until it fitted her.

Don't think I'm vain about the little sketch. It's only the method I wanted to explain. I often wonder whether other writers do the same – If a thing has really come off it seems to me there mustn't be one single word out of place, or one word that could be taken out. That's how I AIM at writing. It will take some time to get anywhere near there.

But you know, Richard, I was only thinking last night people have hardly begun to write yet. Put poetry out of it for a moment and leave out Shakespeare – now I mean prose. Take the very best of it. Aren't they still cutting up sections rather than tackling the whole of a mind? I had a moment of absolute terror in the night. I suddenly thought of *a living mind* – a whole mind – with absolutely nothing left out. With *all* that one knows how much does one not know? I used to fancy one knew all but some kind of mysterious core (or one could). But now I believe just the opposite. The unknown is far, far greater than the known. The known is only a mere shadow. This is a fearful thing and terribly hard to face. But it must be faced.

To Sylvia Lynd

[*January 1921*]

. . . I find my great difficulty in writing is to learn to submit. Not that one ought to be without resistance – of course I don't mean that. But when I am writing of 'another' I want so to lose myself in the soul of the other that I am not . . .

I wish we could have a talk about writing one of these days.

Was there really a new baby in your letter? Oh dear, some people have all the babies in this world. And as sometimes happens to us women just before your letter came, I found myself tossing a little creature up in the air and saying, 'Whose boy are you?' But he was far too shadowy, too far away to reply.

So tell me about *your* baby, will you? And when I do get out of this old bed I shall drive to the lace shop and buy a cobweb to make a cap for himher. Farewell. May the fairies attend you. No, dear woman, it is grim work – having babies. Accept my love and my sympathy.

Journal

[*1921*]

January 30 J. accused me of always bagging his books as soon as he had begun to read them. I said: 'It's like fishing. I see you've got a bite. I want your line. I want to pull it in.'

*

The Cat

Today, passing the kitchen, the door was open. Charles sat up to the table darning socks. And there sat beside the ball of wool a large black cat with an old bow round its neck. When he took up the scissors, the cat squeezed up its eyes as if to say 'That's quite right', and when he put the scissors down it just put out its paw as if to straighten them, but then it drew its paw back, deciding that it wasn't worth it.

To Richard Murry

[3 February 1921]

... Don't worry about the fare. When the time comes just put your toospeg brush, pyjamas and a collar (for Sundays and fête days) into a handkerchief and I'll send along the ticket and a dotted line for you to follow. Seriously a rucksack is all you'll need. My grandpa said a man could travel all over the world with a clean pair of socks and a rook rifle. At the age of 70 odd he started for England thus equipped but Mother took fright and added a handkerchief or two. When he returned he was shorn of everything but a large watering can which he'd bought in London for his young marrows ...

To Ida Baker

[March 1921]

This is just a note to let you know that *tout va bien a la maison.* It is the late afternoon of an exquisite day. That heavy, evening rain that made waterspouts of Jack's trousers fell like a blessing upon the garden. When I went out today the air smelt like moss, and there was a bee to every wallflower. The peach leaves are like linnet wings; the branches of the fig are touched with green, the bush of may is just not in flower. I had to lift up the daffodils and set them on their legs again and to give a finger to the reclining freezias. But nothing has come to harm. As to that white rose bush over the gate and the gas meter it is sprinkled with thousands of tiny satin-fine clusters. This is a darling little garden when one can get out of ones shell and look at it. But what does it profit a man to look at anything if he is not *free*? Unless one is free to offer oneself up wholly and solely to the pansy – one receives nothing. Its promiscuous love instead of a living relationship – a dead thing. But there it is — And my gland is a great deal more swollen for some reason. The blood goes on tapping squeezing through like a continual small hammering, and all that side of my head is numb. Its a vile thing.

I hope you had a good journey. Will you please wire me immediately if you want any money and I'll wire it to you. I am now v. serious. Don't go to other people first. I can so easily overdraw for now; I don't care a button. But you must feed properly in London – eat nourishing food – not scones and coffee – and you must take taxis. Don't buy things in bags and eat them. Make Violet cook you porridge, bacon and eggs and toast for breakfast. That climate is the devil. And wear a thick scarf when you go out and change your shoes and stockings when you come in. And burn the anthracite. And get people to come and see you if you want to see them and make Violet cook for them. I feel you will never be sensible enough to keep warm, dry shod and fed. I have no confidence in you . . .

To Lady Ottoline Morrell

[*14 March 1921*]

. . . Even now I can't explain. Something happened, a kind of earthquake that shook everything and I lost faith and touch with everybody. I cannot write what it was. And perhaps I shall never meet you again so that I can tell you. This is sad. Blame me if you must. How can you do otherwise? I expect this all sounds fantastic. I hate people who hint at secrets in letters. You will hate this. Let me say I was almost out of my mind with misery last year –

M. is here for the moment. He goes back to England at the end of April. His typewriter ticks away here. I have just been looking at the Keats Memorial Volume. It is simply *indescribable* in its vulgarity. But there's a letter by Keats in it – so full of power, gaiety, 'fun' that it mocks the book as he would have mocked it! . . .

To the Hon. Dorothy Brett

[*20 April 1921*]

... Here it is so cold that it might be November. We are both frozen, we shiver all day. I get up from 11–5.30 and turn the clock round so as to get back to bed more quickly. I've been spitting blood since last Tuesday too – which is horrid. It makes one feel that while one sits at the window the house is on fire. And the servants have gone mad or bad or both. One has completely disappeared, only her feather duster remains. She wasn't a little one either. But I expect we shall come across her one day. I have a fancy she is in one of the chimneys. All our flags are pinned on Switzerland. Meadows, trees, mountings, and kind air. I hope we shall get there in time ...

13

Switzerland, May–October 1921

By May 1921 Katherine Mansfield was ready to leave Menton. Her writing spell there seemed to have ended; one of her doctors considered its summer climate too enervating for her lungs; Miss Beauchamp and Miss Fullerton, from whom she had been renting Isola Bella, decided the villa was needed for another friend; and there was a new treatment for T.B. being spoken about in Switzerland.

In May the Murrys left Menton, he for Oxford where he was to deliver some lectures, she for Baugy in Switzerland. She moved from Baugy to Sierre where Murry joined her in June. At the end of June they moved further up the mountains to the Chalet des Sapins, Montana, at 5000 feet above sea-level. The period there from July to October was the most successful of K.M.'s writing life, and fruitful for Murry too. It was not quite a repetition of that early happiness they had experienced in Bandol: she was too seriously ill for that. But they achieved once again the companionship – the marriage of true minds – which had always been the foundation of their relationship. It gave her the security she needed if she was to concentrate on her writing. In just a few months she wrote 'At the Bay', 'The Garden Party', 'The Doll's House', 'The Voyage', and a number of other stories including the brilliant but unfinished 'A Married Man's Story' (hitherto wrongly supposed to have been written at Looe in Cornwall in 1918).

To J. M. Murry

Baugy   [*7 May 1921*]

I have been walking round and round this letter, treading on my toes and waving my tail and wondering where to settle. There's *too* much to say! Also, the least postcard or letter penned within view of these mountains is like presenting one's true account to one's Maker. Perhaps their effect will wear off. But at present, Boge . . . one keeps murmuring that about cats looking at Kings, but one feels a very small cat, sneezing, licking one's paw, making a dab or two at one's tail in the eye of Solemn Immensities. However, the peasants don't mind, so why should I? They are cutting the long brilliant grass; they are wading waist high through the field with silver stars – their scythes, winking bright in the sun – over their shoulders. A cart drawn by a *cow* (I'm sure it is a cow) drags over a little bridge, and the boy driver, lying like a drunken bee on his fresh green bed, doesn't even *try* to drive. It's a perfect, windless day. I'm, as you have gathered, sitting on the balcony outside my room. The sun is wonderfully warm, but the air is just a little too clean not to be chill. The cleanliness of Switzerland! Darling, it is frightening. The chastity of my lily-white bed! The waxy fine floors! The huge bouquet of white lilac, fresh, crisp from the laundry, in my little salon! Every daisy in the grass below has a starched frill – the very bird-droppings are dazzling.

Boge: 'But, Wig, this is all jolly fine, but why don't you tell me things? Get down to it!'

I'm sorry, my precious; I'll have another try. You got my telegram? The journey was excellent. The *lits salons* were horrid – when they unfolded they were covered thickly with buttons so that one felt like a very sensitive bun having its currants put in. But it was soon morning, and my mountains appeared as of yore with snow, like silver light, on their tops, and beautiful clouds above, rolling solid white masses. We passed little watery villages clinging to the banks of rivers, it was raining, the trees dripped, and everybody carried a gleaming umbrella. Even the fishers fished under umbrellas, their line looked like the huge feeler of a large water beetle. And then the rain stopped, the cows began to fatten, the houses had broad eaves, the women at the bookstalls got broader and broader, and it was Switzerland.

I sat on a neat green velvet chair in Geneva for three hours.

L.M. brought tea on a tray. Do you see her, coming from afar, holding the tray high, her head bent, a kind of reverent beam on her face, and the smoke of the teapot rising like the smoke of sacrifices?

Then we mounted an omnibus train and *bümmelt*ed round the Lake. The carriage was full of Germans; I was imbedded in huge ones. When they saw a lilac bush, Vater und die Mamma and even little Hänse all cried: 'Schön!' It was very old-world. Also they each and all read aloud the notice in the carriage that a cabinet was provided for the convenience of passengers! (What other earthly reason would it have been there for?) We reached Clarens at 7. The station clock was chiming. It was a cuckoo clock. Touching – don't you think, darling? I was *very* touched. But I didn't cry. And then a motor car, like a coffee-mill, flew round and round the fields to Baugy. The manager, who is very like a goldfish, flashed through the glass doors and our journey was over . . .

This hotel is admirable. The food is prodigious. At breakfast one eats little white rolls with butter and fresh plum jam and cream. At lunch one eats – but no, I can't describe it. It could not be better though. I suppose in the fullness of time, I shall take soup at midday, too. But at present I can only watch and listen . . . My rooms are like a small appartement. They are quite cut off and my balcony is as big as another room. The sun rises in the morning vers les sept heures, and it sets, or it begins to set, for it takes its setting immensely seriously here, at seven in the evening. It has no connection whatever with the South of France sun. This is le soleil père – and she's a wanton daughter whose name is never mentioned here.

The air, darling, is all they say. I am posing here as a lady with a weak heart and lungs of Spanish leather-o. And so far, I confess I hardly cough except in the morning. One mustn't be too enthusiastic though. Perhaps it is the hypnotic effect of *knowing* one is so high up. But the air is amazing!

It's all very German. Early German. Fat little birds, tame as can be – they look as though their heads unscrewed and revealed marzipan tummies – fat little children, peasants, and – I regret to say – ugly women. In fact, everybody seems to me awfully ugly. Young men with red noses and stuffy check suits and feathers in their hats ogling young females in mackintoshes with hats tied with ribbons under the chin! Oh weh! Oh weh! And if they try to be 'chic' – to be French – it's worse still. Legs – but legs of mutton, Boge, in silk stockings and powder which one feels sure is die Mamma's icing sugar.

Of course, I quite see the difficulty of being chic in this landscape. I can't quite see . . . yet. Perhaps a white woollen dress, a Saint Bernard, a woollen Viking helmet with snowy wings. And for your . . . ? More wool, with your knees bare, dearest, and boots with fringèd tongues . . . But I don't know – I don't know . . .

I am sure you will like Switzerland. I want to tell you nicer things. What shall I tell you? I should like to dangle some very fascinating and compelling young carrots before your eminent nose . . . The furniture of my salon is green velvet inlaid with flesh pink satin, and the picture on the wall is *Jugendidylle*. There is also an immense copper jug with lovely hearts of imitation verdigris . . .

Goodbye, my darling. I love you v. much and I'm fond of you and I long to hear from you.

To Anne Estelle Rice

[*19 May 1921*]

I saw the biggest specialist in Switzerland on Saturday, Anne. That's what made your letter so wonderfully good just at the moment. It seemed to bring Life so near again. After I'd seen this man it was just as if the landscape – everything – changed a little – moved a little *further off*. I always expect these doctor men to say: 'Get better? Of course you will. We'll put you right in no time. Six months at the very most and you'll be fit as a fiddle again.' But though this man was extremely nice he would not say more than

'I still had a chance.' That was all. I tried to get the word 'Guéri' but it was no good. All I could wangle out of him was 'If your digestion continues good, you still have a chance.'

It's an infernal nuisance to love life as I do. I seem to love it more as time goes on rather than less. It never becomes a habit to me – it's always a marvel. I do hope I'll be able to keep in it long enough to do some really good work. I'm sick of people dying who promise well. One doesn't want to join that crowd at all. So I shall go on lapping up jaunes d'œufs and de la crême . . .

To J. M. Murry

[*19 May 1921*]

. . . Of course, I remember old Grundy.[1] It was Goodyear's laugh I heard when I read his name – a kind of snorting laugh, ending in a chuckle and then a sudden terrific *frown* and he got very red. Do you remember? And you remember the stick he brought from Bombay? He was very pleased with that stick. Your mention of Grundy gave me Goodyear again – living, young, a bit careless and *worried*, but enjoying the worry, in the years before the war, when a pale moon shone above Piccadilly Circus and we three stood at the corner and didn't want to separate or to go home . . .

[*21 May 1921*]

. . . Thank you for Tcheh[ov.] Came tonight. I am simply captivated by Chaucer just now. I have had to throw a bow window into my cœur petit to include him with Shakespeare. Oh, dear! His *Troilus and Cressid*!! And my joy at finding your remarks and your pencil-notes.

I read today *The Tale of Chaunticleer and Madame Perlicote*: it's the Pardouner's tale. Perfect in its way. But the *personality* – the *reality* of the man. How his impatience, his pleasure, the

1. Dr. G. B. Grundy of Oxford.

very tone rings through. It's deep delight to read. Chaucer and Marlowe are my two at present. I don't mean there's any comparison between them. But I read *Hero and Leander* last night. That's incredibly lovely. But how extremely amusing Chapman's *finish* is! Taking up that magical poem and putting it into a body and skirt. It's *v.* funny . . .

[*24 May 1921*]

. . . During the past two nights I have read *The Dynasts.* Isn't it queer how a book eludes one. And then suddenly it opens for you? I have looked into this book before now. But the night before last when I opened it I suddenly understood what the poet meant, and how he meant it should be read! *The point of view* which is like a light streaming from the imagination and over the imagination – over one's head as it were – the chorus and the aerial music . . .

To Lady Ottoline Morrell

[*June 1921*]

. . . I know I *ought* to love – and she is such a 'brick,' as they say. But when that brick comes flying in my direction – Oh, I DO want to dodge it!

I read less and less, or fewer and fewer books. Not because I don't want to read them, I do – but they seem so high up on the tree. It's so hard to get at them and there is nobody near to help . . . On my bed at night there is a copy of Shakespeare, a copy of Chaucer, an automatic pistol and a black muslin fan. This is my whole little world . . .

To Richard Murry

[*20 June 1921*]

... About the old masters. What I feel about them (all of them – writers too, of course) is the more one *lives* with them the better it is for one's work. It's almost a case of living *into* one's ideal world – the world that one desires to express. Do you know what I mean? For this reason I find that if I stick to men like Chaucer and Shakespeare and Marlowe and even Tolstoi I keep much nearer what I want to do than if I confuse things with reading a lot of lesser men. I'd like to make the old masters my *daily* bread – in the sense in which it's used in the Lord's Prayer, really – to make them a kind of essential nourishment. All the rest is – well – it *comes after* ...

To William Gerhardi

[*23 June 1921*]

... I cannot tell you how happy I am to know that *The Daughters of the Late Colonel* has given you pleasure. While I was writing that story I lived for it but when it was finished, I confess I hoped very much that my readers would understand what I was trying to express. But very few did. They thought it was 'cruel'; they thought I was 'sneering' at Jug and Constantia; or they thought it was 'drab'. And in the last paragraph I was 'poking fun at the poor old things.'

It's almost terrifying to be so misunderstood. There was a moment when I first had 'the idea' when I saw the two sisters as *amusing*; but the moment I looked deeper (let me be quite frank) I bowed down to the beauty that was hidden in their lives and to discover that was all my desire ... All was meant, of course, to lead up to that last paragraph, when my two flowerless ones turned with that timid gesture, to the sun. 'Perhaps *now* ...' And after that, it seemed to me, they died as surely as Father was dead ...

To the Countess Russell[1]

[June–July 1921]

... My only trouble is John. He ought to divorce me, marry a really gay young healthy creature, have children, and ask me to be godmother. I shall never be a wife and I feel such a fraud when he believes that one day I shall turn into one. Poor John! Its hellish to live with a femme malade. But its also awfully hard to say to him 'You know darling I shall never be any good' ...

Journal

[1921]

July   I finished *Mr and Mrs Dove* yesterday. I am not altogether pleased with it. It's a little bit made up. It's not inevitable. I mean to imply that those two may not be happy together – that that is the kind of reason for which a young girl marries. But have I done so? I don't think so. Besides, it's not *strong* enough. I want to be nearer – far, far nearer than that. I want to use all my force even when I am taking a fine line. And I have a sneaking notion that I have, at the end, used the Doves *unwarrantably*. *Tu sais ce que je veux dire.* I used them to round off something – didn't I? Is that quite my game? No, it's not. It's not quite the kind of truth I'm after. Now for *Susannah*. All must be *deeply felt*.

But what is one to do, with this wretched cat and mouse act? There's my difficulty! I must try to write this afternoon instead. There is no reason why I shouldn't! No reason, except the after-effects of pain on a weakened organism.

*

1. K.M.'s cousin, born Mary Annette Beauchamp, in Sydney, Australia, author of the best-selling *Elizabeth in her German Garden* (1898) married the Count von Arnim, and, after his death, Lord Russell.

July 23　Finished *An Ideal Family* yesterday. It seems to me better than *The Doves*, but still it's not good enough. I worked at it hard enough, God knows, and yet I didn't get the deepest truth out of the idea, even once. What *is* this feeling? I feel again that this kind of knowledge is too easy for me; it's even a kind of trickery. I know so much more. This looks and smells like a story, but I wouldn't buy it. I don't want to possess it – to live with it. NO. Once I have written two more, I shall tackle something different – a long story: *At the Bay*, with *more difficult relationships. That's the whole problem.*

*

A Welcome
And because, when you arrive unexpected, there is so often a cold gleam in the hussif's eye which means: 'I can manage the sheets perfectly, but the blankets are certainly going to be a problem,' I would have you met in the doorway by a young creature carrying a not too bright lamp, it being, of course, late evening, and chanting, as you brush under the jasmine porch:

> Be not afraid, the house is full of blankets,
> Red ones and white ones, lovely beyond dreaming,
> Key-pattern, tasselled, camel-hair and woolly,
> Softer than sleep or the bosom of a swan.

*

The following was written in the middle of the manuscript of 'Her First Ball.'

July 25　All this! All that I write – all that I am – is on the border of the sea. It's a kind of playing. I want to put *all* my force behind it, but somehow, I *cannot!*

To the Hon. Dorothy Brett

[*29 July 1921*]

I am deeply interested in what you feel about Manet. For years he has meant more to me than any other of those French painters. He satisfies something deep in me. There is a kind of beautiful real *maturity* in his painting, as though he had come into his own, and it is a rich heritage. I saw a reproduction of a very lovely Renoir the other day, a young woman – profile – a three-quarter with the arm lazily out-stretched, lovely throat, bosom, shoulder – such grace. But I think that in his later paintings he is so often muzzy. I can't appreciate the queer woolly outline, and I feel it was so often as like as not *rheumatism* rather than *revelation*. But I don't know. I'd like to have a feed of paintings one day – go from here to Madrid, say, and have a good look. I shall. Once one is out of England I always feel every *thing* and *place* is near. We are only four hours from Milan here. Well, even tho' we don't go – there it *is*. One *could* start on Saturday morning and be there for the opera that evening. It's the channel which is such a dividing line.

[*8 August 1921*]

... I must stop this letter and get on with my new story. It's called *At the Bay* and it's (I hope) full of sand and sea-weed, bathing dresses hanging over verandas, and sandshoes on window sills, and little pink 'sea' convolvulus, and rather gritty sandwiches and the tide coming in. And it smells (oh, I *do* hope it smells) a little bit fishy.

To Richard Murry

[*9 August 1921*]

... The weather is superb, here. There has been a Battle of

the Wasps. Three hosts with their citadels have been routed from my balcony blind. In the swamps, still white with cotton grass, there are hundreds of grasshoppers. J. saw an *accident* to one the other day. He jumped by mistake into a stream and was borne away. Body not recovered. When we thought about it – it was the first real accident to an insect that we remembered . . .

Journal

[*1921*]

August 11 I don't know how I may write this next story. It's so difficult. But I suppose I shall. The trouble is I am so infernally cold.

To the Hon. Dorothy Brett

[*29 August 1921*]

. . . As soon as I can get well enough to go downstairs I shall engage our one original cab and go for a drive behind the old carthorse with his jingle-bells. The driver – as a great honour – throws the footmat over the back when one goes for a party of pleasure. He seems to think that is *very* chic! But this is such a beautiful country – Oh! it is so marvellous. Never looks the same – the air like old, still wine – sound of bells and birds and grasshoppers playing their fiddles and the wind shaking the trees. It rains and the drops on the fir trees afterwards are so flashing – bright and glowing that one feels all is enchanted. It is cloudy – we live in fine white clouds for days and then suddenly at night all is crystal clear and the moon has gold wings. They have just taken the new honey from the hives, I wish I could send you a jar. All the summer is shut up in a little pot.

*

What makes Lawrence a *real* writer is his passion. Without passion one writes in the air or on the sand of the seashore. But L. has got it all wrong, I believe. He is right, I imagine – or how shall I put it . . . ? It's my belief that nothing will save the world but love. But his tortured, satanic demon love I think is all wrong.

*

I am at present embedded in a terrific story[1] but it still frightens me.

To Ida Baker

[*29 August 1921*]

. . . Perhaps Jack is right; I *am* a tyrant. But . . . look here (a) Will you please either date your letters or put the day at the top.
(b) Do you mind cutting out the descriptions as much as you *can*? That kind of yearning sentimental writing about a virginia creeper and the small haigh voices of tainy children is more than I can stick. It makes me hang my head; it makes Jack play the mouth organ whenever we meet it in females. But I shall say no more. This is where the tyrant comes in. It's so much worse when the spelling is wrong, too. Brett is just exactly the same in this respect . . . It's very queer . . .

I don't like any of the stuff. Will you go to *Lewis, Evans, Selfridge* or *Debenham*. Number the patterns and I'll wire a reply. Miss Read won't get them done, of course, but arrange with her to send them over. Try for ROYAL blue instead of cornflower. These are either 2 dark or 2 light – try for soft smoky checks on any coloured ground instead – like the red and black check we saw in Menton? You remember? That's the kind of stuff I meant, too. They had both better be lines with silver grey *viyella* or cashmere, I think. And tell miss Read to cut them on the big side so that I can wear my

1. Almost certainly 'A Married Man's Story'.

woollen jumpers underneath if necessary. I'd rather have
nothing than those ugly dull stuffs. I am a very MODERN
woman. I like life in my clothes. It's no good going to
Liberty for plain colours – ever. Try and think of a picture
or a French pattern book or a figure on the stage – can't
you?

Sorry to give you so much trouble. I'd no idear it would be
all so *very* difficult. My advice is to 'concentrate more' and
not to worry about the golden leaves so much. Fall they will!
I am up. I am better and at work again. Cheer up!

Journal

[*1921*]

September   September is different from all other months.
It is more magical. I feel the strange chemical change in the
earth which produces mushrooms is the cause, too, of this
extra 'life' in the air – a resilience, a sparkle. For days the
weather has been the same. One wakes to see the trees outside bathed in green-gold light. It's fresh – not cold. It's
clear. The sky is a light pure blue. During the morning the
sun gets hot. There is a haze over the mountains. Occasionally a squirrel appears, runs up the mast of a pine-tree, seizes
a cone and sits in the crook of a branch, holding it like a
banana. Now and again a little bird, hanging upside-down,
pecks at the seed. There is a constant sound of bells from the
valley. It keeps on all day, from early to late.

Midday – with long shadows. Hot and still. And yet there's
always that taste of a berry rather than scent of a flower in the
air. But what can one say of the afternoons? Of the evening?
The rose, the gold on the mountains, the quick mounting
shadows? But it's soon cold. Beautifully cold, however.

*The following occurs in the middle of an unfinished MS. called 'By
Moonlight'. Karori was the novel of which 'Prelude' and 'At
the Bay' were at one time to have formed parts.*

I am stuck beyond words, and again it seems to me that what I am doing has *no form*! I ought to finish my book of *stories first* and then, when it's gone, really get down to my novel, *Karori*.

Why I should be so passionately determined to disguise this, I don't quite know. But here I lie, pretending, as Heaven knows how often I have before, to write. Supposing I were to give up the pretence and really did try? Supposing I only wrote half a page in a day – it would be half a page to the good; and I should at least be training my mind to get into the habit of regular performance. As it is, every day sees me further off my goal *And*, once I had this book finished, I'm free to start the real one. *And* it's a question of money.

But my idea, even of the short story, has changed rather, lately – That was lucky! Jack opened the door softly and I was apparently really truly engaged ... And – no, enough of this. It has served its purpose. It has put me on the right lines.

At the end of the same unfinished MS. is the following note.

This isn't bad, but at the same time it's not good. It's too easy ... I wish I could go back to N.Z. for a year. But I can't possibly just now. I don't see why not, in two years' time though.

Journal

[*1921*]

September   It's nothing short of loathsome' to be in my state. Two weeks ago I could write anything. I went at my work each day and at the end of each day so much was written. Whereas *now* I can't say a word!

*

(Tchehov: *Misery*.)

I would see every single French short story up the chimney for this. It's one of the masterpieces of the world.

To the Hon. Dorothy Brett

[September 1921]

The Cezanne book, Miss, you won't get back until you send a policeman or an urgent request for it. It is fascinating, and you can't think how we enjoy such a book on our mountain tops. It's awfully sympathetic to me. I am absolutely uneducated about painting. I can only look at it as a writer, but it seems to me the real thing. It's what one is aiming at. One of his men gave me quite a shock. He's the *spit* of a man I've just written about, one Jonathan Trout. To the life. I wish I could cut him out and put him in my book.

I've just finished my new book. Finished last night at 10.30. Laid down the pen after writing 'Thanks be to God.' I wish there was a God. I am longing to (1) praise him, (2) thank him. The title is *At the Bay*. That's the name of the very long story in it – a continuation of *Prelude*. It's about 60 pages. I've been at it all last night. My precious children have sat in here, playing cards. I've wandered about all sorts of places – in and out – I hope it is good. It is as good as I can do, and all my heart and soul is in it . . . every single bit. Oh God, I hope it gives pleasure to someone . . . It is so strange to bring the dead to life again. There's my Grandmother, back in her chair with her pink knitting, there stalks my uncle over the grass; I feel as I write, 'You are not dead, my darlings. All is remembered. I bow down to you. I efface myself so that you may live again through me in your richness and beauty.' And one feels *possessed*. And then the place where it all happens. I have tried to make it as familiar to 'you' as it is to me. You know the marigolds? You know those pools in the rocks, you know the mouse trap on the washhouse window-sill? And too, one tries to go deep – to speak to the secret self we all have – to acknowledge that. I mustn't say any more about it.

No, we certainly shan't be back in England for years. Sometimes, in bed at night, we plan one holiday a year, but everywhere else feels nearer than England. If we can get the money we shall build here in two or three years' time. We have already chosen the way to look – the way the house shall face. And it is christened *Chalèt Content*. We are both most fearful dreamers, especially when it's late and we lie staring at the ceiling. It begins with me. M. declares he won't talk. It's too late. Then I hear: 'Certainly not more than two floors and a large open fireplace.' A long pause. *K.:* 'What about bees?' *M.:* 'Most certainly bees and I aspire to a goat.' And it ends with us getting fearfully hungry and M. going off for two small whacks of cake while I heat two small milks on the spirit stove.

You know Wingley? The Mountain brought him over. He arrived with immense eyes after having flown through all that landscape and it was several hours before the famous purr came into action. Now he's completely settled down and reads Shakespeare with us in the evenings. I wonder what cat-Shakespeare is like. We expect him to write his reminiscences shortly. They are to be bound in mouse skin . . .

Goodbye. I am taking a holiday today after my labours last week. I wrote for nine solid hours yesterday.

Who do you think turned up at the end of this letter? Mrs H.G. Wells and two young H.G. Wells. *Very* nice boys. We are full of gaiety.

[*1921*]

At the end of the manuscript of 'The Garden Party', finished 14 October 1921, K.M. wrote the following note.

This is a moderately successful story, and that's all. It's somehow, in the episode at the lane, scamped.

Journal

[*1921*]

October 16 Another radiant day. J. is typing my last

story, *The Garden Party*, which I finished on my birthday. It took me nearly a month to 'recover' from *At the Bay*. I made at least three false starts. But I could not get away from the sound of the sea, and Beryl fanning her hair at the window. These things would not *die down*. But now I am not at all sure about that story. It seems to me it's a little 'wispy' – not what it might have been. The *G.P.* is better. But that is not *good enough*, either . . .

The last few days what one notices more than anything is the blue. Blue sky, blue mountains, all is a heavenly blueness! And clouds of all kinds – wings, soft white clouds, almost hard little golden islands, great mock-mountains. The gold deepens on the slopes. In fact, in sober fact, it is perfection.

But the late evening is the time – of times. Then with that unearthly beauty before one it is not hard to realize how far one has to go. To write something that will be worthy of that rising moon, that pale light. To be 'simple' enough, as one would be simple before God . . .

*

October I wonder why it should be so difficult to be humble. I do not think I am a good writer; I realise my faults better than anyone else could realise them. I know exactly where I fail. And yet, when I have finished a story and before I have begun another, I catch myself *preening* my feathers. It is disheartening. There seems to be some bad old pride in my heart; a root of it that puts out a thick shoot on the slightest provocation . . . This interferes very much with work. One can't be calm, clear, good as one must be, while it goes on. I look at the mountains, I try to pray and I think of something *clever*. It's a kind of excitement within one, which shouldn't be there. Calm yourself. Clear yourself. And anything that I write in this mood will be no good; it will be full of *sediment*. If I were well, I would go off by myself somewhere and sit under a tree. One must learn, one must practise, to *forget* oneself. I can't tell the truth about Aunt Anne unless I am free to enter into her life without selfconsciousness. Oh

God! I am divided still. I am bad. I fail in my personal life. I lapse into impatience, temper, vanity, and so I fail as thy priest. Perhaps poetry will help.

I have just thoroughly cleaned and attended to my fountain pen. If after this it leaks, then it is *no* gentleman!

To the Countess Russell

[*October 1921*]

... I have turned to Milton all last week. There are times when Milton seems the only food to me. He is a most blessed man.

> '... Yet not the more
> Cease I to wander where the Muses haunt
> Cleer Spring, or shadie Grove, or sunnie Hill.
> Smit with the love of sacred song;'

But the more poetry one reads the more one longs to read! This afternoon J., lying on my furry rug, has been reading aloud Swinburne's *Ave Atque Vale* – which did not sound fearfully good. I suspect those green buds of sin and those gray fruits of shame. And try as one may, one can't see Baudelaire. Swinburne sits so very tight on the tomb. Then we read Hardy's poem to Swinburne, which J. adored. I, being an inferior being, was a little troubled by the picture of Sappho and Algernon meeting en plein mer (if one can say such a thing) and he begging her to tell him where her manuscript was. It seemed such a watery rendezvous. But we went on reading Hardy. How exquisite, how marvellous some of those poems are! They are almost intolerably near to one. I mean I always long to weep ... that love and regret touched so lightly – that autumn tone, that feeling that 'Beauty passes though rare, rare it be ...'

But speaking of autumn, it is here. Yesterday, soft, silky, sweet-smelling summer kissed the geraniums, and waving the loveliest hand, *went*. To-day it is cold, solemn, with the first snow falling. Oh, Elizabeth, how I longed for you this morning on my balcony! The sun came through, a silver star. In the folds of the mountains little clouds glittered like Dorothy Wordsworth's sheep. And all that paysage across the valley was a new land. The colour is changed since you were here. The green is gold, a very deep gold like *amber*. On the high peaks snow was falling. And the Wind walking among the trees had a new voice. It was like land seen from a ship. It was like arriving in the harbour, and wondering, half frightened and yet longing, whether we would go ashore. But no, I can't describe it. Soon after all was grey and down came the white bees. The feeling in the house changed immediately. Ernestine became mysterious and blithe. The Faithful One ran up and down as though with cans of hot water. One felt the whisper had gone round that the pains had begun and the doctor had been sent for.

I am just at the beginning of a new story, which I may turn into a serial. Clement Shorter wants one. But he stipulates for 13 'curtains' and an adventure note! Thirteen curtains! And my stories haven't even a wisp of blind cord as a rule. I have never been able to manage curtains. I don't think I shall be able to see such a wholesale *hanging* through.

The knitting becomes almost frenzied at times. We may be sober in our lives, but we shall be garish in our shrouds and flamboyant in our coffins if this goes on. J. now *mixes* his wools thereby gaining what *he* calls a 'superb astrachan effect.' Chi lo sa! I softly murmur over my needles. I find knitting turns me into an imbecile. It is the female tradition, I suppose.

To Violet Schiff

[*October 1921*][1]

... My book is to lie in Constable's bosom until after the New Year. Its called, after all, *The Garden Party*. I hope you

1. Wrongly dated in the *Letters* (1928), vol. II, p. 137.

like the title. The Mercury is publishing one of the stories in a month or two. Terribly long. Too long for the Mercury . . . Murry is re-reading Proust – all from the beginning. So far he likes it infinitely more than the first time. I've been reading the book of Job! There are times when I turn to the bible. It is marvellous!

As for papers. I wonder what you read? The Dial? It is improved, I think. It's a mixed lot but on the whole there is always something in it. I thought Lawrence was good this month – so warm – so living. In spite of everything Lawrence's feeling for life is there.

Poor Eliot sounds tired to death. His London letter is all a maze of words. One feels the awful effort behind it – as though he were being tortured.[1]

1. Shortly after this was written T. S. Eliot suffered some kind of 'breakdown', the experience of which set off the writing of 'The Waste Land'.

14

Switzerland, November 1921–January 1922

*By November the most prolific and brilliant three months of
Katherine Mansfield's writing life were behind her. She was to write
only one further story that ranks with her best ('The Fly'). Now a
new restlessness began to take hold of her. Enjoying life again, enjoying her success as a writer and the companionship of her husband,
she found it harder than ever to accept her invalid role. She wanted a
cure – a miracle – and began to fix her mind on the Russian émigré
doctor Manoukhin, who practised in Paris and who claimed to cure
advanced cases of tuberculosis by bombarding the spleen with X-rays.*

To the Hon. Dorothy Brett

[*11 November 1921*]

. . . But all agree the snow is not serious yet. It falls, small and
light like confetti, or it swarms like white bees – M. comes
back from his walks hung with real icicles . . . Have I told
you about my balcony? It is as big as a small room, the sides
are enclosed and big double doors lead from it to my workroom. Three superb geraniums still stand on the ledge when
it's fine, and their rosy masses of flowers against *blue space*
are wonderful. It is so high up here that one only sees the
tops and half way down of the enormous mountains opposite,
and there's a great sweep of sky as one only gets at sea – on a
ship – anchored before a new, undiscovered country. At
sunset, when all the clouds are really too much to bear alone
I call out, 'Mountains on your right a deep blue,' and M.
shouts from below, 'Right!' and I hear him go out on *his*
balcony to observe. But it's most beautiful at night. Last
night, for instance, at about 10 o'clock, I wound myself up

in wool and I came out here and sat watching. The world was like a huge ball of ice. There wasn't a sound. It might have been ages before man . . .

Tchehov *said* over and over again, he protested, he begged, that he had no problem. In fact, you know, he thought it was his weakness as an artist. It worried him, but he always said the same. No problem. And when you come to think of it, what was Chaucer's problem or Shakespeare's? The 'problem' is the invention of the 19th Century. The artist takes a long look at life. He says softly, 'So this is what life is, is it?' And he proceeds to express that. All the rest he leaves. Tolstoi even had no problem. What he had was a propaganda and he is a great artist in spite of it.

[*12 November 1921*]

It's very late at night and I ate such a stupid man with my tea – I can't digest him. He is bringing out an anthology of short stories and he said the more 'plotty' a story I could give him the better. What about that for a word! It made my hair stand up in prongs. A nice 'plotty' story, please. People *are* funny.

The Fat Cat sits on my Feet.

Fat is not the word to describe him by now. He must weigh pounds and pounds. And his lovely black coat is turning white. I suppose it's to prevent the mountains from seeing him. He sleeps here and occasionally creeps up to my chest and pads softly with his paws, singing the while. I suppose he wants to see if I have the same face all night. I long to surprise him with terrific disguises.

M. calls him 'My *Breakfast* Cat' because they share that meal, M. *at* the table and Wingley *on*. It's awful the love one can lavish on an animal. In his memoirs which he dictates to me M.'s name is always Masteranman – one word – my name is Grandma Jaegar – the Mountain is always called 'Fostermonger' and for some reason our servant he refers to as The Swede. He has rather a contempt for her.

Journal

[*November 1921*]

November 21 ... A bad spell has been on me. I have begun two stories, but then I told them and they felt betrayed. It is absolutely fatal to give way to this temptation ... To-day I began to write, seriously, *The Weak Heart*, – a story which fascinates me *deeply*. What I feel it needs so peculiarly is a very subtle variation of 'tense' from the present to the past and back again – and softness, lightness, and the feeling that all is in bud, with a play of humour over the character of Ronnie. And the feeling of the Thorndon Baths, the wet, moist, oozy ... no, I know how it must be done.

November 24 Why am I haunted every single day of my life by the nearness of death and its inevitability? I am really diseased on that point! And I can't speak of it. If I tell J. it makes him unhappy. If I don't tell him, it leaves me to fight it. I am tired of the battle. No one knows how tired.

To-night, when the evening-star shone through the side-window and the pale mountains were so lovely, I sat there thinking of death. Of all there was to do – of Life, which is so lovely – and of the fact that my body is a prison. But this state of mind is *evil*. It is only by acknowledging that I, being what I am, had to suffer *this* in order to do the work I am here to perform – it is only by acknowledging it, by being thankful that work was not taken away from me, that I shall recover. I am weak where I must be strong.

*

Why must thinking and existing be ever on two different planes? Why will the attempt of Hegel to transform subjective processes into objective world-processes not work out? 'It is the special art and object of thinking to attain existence by quite other methods than that of existence itself.' That is to say, reality cannot become the ideal, the dream; and it is not the business of the artist to grind an axe, to try to impose his vision of life upon the existing world. Art is not an attempt of the artist to reconcile existence with his vision; it is an attempt to create his own world *in* this world. That which suggests the subject to the artist is the *unlikeness* to what we accept as reality. We single out – we bring into the light – we put up higher.

All's Well that Ends Well

The First Lord is worth attending to. One would have thought that his speeches and those of the Second Lord would have been interchangeable; but he is a very definite, quick-cut character. Take, for example, the talk between the two in Act IV Scene III. The Second Lord asks him to let what he is going to tell dwell darkly with him.

First Lord: 'When you have spoken it, 'tis dead, and I am the grave of it.'

And then his comment:

'How mightily sometimes we make us comforts of our losses.'

And this is most excellent:

'The web of our life is of a mingled yarn, good and ill together; our virtues would be proud if our faults whipped them not; and our faults would despair if they were not cherished by our virtues.'

I like the temper of that extremely – and does it not reveal the man? Disillusioned and yet – amused – worldly, and yet he has feeling. But I see him as – quick, full of life, and marvellously at his ease with his company, his surroundings, his own condition, and the whole small, solid earth. He is like a man on shipboard who is inclined to straddle just to show (but not to *show off*) how well his sea-legs serve him . . .

The Clown – 'a shrewd knave and an unhappy' – comes to tell the Countess of the arrival of Bertram and his soldiers.

'Faith, there's a dozen of 'em, with delicate fine hats, and most courteous feathers, that bow and nod the head at every man.'

In that phrase there is all the charm of soldiers on prancing, jingling, dancing horses. It is a veritable little pageant. With what an air the haughty (and intolerable) Bertram wears his two-pile velvet patch – with what disdain his hand in the white laced French glove tightens upon the tight rein of his silver charger. Wonderfully sunny, with a little breeze. And the Clown, of course, sees the humour of his conceit . . .

Parolles is a lovable creature, a brave little cock-sparrow of a ruffian.

. . . .'I am now sir, muddied in Fortune's mood, and smell somewhat strong of her strong displeasure.'

I must say Helena is a terrifying female. Her virtue, her persistence, her pegging away after the odious Bertram (and disguised as a pilgrim – so typical!) and then telling the whole story to that *good* widow-woman! And that tame fish Diana. As to lying in Diana's bed and enjoying the embraces meant for Diana – well, I know nothing more sickening. It would take a respectable woman to do such a thing. The worst of it is I can so well imagine . . . for instance acting in precisely that way, and giving Diana a present afterwards. *What* a cup of tea the widow and D. must have enjoyed while it was taking place, or did D. at the last moment want to cry off the bargain? But to forgive such a woman! Yet Bertram would. There's an espèce de mothers-boyisme in him which makes him stupid enough for anything.

The Old King is a queer old card – he seems to have a mania for bestowing husbands. As if the one fiasco were not enough, Diana has no sooner explained herself than he begins:

> 'If thou be'st yet a fresh uncropped flower
> Choose thou thy husband, and I'll pay thy dower.'

I think Shakespeare must have seen the humour of that. It just – at the very last moment of the play, puts breath into the old fool.

Hamlet

Coleridge on Hamlet. 'He plays that subtle trick of

pretending to act only when he is very near being what he acts.'

. . . So do we all begin by acting and the nearer we are to what we would be the more perfect our *disguise*. Finally there comes the moment when *we are no longer acting;* it may even catch us by surprise. We may look in amazement at our no longer borrowed plumage. The two have merged; that which we put on has joined that which was; acting has become action. The soul has accepted this livery for its own after a time of trying on and approving.

To act . . . to see ourselves in the part – to make a larger gesture than would be ours in life – to declaim, to pronounce, to even exaggerate. To persuade ourselves? Or others? To put ourselves in heart? To do more than is necessary in order that we may accomplish ce qu'il faut.

And then Hamlet is lonely. The solitary person always acts.

But I could write a thousand pages about Hamlets.

Mad Scene. If one looks at it with a cold eye is really very poor. It depends entirely for its effect upon wispy Ophelia. The cardboard King and Queen are of course only lookers-on. They don't care a halfpenny. I think the Queen is privately rather surprised at a verse or two of her songs . . . And who can believe that a solitary violet withered when that silly fussy old pomposity died? And who can believe that Ophelia really loved him, and wasn't thankful to think how peaceful breakfast would be without his preaching?

The Queen's speech after Ophelia's death is exasperating to one's sense of poetic truth. If no one saw it happen – if she wasn't found until she was drowned, how does the Queen know how it happened? Dear Shakespeare has been to the Royal Academy . . . for his picture.

Antony & Cleopatra
Act I. Scene 4.

> Like to a vagabond flag upon the stream
> Goes to and back, lackeying the varying tide,
> To rot itself with motion.

Marvellous words! I can apply them. There is a short story. And then it seems that the weed gets caught up and then sinks; then it is gone out to sea and lost. But comes a day, a like tide, a like occasion, and it reappears more sickeningly rotten still! Shall he? Will he? Are there any letters? No letters? The post? Does he miss me? No. Then sweep it all out to sea. Clear the water for ever! Let me write this one day.

'Thy cheek so much as lanked not.' The economy of utterance.

*

Scene 5. '*Tawny*-finned fishes . . . their *shiny* jaws . . .' and the adjectives seem part of the nouns when Shakespeare uses them. They grace them so beautifully, attend and adorn so modestly, and yet with such skill. It so often happens with lesser writers that we are more conscious of the servants than we are of the masters, and quite forget that their office is to serve, to enlarge, to amplify the power of the master.

> Ram thou thy fruitful tidings in my ears
> That long time have been barren.

Good lines! And another example of the choice of the place of words. I suppose it was instinctive. But 'fruitful' seems to be just where it ought to be, to be resolved (musically speaking) by the word 'barren'. One reads 'fruitful' expecting 'barren' almost from the 'sound-sense.'

To the Hon. Dorothy Brett

[*5 December 1921*]

Wasn't that Van Gogh shown at the Goupil ten years ago? Yellow flowers, brimming with sun, in a pot? I wonder if it is the same. That picture seemed to reveal something that I hadn't realized before I saw it. It lived with me afterwards. It still does. That and another of a sea-captain in a flat cap. They taught me something about writing, which was queer, a kind of freedom – or rather, a shaking free. When one has been working for a long stretch one begins to narrow one's vision a bit, to fine things down too much. And it's only when something else breaks through, a picture or something seen out of doors, that one realizes it. It is – literally – years since I have been to a picture show. I can *smell* them as I write.

To S. S. Koteliansky

[*5 December 1921*]

Thank you. I have written to M. today. Whatever he advises that will I do. It is strange – I have faith in him. I am sure he will not have the kind of face one walks away from. Besides – Think of being '*well*.' Health is as precious as life – no less. Do you know I have not walked since November 1920? Not more than to a carriage and back. Both my lungs are affected; there is a cavity in one and the other is affected through. My heart is weak, too. Can all this be cured. Ah, Koteliansky – wish for me!

The 'M.' referred to in the above letter was the Russian émigré doctor Manoukhin (see above). K.M. had begun to persuade herself that this was the 'miracle' she knew was needed to save her life.

To Sydney Schiff

[*28 December 1921*]

... I have chosen today to write because Manoukhine has come a great deal nearer. He has told me that if I go to Paris he will treat me by his new method and there is the word *guérison* shining in his letter. I believe every word of it; I believe in him implicitly. As soon as I am out of bed (the cold has been *too* cold) Jones[1] will pack the boxes and I shall go to see him and arrange to return to him in May. I want to spend the winter here. But in May I shall go to Paris for the course of treatment which takes 15 weeks – (Manoukhine is not only a doctor, he is a whole new stage of the journey. I hardly know why.) His treatment consists of applications of Rayons X.

One word I must say about Joyce. Having re-read the Portrait it seems to me on the whole awfully *good*. We are going to buy *Ulysses*. But Joyce is (if only Pound didn't think so too) immensely important. Sometime ago I found something so repellant in his work that it was difficult to read it – It shocks me to come upon words, expressions and so on that I'd shrink from in life. But now it seems to me the *new novel*, the seeking after Truth is so by far and away the most important thing that one must conquer all minor aversions. They are unworthy.

To S. S. Koteliansky

[*December 1921*]

I want to write to you at this time in memory of that other Christmas when Lawrence gave his party in the top room of Elsie Munay's [?] cottage . . .

Wasn't Lawrence awfully nice that night. Ah, one must always love Lawrence for his 'being'. I could love Frieda too, tonight, in her Bavarian dress, with her face flushed as though she had been crying about the 'children'. It is a pity that all things must pass. And how strange it is, how in spite of everything, there are certain people, like Lawrence, who remain in one's life for ever, and others who are forever shadowy.

You, for instance, are part of my life like that.

1. Ida Baker.

Journal

[*1922*]

January 1   I dreamed I sailed to Egypt with Grandma – a very white boat.

Cold, still. The gale last night has blown nearly all the snow off the trees; only big, frozen-looking lumps remain. In the wood where the snow is thick, bars of sunlight lay like pale fire.

*

Wrote *The Doves' Nest* this afternoon. I was in no mood to write; it seemed impossible. Yet when I had finished three pages, they were 'all right'. This is a proof (never to be too often proved) that once one has thought out a story nothing remains but the *labour*.

*

I want to remember how the light fades from a room – and one fades with it, is *expunged*, sitting still, knees together, hands in pockets . . .

*

January 2   Little round birds in the fir-tree at the side window, scouring the tree for food. I crumbled a piece of bread, but though the crumbs fell in the branches only two found them. There was a strange remoteness in the air, the scene, the winter cheeping. In the evening, for the first time for — I felt rested. I sat up in bed and discovered I was singing within. Even the sound of the wind is different. It is joyful, not ominous. And black dark looks in at the window and is only black dark. In the afternoon it came on to pour with rain, long glancing rain, falling aslant.

I have not done the work I should have done. I shirk the lunch party [see *The Doves' Nest*]. This is very bad. In fact I am disgusted with myself. There must be a change from now on. What I chiefly admire in Jane Austen is that what she promises, she performs, *i.e.* if Sir T. is to arrive, we have his arrival at length, and it's excellent and excels our expectations. This is rare; it is also my very weakest point. Easy to see why . . .

To the Hon. Dorothy Brett

[*9 January 1922*]

This awful writing is frozen writing, Brett. I am writing with two icicles for fingers. We have 6 foot of snow here, all is frozen over and over, even the bird's tails. Is not that hideous cruelty? I have a large table for these precious atoms daily, and the first cocoanut in Switzerland is the Big Joint. They can't yet believe in the cocoanut. It overwhelms them. A special issue of the *Bird Times* is being issued, the bird who discovered it is to be photographed, interviewed and received at Pluckingham Palace and personally conducted tours are being arranged. What with them and my poor dear pussy-wee, who got out today and began to scratch, scratched away, kept at it, sat up, took a deep breath, scratched his ear, wiped his whiskers, scratched on, SCRATCHED, until finally only the tip of a quivering tail was to be seen and he was rescued by the gentle Ernestine. He wrung his little paws in despair. Poor lamb! to think he will not be able to scratch *through* until April. I suppose snow is beautiful. I hate it. It always seems to me a kind of humbug – a justification of mystery, and I hate mystery. And then there is no movement. All is still, white, cold, deathly, eternal. Every time I look out I feel inclined to say I *refuse* it. But perhaps if one goes about and skims over, all is different.

I'm working at such a big story that I still can only just see the end in my imagination . . . the longest by far I've ever written. It's called *The Doves' Nest*. But winter is a bad black time for work, I think. One's brain gets congealed. It is very hard.

Journal

[*1922*]

January 9 Read and knitted and played cards. A long letter from Sydney [Schiff]. I want to believe all he says about my story. He *does* see what I meant. He does not see it as a set of trivial happenings just thrown together. This is enough to be deeply grateful for – more than others will see. But I have this continual longing to write something with all my power, all my force in it.

January 10 Dreamed I was back in New Zealand.

Got up today. It was fine. The sun shone and melted the last trace of snow from the trees. All the morning big drops fell from the trees, from the roof. The drops were not like rain-drops, but bigger, softer, more *exquisite*. They made one realise how one loves the fertile earth and hates this snow-bound cold substitute.

The men worked outside on the snowy road, trying to raise the telegraph pole. Before they began they had lunch out of a paper, sitting astride the pole. It is very beautiful to see people sharing food. Cutting bread and passing the loaf, especially cutting bread in that age-old way with a clasp-knife. Afterwards one got up in a tree and sat among the branches working from there, while the other lifted. The one in the tree turned into a kind of bird, as all people do in trees – chuckled, laughed out, peered from among the branches, careless. *At-tend! Ar-rêt! Al-lez!*

January 11 In bed again. Heard from Pinker *The Dial* has taken *The Doll's House*. Wrote and finished *A Cup of Tea*. It took about 4–5 hours. In the afternoon Elizabeth came. She looked fascinating in her black suit, something between a Bishop and a Fly. She spoke of my 'pretty little story' in the *Mercury*. All the while she was here I was conscious of a falsity.

*

There is no feeling to be compared with the joy of having written and finished a story. I did not go to sleep, but nothing mattered. There it was, *new* and complete.

To Sydney Schiff

[*January 1922*]

... I remember once talking it over with Lawrence and he said 'We must swear a solemn pact of friendship. Friendship is as binding, as solemn as marriage. We take each other for life, through everything – for ever. But it's not enough to say we will do it. We must *swear*.' At the time I was impatient with him. I thought it extravagant – fanatic. But when one considers what this world is like I understand perfectly why L. (especially being L.) made such claims ... I think, myself, it is pride which makes friendship most difficult. To submit, to bow down to the other is not easy, but it must be done if one is to really understand the being of the other. Friendship isn't *merging*. One doesn't thereupon become a shadow and one remain a substance ...

To Lady Ottoline Morrell

[*January 1922*]

... I am so glad you liked *The Veil*.[1] There is one poem:

> Why has the rose faded and fallen
> And these eyes have not seen ...

It haunts me. But it is a state of mind I know so terribsy well – That regret for what one has not seen and felt – for what has passed by – unheeded. Life is only given once and then I *waste* it. Do you feel that?

1. Walter de la Mare, *The Veil and Other Poems*, London, 1921.

Journal

[*1922*]

January 17 Tchehov made a mistake in thinking that if he had had more time he would have written more fully, described the rain, and the midwife and the doctor having tea. The truth is one can get only *so much* into a story; there is always a sacrifice. One has to leave out what one knows and longs to use. Why? I haven't any idea, but there it is. It's always a kind of race to get in as much as one can before it *disappears*.

But time is not really in it. Yet wait. I do not understand even now. I am pursued by time myself. The only occasion when I ever felt at leisure was while writing *The Daughters of the Late Colonel*. And then at the end I was so terribly unhappy that I wrote as fast as possible for fear of dying before the story was sent. I should like to prove this, to work at *real leisure*. Only thus can it be done.

January 22 Lumbago. This is a very queer thing. So sudden, so painful. I must remember it when I write about an old man. The start to get up – the pause – the slow look of fury – and how, lying at night, one seems to get *locked*. To move is an agony; till finally one discovers a movement which is possible. But the helpless feeling about with the legs first!

January 23 ... To remember the sound of wind – the peculiar wretchedness one can feel while the wind blows. Then the warm soft wind of spring searching out the heart. The wind I call the Ancient of Days which blows here at night. The wind that shakes the garden at night when one runs out into it.

Dust. Turning one's back on a high, tearing wind. Walking along the Esplanade when the wind carries the sea over. The wind of summer, so playful, that rocked and swung in the trees here. And wind moving through grass so that the grass

quivers. This moves me with an emotion I don't ever understand. I always see a field, a young horse – and there is a very
fair Danish girl telling me something about her step-father.
The girl's name is Elsa Bagge.

January 24　Wrote and finished *Taking the Veil*. It took
me about 3 hours to write finally. But I had been thinking
over the *décor* and so on for weeks – nay, months, I believe. I
can't say how thankful I am to have been born in N.Z., to
know Wellington as I do, and to have it to range about in.
Writing about the convent seemed so natural. I suppose I
have not been in the grounds more than twice. But it is one
of the places that remains as vivid as ever. I must not forget
the name of *Miss Sparrow*, nor the name *Palmer*.

January 29　H. came. He says my right lung is practically
all right. Can one believe such words? The other is a great
deal better. *He* thinks my heart will give me far less trouble
at a lower level.[1] Can this be true? He was so hopeful today
that T.B. seemed no longer a scourge. It seemed that one
recovered more often than not. Is this fantastic?

Tidied all my papers. Tore up and ruthlessly destroyed
much. This is always a great satisfaction. Whenever I prepare
for a journey I prepare as though for death. Should I never
return, all is in order. This is what life has taught me.

In the evening I wrote to Orage about his book. It has
taken me a week to write the letter. J. and I seem to have
played cribbage off and on all day. I feel there is much love
between us. Tender love. *Let it not change!*

1. i.e. of altitude.

15

Paris, February–May 1922

Katherine Mansfield left the Chalet des Sapins on January 30 to see Dr Manoukhin in Paris. He told her he could cure her (see Journal entry below) and despite her doubts about him she decided to begin at once. At first Murry would not leave Switzerland – according to his own account because he believed (probably rightly) that the regular life they had led there represented her best chance for survival. He soon yielded to pressure, however, and joined K.M. in Paris on 11 February. For four months they lived together in a hotel while she underwent the treatment, her faith in its efficacy declining all the time. On 20 February she completed 'The Fly' – her most sombre story and the one which has received probably more frequent and detailed critical attention than any other she wrote. In the same month her third book, The Garden Party, *was published. It was an immediate success.*

Journal

[*1922*]

January 30 There was a tremendous fall of snow on Sunday night. Monday was the first *real* perfect day of the winter. It seemed that the happiness of Bogey and of me reached its zenith on that day. We could not have been happier; that was the feeling. Sitting one moment on the balcony of the bedroom, for instance, or driving in the sleigh through masses of heaped-up snow. He looked so beautiful, too – hatless, strolling about with his hands in his pockets. He weighed himself. 10 stone. There was a harmonium in the waiting-room. Then I went away, after a quick but not hurried kiss . . .

It was very beautiful on the way to Sierre. Then I kept wondering if I was seeing it all for the last time – the snowy bushes, the leafless trees. 'I miss the buns.'

Pinker told me *The Westminster* had taken *The Garden Party*.

January 31 Travelling is terrible. All is so sordid, and the train shatters one. Tunnels are *hell*. I am frightened of travelling.

We arrived in Paris late, but it was very beautiful – all emerging from water. In the night I looked out and saw *the men with lanterns*. The hotel all sordid again, – fruit peelings, waste-paper, boots, grime, ill-temper. In the evening I saw Manoukhin. But on the way there, nay, even before, I realized my heart was not in it. I feel divided in myself and angry and without virtue. Then L.M. and I had one of our famous quarrels, and I went to the wrong house. Don't forget, as I rang the bell, the scampering and laughter inside. M. had a lame girl there as interpreter. He said through her he could cure me completely. But I did not believe it. It all seemed suddenly unimportant and ugly. But the flat was nice – the red curtains, marble clock, and pictures of ladies with powdered hair.

February 1 I have the feeling that M. is a really good man. I have also a sneaking feeling (I use that word 'sneaking' advisedly) that he is a kind of unscrupulous impostor.

To J. M. Murry

[*7 February 1922*]

. . . Have you read that Goethe-Eckermann? I shall give it to Ida to return to you. But I mean to order a whole one for myself. That taste has given me *such* an appetite. It's a mystery to me that so fascinating a book should be so little talked of. In fact it's one of those books which, once discovered, abides for ever. It's such a whole (even in part, as I have it). These two men live and one is carried with them. The slight absurdity and the sentimental bias of Eckermann I wouldn't have not there! Delightfully human – one smiles but one can't help smiling always tenderly. And then outside sounds come in – the bells of Weimar ringing in the evening – the whisper of the wheat as the friends walk together, the neighbours' little children calling like birds. But all this human interest (Ah! how it draws one) apart, there is Goethe talking, and he did say marvellous things. He was great enough to be simple enough to say what we all feel and don't say. And his attitude to Art was noble. It does me good to go to Church in the breasts of great men. Shakespeare is my Cathedral, but I'm glad to have discovered this other. In fact, isn't it a joy – there is hardly a greater one – to find a *new book*, a living book, and to know that it will remain with you while life lasts? ...

To the Countess Russell

[*21 February 1922*]

... John, after his beating at chess has had the satisfaction of teaching me. If he wallops me absolutely he remarks 'A good game. You're getting on.' If it is a draw he exclaims 'My God I'm a complete idiot. I've lost my head completely.' This strikes me as very male. The gentle female would never be so brutal. There is a look of Bertie[1] about the knight – don't you think? ...

To Lady Ottoline Morrell

[*4 March 1922*]

... It's a joy to know that *The Garden Party* has given you pleasure and especially that you like my poor old girls, the

1. Bertrand Russell, the Countess Russell's brother-in-law.

'Daughters.' I shall never forget lying on that wretched little sofa in Mentone writing that story. I couldn't stop. I wrote it all day and on my way back to bed sat down on the stairs and began scribbling the bit about the meringues . . .

To Ida Baker

[*7 March 1922*]

I have had letters from Elizabeth, Chaddie Waterlow about the book[1] which are a great joy. Letters from strangers, too, and 'my' undergraduate[2] (*pages* from him) and Clement Shorter the Sphere man who asked for a portrait for publication and has ordered 12 stories to be ready in July. This is no less than staggering. I enclose the *Times* review. Please return it. Jack, who read my card to you, said off his own bat he'd order you a copy to be sent direct from London. He also said off his own bat, 'of course she won't believe it was I who did it'. Well, it was.

Thank you for the grey satin top with all its little blanket stitches. They made me smile. My writing case looks excessively sumptuous here. It reminds me of the Ida I love. Not because of what it cost. *No.* But the 'impulse' – the gesture – what you call the 'perfect thing'! It carries me back to Isola Bella. Oh, memory! And back I go to the Casetta and the olive tree before and the cotton tree along the twisted fence and the red roses and big starry-eyed daisies. Menton seems to hold years of life. How hard it is to escape from places. However carefully one goes they hold you – you leave little bits of yourself fluttering on the fences – little rags and shreds of your very life. But a queer thing is – this is personal – however painful a thing has been when I look back it is no longer painful – or no more painful than music is. In fact it is just that. *Now* when I hear the sea at the Casetta its unbearably beautiful.

1. *The Garden Party*, published February 1922.
2. William Gerhardi.

I must begin working. I'll never be a Wealthy Woman. I write like this because I write at such a pace. I can't manage it otherwise. Here is some money. Be well! Be happy! Eat! Sleep!

To the Hon. Dorothy Brett

[*9 March 1922*]

. . . France is a remarkable country. It is I suppose the most civilized country in the world. Bookshops swarm in Paris and the newspapers are written in a way that English people would not stand for one moment. There's practically *no* police news. True, they did write about Landru's execution, but so well it might have been de Maupassant! They are corrupt and rotten politically, that's true. But oh, how they know how to live! And there is always the feeling that Art has its place . . . is accepted by everybody, by the servants, by the rubbish man as well as by all others as something important, necessary, to be proud of. That's what makes living in France such a rest. If you stop your taxi to look at a tree the driver says, 'En effet c't' arbre est bien jolie,' and ten to one moves his arms like branches. I learnt more about France from my servant at Mentone than anywhere. She was *pure* French, highly highly civilised, nervous, eager, and she would have understood anything on earth you wished to explain to her, in the artistic sense. The fact is they are always *alive*, never indifferent as the English are. England has political freedom (a terrific great thing) and poetry and lovely careless lavish green country. But I'd much rather admire it from afar. English people are I think superior Germans. (10 years hard labour for that remark.) But it's true. They are the German ideal. I was reading Goethe on the subject the other day. He had a tremendous admiration for them. But all through it one feels 'so might we Germans be if we only knocked the heads of our police off.' It's fascinating to think about nations and their 'significance' in the history of the world. I mean in the spiritual history. Which reminds me I've read lately 2 amazing books about present-day Russia. One by Merejkovski and Zinaida Hippius and the other by Bunin. It is a very extraordinary thing that Russia can be there at our back door at furthest, and we know nothing, pay no attention, hear nothing in English. These books were in French. Both were full of *threats*. 'You may think you have escaped. But you have not escaped. What has happened to us will happen to you. And worse. Because you have not heard our prayers.' The ghastly horror and terror of that life in Petrograd is impossible to imagine. One must read it to know about it. But English people, people like us, would never survive as some of these Russian intellectuals have survived. We would die of so many things, vermin, fright, cold, hunger, even if we were not assassinated. At this present moment life in Russia is rather like it was four centuries ago. It has simply gone back four centuries. And anyone who sympathises with Bolshevism has much to answer for . . .

To William Gerhardi

[*13 March 1922*]

. . . I've been wanting to say – how strange, how delightful it is you should feel as you do about *The Voyage*. No one has mentioned it to me but Middleton Murry. But when I wrote that little story I felt that I was on that very boat, going down those stairs, smelling the smell of the saloon. And when the stewardess came in and said, 'We're rather empty, we may pitch a little,' I can't believe that my sofa did not pitch. And one moment I had a little bun of silk-white hair and a bonnet and the next I was Fenella hugging the swan neck umbrella. It was so vivid – terribly vivid – especially as they drove away and heard the sea as slowly it turned on the beach. Why – I don't know. It wasn't a memory of a real experience. It was a kind of *possession*. I might have remained the grandma for ever after if the wind had changed that moment. And that would have been a little bit embarrassing for Middleton Murry . . .

*

And yes, that is what I tried to convey in *The Garden Party*. The diversity of life and how we try to fit in everything, Death included. That is bewildering for a person of Laura's age. She feels things ought to happen differently. First one and then another. But life isn't like that. We haven't the ordering of it. Laura says, 'But all these things must not happen at once.' And Life answers, 'Why not? How are they divided from each other.' And they *do* all happen, it is inevitable. And it seems to me there is beauty in that inevitability . . .

To Ida Baker

[*15 March 1922*]

. . . We cannot live together in any sense until we – *I* – are am stronger. It seems to me it is my job, my fault, and not yours. I am simply unworthy of friendship, as I am. I take advantage of you – demand perfection of you – crush you – And the devil of it is that even though that is true as I write it I want to laugh. A deeper self looks at you and a deeper self in you looks back and we laugh and say 'what nonsense'. Its very queer, Jones, isn't it? Can you believe it – that looking back upon our times in Italy and Garavan – even the afternoon when you were raking the garden and I was proving our purely evil effect on each other I keep on remembering that it was a lovely day or that the button daisies were ducks. How nice – how very nice it would be to bowl along in one of those open cabs with the wind ruffling off the sea and a smell of roasting coffee and fresh lemons from the land. Oh dear! Oh dear! And do you remember standing at your window in your kimono one morning at five o'clock while I sat up in bed behind the mosquito curtains and talked of decomposition? No, we can't simply live apart for all our lives from now on. We shall have to visit at least. How can we live? What is the best plan? The future is so wrapt in mystery. Until I am well its foolishness for us to be together . . .

To Sir Harold Beauchamp[1]

[*18 March 1922*]

I have found it almost impossible to do any work so far, as the treatment is exceedingly tiring. But my new book has been a success and that is a comfort. It is extraordinary the letters I receive from strangers – all kinds of people. I have certainly been most fortunate as a writer. It is strange to remember buying a copy of *The Native Companion* on Lambton Quay and standing under a lamppost with darling Leslie to see if my story had been printed.

The more I see of life the more certain I feel that it's the people who live remote from cities who inherit the earth. London, for instance, is an awful place to live in. Not only is the climate abominable but it's a continual chase after distraction. There's no peace of mind – no harvest to be reaped out of it. And another thing is the longer I live the more I turn to New Zealand. I thank God I was born in New Zealand. A young country is a real heritage, though it takes one time to recognize it. But New Zealand is in my very bones. What wouldn't I give to have a look at it!

To Richard Murry

[*29 March 1922*]

. . . I wish you read German. Goethe's *Conversations with Eckermann* is one of those books which become part of one's life and what's more, enrich one's life for ever. Our edition

1. K.M's father.

is in two volumes. We lie in bed each reading one – it would
make a funny drawing . . .

To the Hon. Dorothy Brett

[*4 April 1922*]

. . . I'm interested in what you say of Wyndham L[ewis]. I've
heard so very very much about him from Anne Rice and
Violet Schiff. Yes, I admire his line tremendously. It's
beautifully obedient to his wishes. But it's queer I feel that as
an artist in spite of his passions and his views and all that he
lacks a real *centre*. I'll tell you what I mean. It sounds personal but we can't help that, we can only speak of what we
have learnt. It seems to me that what one aims at is to work
with one's mind and one's soul *together*. By soul I mean the
'thing' that makes the mind really important. I always
picture it like this. My mind is a very complicated, capable
instrument. But the interior is dark. It *can* work in the dark
and throw off all kinds of things. But behind that instrument
like a very steady gentle light is the soul. And it's only when
the soul *irradiates* the mind that what one does matters . . .
What I *aim* at is that state of mind when I feel my soul
and my mind are one. It's awfully, terribly difficult to get at.
Only solitude will do it for me. But I feel Wyndham Lewis
would be inclined to call the soul tiddley-om-pom. It's a
mystery, anyway. One aims at perfection – knows one will
never achieve it and goes on aiming as though one knew the
exact contrary.

To Ida Baker

[*April 1922*]

When you wrote Thursday with icicles, it was warm, really
hot here and sunny. I had a most extraordinary afternoon.
Got ready to go to Cox's and lost my cheque book – spent an

hour with Jack turning the whole room into a hay stack. No sign. Went off to Cox's – to stop all cheques. I had to wait to explain, to see my entire account, to go to the intelligence department where my name 'Mansfield' was cried like a vegetable and finally escaping prison by a hair we went off to the Bon Marché to buy a very simple light hat. Have you been there? Its one of the wonders of the world. Having fought to the lift we got out on to an open gallery with about 5,000 hats on it 10,000 dressing gowns, and so on. But the gallery looked over the entire ground floor and the whole of the ground floor was taken up with untrimmed 'shapes' and litera[ll]y, hundreds and hundreds of women – nearly all in black wandered from table to table turning and turning over these shapes. They were like some terrible insect swarm – not ants more like blow flies. Free balloons were given away that day and fat elderly women with little eyes and savage faces carried them. It was exactly like being in hell. The hats were loathsome. Jack as usual on such occasions would not speak to me and became furious. If I said 'Do you like that?' he replied 'No. Horribly vulgar!' If I timidly stretched out a hand he hissed 'Good God!' in my ear. We got out of the place at last. Then while waiting for a taxi a woman tried to commit suicide by flinging herself at his umbrella with which he was prodding the pavement. *She* was violently angry. I ran away to where a man was selling easter chickens that cheeped when you blew a whistle. The taxi came and Jack had by this time lost me. Finally both of us raging we got in, drove to the hotel, got out, got in again, and drove to another hat shop. 'Get this damned thing over!' was Jack's excuse. There [was] a quiet shop we both knew. We found only about 25 people and hats flying through the air. One woman put on another woman's old dead hat with the pins in it and walked off to pay the cashier. The owner dashed after her, with a face of fury and snatched it off her astonished head. My one stipulation was I didn't mind what kind of hat I bought but it must have no feathers. And I finally decided on a little fir cone with 2 whole birds on it!

To the Hon. Dorothy Brett

[*1 May 1922*]

About Joyce – Don't read it unless you are going to really worry about it. It's no joke. It's fearfully difficult and obscure and one needs to have a really vivid memory of the Odyssey and of English Literature to make it out at all. It is wheels within wheels within wheels. Joyce certainly had not one grain of a desire that one should read it for the sake of the coarseness, though I confess I find many 'a ripple of laughter' in it. But that's because (although I don't *approve* of what he's done) I do think Marian Bloom and Bloom are superbly seen at times. Marian is the complete complete female. There's no denying it. But one has to remember she's also Penelope, she is also the night and the day, she is also an image of the teeming earth, full of seed, rolling round and round. And so on and so on. I am very surprised to hear a Russian has written a book like this. It's most queer that it's never been heard of. But has Kot *read* Ulysses? It's not the faintest use considering the coarseness except purely critically.

I am very interested that Koteliansky thinks the German– Russian treaty really good.

I must say I never in my life felt so entangled in politics as I do at this moment. I hang on the newspapers. I feel I dare not miss a speech. One begins to feel, like Gorky feels, that it's one's duty to what remains of civilization to care for those things and that writers who do not are traitors. But it's horrible. It's like jumping into a treacle pot. However, perhaps tomorrow one will stop reading the papers or caring a fig.

> ABC
> Tumble down D
> The cat's in the cupboard
> And can't see me . . .

To Ida Baker

[*May 1922*]

Its less fearfully hot here. There is a breeze. It has been terrifically hot until tonight (Saturday). I went to the Louvre this afternoon and looked at Greek sculpture – wonderfully beautiful. The difference between the Greek and the Roman stuff is extraordinary; the Greek lives, breathes, floats; it is like life imprisoned, except that imprisonment sounds like unhappiness and there is a kind of radiant peace in the best of it. – Scraps of the Parthenon frieze – figures greeting, and holding fruits and flowers and so on are simply divine. I never realized what drapery was until today. I had a good stare at the Venus de Milo with all the other starers, and she is lovely as ever – the balance is most marvellous. Its intensely fascinating to see the development of that perfection – to trace it from heads that are flat as flat irons with just one dab for a nose – then to the period of tree worship when all the bodies are very round and solid like the trunks of trees, then through the Egyptian influence when they begin to have stiff and terrible wings, and at last that perfect flowering flower. It makes one in love with the human body to wander about there – all the lovely creases in the belly and the roundness of knees and the beauty of thighs.

16
Switzerland again, June–August 1922

After four months the first round of the Manoukhin treatment was over and on 4 June 1922 Katherine Mansfield returned with Murry to Switzerland. But now, according to Murry, a deep restlessness had taken hold of her. She found it almost impossible to write; her last hope of a medical or 'scientific' cure for her illness was gone; and her mind turned more and more towards the ideas of Gurdjieff and 'the attainment of such psychic control as would allow her to ignore her bodily condition'. These were ideas Murry could not share. He saw them as 'occultism', and to this difference between them he ascribes the fact that they began to have 'a depressing effect upon one another' and separated, he living at Randogne, she further down the mountain at Sierre. He visited her at weekends, however, they telephoned daily, and she wrote occasional notes, addressing him as 'Betsy' but assuring him 'I like you awfully'.

By August the possibility of death must have seemed very real to her. On 7 August she wrote a letter left for Murry to read in the event of her death; and on 14 August she made her will.

To Ida Baker

[5 June 1922]

I am at last on the balcony overlooking the same mountains. It's hot with a small wind: grasshoppers are playing their small tambourines and the church bells of Old Montana are ringing. How we got here I shall never know! Every single thing went wrong. The laundry didn't come back in time. We were off late. Brett was laden with large parcels which we could not pack and which she promised to store for us – until when? And only when we got to the [Gare] de Lyon we remembered that it was Whitsun. *No* porters. People wheeling their own luggage. Swarms and thousands of people. Fifteen thousand young Gymnastes de Provence arriving and pouring through one. Poor Jack who had my money gave away a 500 note instead of a 50. And at last arrived at the Couchettes we found ordinary 1st class carriage with 3 persons a side. No washing arrangements – nothing. It was the cursed *Fete de Narcisse* at Montreux yesterday so conducted parties crammed the train. What a night! And the grime! At Lausanne we both looked like Negroes. Then came a further rush for the Sierre train (registered luggage tickets lost) and finally two hours late we arrived at the Belle Vue, starving, as we had no food with us and there was no food on the train. But that enchanted hotel was more exquisite than ever. The people so kind and gentle, the waving branches outside the windows, a smell of roses and lime blossom. After a very powerful wash and an immaculate lunch – how do the glasses and spoons shine so? – I lay down and went to sleep and Jack went out. The next thing was: *La voiture est là Madame.* Heavens! Nothing was packed. Jack had not come back. The bill was not paid and so on. I am quite out of the habit of these rushes. Finally we found Jack at the Post Office and just got to the station in time. Then at Randogne there was no room for our luggage in the cart. So we went off without it. (Last bulletin de bagage lost, Jack simply *prostrate*) and, we'd scarcely left the station when it began to pour with rain. Sheets, spouts of cold mountain rain. My mole coat and skirt was like a mole skin. We got soaked and the road which hasn't been remade yet after the winter was exactly like the bed of a river. But the comble was to get here and to see these small poky little rooms waiting us. We took the ground floors three as you said they were so *big* and so *nice*. Good God! whatever made you tell such bangers. They are small single rooms and really they look quite dreadful. Also the woman told us she had *no* servants. She and her sister were alone, to do everything. I thought at first we'd have to drive off again. But that was impossible. So I decided to accept it as a kind of picnic: 'the kind of place R. L. Stevenson might have stayed at' – or 'some little hotel in Russia'. Jack looked much happier then. But there wasn't even an armchair or a glass in my room. No wash table in his. I made the old woman get in these things. She is amiable and kind and poor soul – very frightened. And before supper the luggage arrived and we unpacked and my room looked much better. We were just settling down when I found Jack had left the dear little square clock in the train. I was devoted to that clock – and he found he had lost his only fountain pen!

To William Gerhardi

[*14 June 1922*]

... If it happens to be sunset, too, I could shew you something very strange. Behind this Hotel there is a big natural lawn, a wide stretch of green turf. When the herds that are being driven home in the evening come to it they go wild with delight. Staid, black cows begin to dance, to leap, to cut capers. Quiet, refined little sheep who look as though buttercups would not melt in their mouths suddenly begin to jump, to spin round, to bound off like rocking-horses. The goats are complete Russian Ballet Dancers; they are almost too brilliant. But the cows are the most surprising and the most näive. You will admit that cows don't look like born dancers, do they? And yet my cows are light as feathers, bubbling over with fun. Please tell dear little Miss Helsingfors that it's quite true they *do* jump over the moon.

Journal

[*June 1922*]

The reason why you find it so hard to write is because you are learning nothing. I mean of the things that count – like the sight of this tree with its purple cones against the blue. How can I put it, that there is gum on the cones? 'Gemmed?' *No.* 'Beaded?' *No.* 'They are like crystals.' Must I? I am afraid so . . .

*

I seem to have lost all power of writing. I can think, in a vague way, and it all seems more or less real and worth doing. But I can't get any further. I can't write it down.

To S. S. Koteliansky

[*4 July 1922*]

Have you read Lawrence's new book? I should like to very much. He is the only writer living whom I really profoundly care for. It seems to me whatever he writes, no matter how much one may 'disagree,' is important. And after all even what one objects to is a *sign of life* in him. He is a living man. There has been published lately an extremely bad collection of short stories – Georgian Short Stories. And *The Shadow in the Rose Garden* by Lawrence is among them. This story is perhaps one of the weakest he ever wrote. But it is so utterly different from all the rest that one reads it with joy. When he mentions gooseberries these are real red, ripe gooseberries that the gardener is rolling on a tray. When he bites into an apple it is a sharp, sweet, fresh apple from the growing tree.

[*17 July 1922*]

I want to talk to you for hours about – *Aaron's Rod,* for instance. Have you read it? There are certain things in this new book of L.'s that I do not like. But they are not important or really part of it. They are trivial, encrusted, they cling to it as snails cling to the underside of a leaf. But apart from them there is the leaf, is the tree, firmly planted, deep thrusting, outspreading, growing grandly, alive in every twig. It is a living book; it is warm, it breathes. And it is written by a living man, with *conviction*. Oh, Koteliansky, what a relief it is to turn away from these little pre-digested books written by authors who have nothing to say! It is like walking by the sea at high tide eating a crust of bread and looking over the water. I am so sick of all this modern seeking which ends in seeking. *Seek* by all means, but the text goes on 'that ye shall find.' And although, of course, there can be no ultimate finding, there is a kind of finding by the way which is enough, is sufficient. But these seekers in the looking glass, these half-female, frightened writers-of-today – You know, darling, they remind me of the greenfly in roses – they are a kind of blight.

To Sir Harold Beauchamp

[28 July 1922]

... J. is still in his lofty perch among the mountains. At the week-ends, whenever the weather is wet, we play billiards. There is a splendid table here and we are both very keen. It's a fascinating game. I remember learning to hold a cue at Sir Joseph Ward's,[1] and I can see now R's super-refinement as if she expected each ball to be stamped with a coronet before she would deign to hit it.

To S. S. Koteliansky

[2 August 1922]

I hope you are better. If you need a doctor, *Sorapure* is a good man – intelligent and quiet. He does not discuss Lloyd George with me, either. This is a great relief. All the other English doctors that I know have just finished reading The Daily Mail by the time they reach me. It is a pity that

1. Prime Minister of New Zealand from 1906 to 1911.

Lawrence is driven so far. I am sure that Western Australia will not help. The desire to travel is a great, real temptation. But does it do any good? It seems to me to correspond to the feelings of a sick man who thinks always 'if only I can get away from here I shall be better.' However – there is nothing to be done. One must go through with it. No one can stop that sick man, either, from moving on and on. But Lawrence, I am sure, will get well.

Perhaps you will be seeing Brett in a few days? She goes back to England tomorrow. I feel awfully inclined to Campbell about her[1] for a little. But it would take a whole book to say all that one feels. She is a terrible proof of the influence ones childhood has upon one. And there has been nothing stronger in her life to counteract that influence. I do not think she will ever be an adult being. She is weak; she is a vine; she longs to cling. She cannot nourish herself from the earth; she must feed on the sap of another. How can these natures ever be happy? By happy I mean at peace with themselves. She is seeking someone who will make her forget that early neglect, that bullying and contempt. But the person who would satisfy her would have to dedicate himself to curing all the results of her unhappiness – her distrust, for instance, her suspicions, her fears. He would have to take every single picture and paint it with her, just as a singer, by singing with his pupil can make that weak voice strong and confident . . . But even then, she would not be *cured*. I believe one can cure nobody, one can change nobody fundamentally. The born slave cannot become a free man. He can only become free-er. I have refused to believe that for years, and yet I am certain it is true, it is even a law of life. But it is equally true that hidden in the slave there are the makings of the free man. And these makings are very nice in Brett, very sensitive and generous. I love her for them. They make me want to help her as much as I can.

1. To 'Campbell' was to ramble on amiably in the manner of their old friend Gordon Campbell (later Lord Glenavy), husband of Beatrice Campbell to whom some of K.M.'s letters are addressed.

I am content. I prefer to leave our meeting to chance. To know you are there is enough. If I knew I was going to die I should even ask you definitely to come and see me. For I should hate to die without one long, uninterrupted talk with *you*. But short of it – it does not greatly matter.

To the Hon. Dorothy Brett

[*11 August 1922*]

I can't arrive before Thursday afternoon. No sleeper before then. Your clouds like Feather Boas are perfeck!

This – yours – is such a very nice letter that it is a good thing we shall meet so soon, I feel inclined to come by the perambulator and have done with it.

Why do things need so many nails? Why can't one use safety pins? They are so much quicker and they are deadly Secure. Once you have clasped yourself to a safety pin human flesh and blood can't separate you.

(Let us go and see Charlie Chaplin when I come. Shall we? On the Fillums, of course, I mean.)

This place is flaming with Gladioli, too. As for the dahlias they are rampant everywhere. The pears which we had for lunch, are iron pears, with little copperplums and a zinc greengage or two.

L.M., smelling the luggage from afar, is in her element. She is hung round with tickets already and almost whistles and shunts when she brings me my tisane. I am moving already myself, the writing table is gliding by, and I feel inclined to wave to people in the garden.

Elizabeth came yesterday with one of the Ladies Fair. I must say she had ravishing deep, deep grey eyes. She seemed, too, divinely happy. She is happy. She has a perfect love, a man. They have loved each other for eight years and it is still as radiant, as exquisite as ever. I must say it *is* nice to gaze at people who are in love. M. has taken up golf. I've always wondered when this would happen . . .

To Richard Murry

[*14 August 1922*]

I did a thing today which it has been in my mind to do for a long time. I made a will, signed it, and got it duly witnessed. In it I left you my large pearl ring. My idea in leaving it to you was that you should give it – if you care to – to your woman whoever she may be. I hope you won't think this ghoulish. But Jack gave me the ring and I feel it would be nice to keep it in the family . . .

17

London, Paris, Fontainebleau,
August 1922–January 1923

Katherine Mansfield had intended to go to Paris to continue the Manoukhin treatment but changed her mind and went to London instead, arriving with Murry on 17 August 1922. In London they continued to live apart. She met her old editor, A. R. Orage, who introduced her to the circle in London to whom P. D. Ouspensky was teaching the ideas of Gurdjieff. On 2 October she returned to Paris, having told her friends, and Murry too, that she was going there for further X-ray treatment. In fact she hoped secretly to be admitted to the Gurdjieff Institute for the Harmonious Development of Man, which had recently moved to Fontainebleau-Avon. On 17 October she was admitted to the Institute. There she found contentment in communal living, though Gurdjieff's strange discipline seems to have involved considerable physical hardship, and her letters are punctuated with 'it is intensely cold here'.

On 31 December she wrote asking Murry to visit her at the Institute on 8 or 9 January. He arrived on 9 January and found her 'very pale, but radiant'. That evening as they climbed the stairs to bed she was seized with a fit of coughing which brought on a haemorrhage. Two doctors attended her at once but she was dead within a few minutes.

She was buried in the communal cemetery at Fontainebleau-Avon.

To J. M. Murry

[20 September 1922]

. . . I had a card from Lawrence today – just the one word 'Ricordi'. How like him! I was glad to get it though . . .

Paris [*3 October 1922*]

... Oh, I meant to suggest to you to ask for Yeats's Memoirs
to review. I think they are coming out this autumn. I believe
you would find them very interesting. He's not a 'sympathetic' person, as far as I know, but he's one of those men who
reflect their time. Such men have a fascination for me.
Haven't they for you?

I wish we lived nearer to each other. I should like to talk
more to you. But there is time. When this jungle of circum-
stances is cleared a little we shall be freer to enjoy each other.
It is not the moment now. Tell me what you can about yourself. Not even you could wish for your happiness more than I
do. Don't forget that dragons are only guardians of treasures
and one fights them for what they keep – not for themselves ...

[*8 October 1922*]

Do not bother to write to me when you are not in the mood.
I quite understand and don't expect too many letters.

Yes, this is where I stayed *pendant la guerre*. It's the quietest
hotel I ever was in. I don't think tourists come at all. There
are funny rules about not doing one's washing or fetching in
one's cuisine from *dehors* which suggest a not rich an' grand
clientèle. What is nice too is one can get a tray in the evening
if one doesn't want to go out. Fearfully good what I imagine is
provincial cooking – all in big bowls, piping hot, brought up
by the garçon who is a v. nice fellow in a red veskit and white
apron and a little grey cloth *cap*! I think some English travel-
ler left it in a cupboard about 1879. The salt and pepper
stand, by the way, is a little glass motor car. Salt is driver and
Pepper Esquire is master in the back seat – the dark fiery one
of the two, so different to plain old Salt ... What a good
fellow he is, though!

Yesterday the wind was nor' north by north by east by due
east by due east-north-east. If you know a colder one, it was
there, too. I had to thaw a one-franc piece to get the change

out of it. (That is a joke for your Sunday paper only!)

I've just read you on Bozzy. You awe me very much by your familiarity with simply all those people. You've always such a vast choice of sticks in the hall-stand for when you want to go walking and even a vaster choice of umbrellas – while I go all unprotected and exposed with only a fearful sense of the heavens lowering.

Lawrence has reached Mexico and feels ever so lively. Father has reached Port Said. He quoted a whole poem by Enid Bagnold to say so. 'I am a sailor sailing on summer seas.' All the same a marvellous wash of the blue crept up the page as I read his letter, which had nothing to do with E.B.

By the way, do you read letters at Selsfield? Do you ever read letters? You never do. You only skate over them. 'Here's a letter!' And down you sit, clamp on your skates, do a dreamy kind of twirl over the pages, and that's all. Or is that libelling you?

Mary! There's a most beautiful magpie on *my* roof. Are magpies still wild? Ah me, how little one knows!

I must go out to lunch. Goodbye, my darling. I hope to send you some MSS to type this next week. Give my love to L.-E. Tell him of this hôtel in case he comes to Paris. I think he'll like it. My room is on the 6ème. Didn't I tell you? I felt sure I did.

I know that water music. It is lovely – so very watery – reminds me too in bits of Spenser's Swans.

To S. S. Koteliansky

[*9 October 1922*]

I have finished the letters;[1] here they are. They are, the more one looks into them, a remarkable revelation of what goes on *behind the scenes*. Except for 'Kiss the foal' and 'buy the children sweets; even doctors prescribe sweets for children,' there is hardly one single statement that isn't pure

1. Dostoyevsky's letters to his wife.

matter-of-fact. The whole affair is like the plot of a short story or small novel by himself; he reacts to everything exactly as he would to a *written* thing. There's no expansion, no evidence of a LIVING man, a REAL man. The glimpse one has of his relationship with Anya is somehow petty and stuffy, essentially a double bed relationship. And then 'Turgenev read so badly'; they say *he* (D.) read so superbly – Oh dear, Oh dear, it would take an Anna Grigorevna to be proud of such letters.

Yet this was a noble, suffering, striving soul, a real hero among men – wasn't he? I mean from his books . . . The one who writes the letters is the house porter of the other. I suppose one ought not to expect to find the master at his own front door as well as in his study. But I find it hard to reconcile myself to that. I do not think these deep divisions in people are necessary or vital. Perhaps it is cowardice in me.

To J. M. Murry

[*11 October 1922*]

. . . All the same, you say 'Tell me about yourself.' I'll have a try. Here goes.

A new way of being is not an easy thing to *live*. Thinking about it, preparing to meet the difficulties and so on, is one thing, meeting those difficulties another. I have to die to so much; I have to make such *big* changes. I feel the only thing to do is to get the dying over – to court it, almost. (Fearfully hard, that.) And then all hands to the business of being re-born again. What do I mean exactly? Let me give you an instance. Looking back, my boat is almost swamped sometimes by seas of sentiment. 'Ah, what I have missed! How sweet it was, how dear, how warm, how simple, how precious!' And I think of the garden at the Isola Bella and the furry bees and the house-wall so warm. But then I remember what we really felt there – the blanks, the silences, the anguish of continual misunderstanding. Were we posi-

tive, eager, real, alive? No, we were not. We were a nothing-
ness shot with gleams of what might be. But no more. Well,
I have to face everything as far as I can and see where I
stand – what *remains*.

For with all my soul I do long for a real life, for truth, and
for real strength. It's simply incredible, watching K.M., to
see how little causes a panic. She's a perfect corker at toppling
over.

[*14 October 1922*][1]

. . . About doing operations on yourself. I know just what
you mean. It is as though one were the sport of circumstance –
one *is*, indeed. Now happy, now unhappy, now fearful, now
confident, – just as the pendulum swings. You see one can
control nothing if one isn't conscious of a purpose – it's like a
journey without a goal. There is nothing that makes you
ignore some things, accept others, order others, submit to
others. For there is no reason why A. should be more important than B. So there one is – involved beyond words – feeling
the next minute I may be bowled over or struck all of a
heap. I *know* nothing.

This is to me a very terrible state of affairs. Because it's the
cause of all the unhappiness (the secret profound unhappiness)
in my life. But I mean to escape and to try to live differently.
It isn't easy. But is the other state easy? And I do believe
with all my being that if one *can* break through the circle one
finds 'my burden is light' . . .

Journal

[*14 October 1922*]

My spirit is nearly dead. My spring of life is so starved
that it's just not dry. Nearly all my improved health is
pretence – acting. What does it amount to? Can I walk?

1. K.M.'s thirty-fourth birthday.

Only creep. Can I do anything with my hands or body? Nothing at all. I am an absolutely hopeless invalid. What is my life? It is the existence of a parasite. And five years have passed now, and I am in straiter bonds than ever.

*

Therefore if the Grand Lama of Thibet promised to help you – how can you hesitate? Risk! Risk anything! Care no more for the opinions of others, for those voices. Do the hardest thing on earth for you. Act for yourself. Face the truth.

True, Tchehov didn't. Yes, but Tchehov died. And let us be honest. How much do we know of Tchehov from his letters? Was that all? Of course not. Don't you suppose he had a whole longing life of which there is hardly a word? Then read the final letters. He has given up hope. If you de-sentimentalise those final letters they are terrible. There is no more Tchehov. Illness has swallowed him.

But perhaps to people who are not ill, all this is nonsense. They have never travelled this road. How can they see where I am? All the more reason to go boldly forward alone. Life is not simple. In spite of all we say about the mystery of Life, when we get down to it we want to treat it as though it were a child's tale . . .

Now, Katherine, what do you mean by health? And what do you want it for?

Answer: By health I mean the power to live a full, adult, living, breathing life in close contact with what I love – the earth and the wonders thereof – the sea – the sun. All that we mean when we speak of the external world. I want to enter into it, to be part of it, to live in it, to learn from it, to lose all that is superficial and acquired in me and to become a conscious, direct human being. I want, by understanding myself, to understand others. I want to be all that I am capable of becoming so that I may be (and here I have stopped and waited and waited and it's no good – there's only one phrase that will do) *a child of the sun*. About helping others, about carrying a light and so on, it seems false to say a single word. Let it be at that. *A child of the sun.*

Then I want to *work*. At what? I want so to live that I work with my hands and my feeling and my brain. I want a garden, a small house, grass, animals, books, pictures, music. And out of this, the expression of this, I want to be writing. (Though I may write about cabmen. That's no matter.)

But warm, eager, living life – to be rooted in life – to learn, to desire to know, to feel, to think, to act. That is what I want. And nothing less. That is what I must try for.

To J. M. Murry

[*15 October 1922*]

. . . About being like Tchekhov and his letters. Don't forget he died at 43. That he spent – how much? of his life chasing about in a desperate search after health. And if one reads 'intuitively' the last letters, they are terrible. What is left of him? 'The braid on German women's dresses . . . bad taste' – and all the rest is misery. Read the last! All hope is over for him. Letters are deceptive, at any rate. It's true he had occasional happy moments. But for the last 8 years he knew no *security* at all. We know he felt his stories were not half what they might be. It doesn't take much imagination to picture him on his deathbed thinking 'I have never had a real chance. Something has been all wrong.'

Journal

[*1922*]

October 15 Nietzsche's Birthday. Sat in the Luxembourg Gardens. Cold, wretchedly unhappy. Horrid people at lunch, everything horrid, from *Anfang bis zum Ende.*

October 17 Laublätter. The Four Fountains. The Red Tobacco Plant. English dog. The funeral procession. Actions
and Reactions. The silky husk, like the inside of the paw of
a cat. 'Darling.'

Fire is sunlight and returns to the sun again in an unending
cycle ... He [Gurdjieff] looks exactly like a desert chief. I
kept thinking of Doughty's *Arabia*.

To be wildly enthusiastic, or deadly serious – both are
wrong. Both pass. One must keep ever present a sense of
humour. It depends entirely on yourself how much you see or
hear or understand. But the sense of humour I have found
true of every single occasion of my life. Now perhaps you
understand what 'indifferent' means. It is to learn not to
mind, and not to show your mind.

October 18 In the autumn garden leaves falling. Little
footfalls, like gentle whispering. They fly, spin, twirl, shake.

To J. M. Murry

Fontainebleau   [*24 October 1922*]

... As for writing stories and being true to one's gift – I
wouldn't write them if I were not here, even. I am at the end
of my source for the time. Life has brought me no FLOW. I
want to write – but differently – far more steadily ...

[*27 October 1922*]

I do hope you are having this glorious weather. Day after
day of perfect sunshine. It's like Switzerland. An *intense* blue
sky, a chill in the air, a wonderful clarity so that you see
people far away, all sharp-cut and vivid.

I spend all the sunny time in the garden. Visit the carpen-
ters, the trench diggers. (We are digging for a Turkish Bath
– not to discover one, but to lay the pipes.) The soil is very
nice here, like sand, with small whitey pinky pebbles in it.

Then there are the sheep to inspect and the new pigs that
have long golden hair – very mystical pigs. A mass of cosmic
rabbits and hens – and goats are on the way, likewise horses
and mules to ride and drive. The Institute is not really started
yet for another fortnight. A dancing hall is being built and
the house is still being organized. But it has started really. If
all this were to end in smoke tomorrow I should have had the
very great wonderful adventure of my life. I've learnt more
in a week than in years là-bas. As to habits. My wretched sense
of order, for instance, which rode me like a witch. It did not
take long to cure that. Mr Gurdjieff likes me to go into the
kitchen in the late afternoon and 'watch'. I have a chair in
a corner. It's a large kitchen with 6 helpers. Madame
Ostrovsky, the head walks about like a queen exactly. She is
extremely beautiful. She wears an old raincoat. Nina, a
big girl in a black apron – lovely, too – pounds things in
mortars. The second cook chops at the table, bangs the saucepans, sings; another runs in and out with plates and pots, a
man in the scullery cleans pots – the dog barks and lies on
the floor, worrying a hearthbrush. A little girl comes in with
a bouquet of leaves for Olga Ivanovna. Mr Gurdjieff strides
in, takes up a handful of shredded cabbage and eats it . . .
there are at least 20 pots on the stove. And it's so full of life
and humour and ease that one wouldn't be anywhere else.
It's just the same all through – *ease* after *rigidity* expresses it
more than anything I know. And yet I realize that as I
write this, it's no use. An old personality is trying to get back
to the outside and observe, and it's not true to the present
facts at all. What I write sounds so petty. In fact, I cannot
express myself in writing just now. The old mechanism isn't
mine any longer and I can't control the new. I just have to
talk this baby talk . . .

[*2 November 1922*]

Ever since my last letter to you I have been so enraged with
myself. It's so like me. I am ashamed of it. But you who know

me will perhaps understand. I always try to go too fast. I always think all can be changed and renewed in the twinkling of an eye. It is most fearfully hard for me, as it is for you, not to be 'intense'. And whenever I am intense (really, this is so) I am a little bit false . . .

[*19 November 1922*]

. . . It is intensely cold here – quite as cold as Switzerland. But it does not matter in the same way. One has not the time to think about it. There is always something happening, and people are a support. I spent the winter afternoon yesterday scraping carrots – masses of carrots – and half way through I suddenly thought of my bed in the corner of that room at the Chalet des Sapins . . . Oh, how is it possible there is such a difference between that loneliness and isolation (just waiting for you to come in and you knowing that I was waiting) and *this*. People were running in and out of the kitchen. Portions of the first pig we have killed were on the table and greatly admired. Coffee was roasting in the oven. Barker clattered through with his milk-pail. I must tell you, darling, my love of cows persists. We now have three. They are real beauties – immense – with short curly hair? fur? wool? between their horns. Geese, too, have been added to the establishment. They seem full of intelligence . . .

[*November 1922*]

. . . Do you ever feel inclined to get into touch with Lawrence again, I wonder? I should like very much to know what he intends to do – how he intends to live now his *Wanderjahre* are over. He and E. M. Forster are two men who *could* understand this place if they would. But I think Lawrence's pride would keep him back. No one person here is more important than another.

*

It is intensely cold here – colder and colder. I have just been brought some small fat pine logs to mix with my *boulets*. Boulets are unsatisfactory; they are too passive. I simply live in my fur coat. I gird it on like my heavenly armour and wear it ever night and day. After this winter the Arctic even will have no terrors for me. Happily, the sun *does* shine as well, and we are thoroughly well nourished. But I shall be glad when the year has turned . . .

[November 1922]

. . . Are you having really perfect weather (except for the cold)? It is absolutely brilliantly sunny – a deep blue sky, dry air. Really, it's better than Switzerland. But I must get some wool-lined over-boots. My footgear is ridiculous when I am where I was yesterday – round about the pigsty. It is noteworthy that the pigs have of themselves divided their sty into two; one, the clean part, they keep clean and sleep in. This makes me look at pigs with a different eye. One must be impartial even about them, it seems . . .

To Ida Baker

[12 December 1922]

. . . It is intensely cold here and very damp. Very rarely the house is heated. I have a fire in my little room though. I live now in the workers' quarters and have the kind of bedroom Gertie Small might have. Bare boards – a scrubbed table for the jug and basin etc. At about 10.30 p.m. we start work in the salon and go to bed at about 1–2 a.m. The windows are like whistling side streets to pass down – icy-cold. My hands are ruined for the present with scraping carrots and peeling onions. I do quite a lot of that kind of kitchenwork. But I shall be very glad to exchange a very grubby washing up cloth for an apron or an overall. This life proves how terribly wrong and stupid all doctors are. I would have been dead 50 times in the opinion of all the medical men whom I have known. And when I remember last year and that bed in the corner week after week and those *trays*. Here there is no more fine food. You eat what you get and that's the end of it. At the same time I have wonderful what shall I call them? friends...

To the Countess Russell

[*31 December 1922*]

I am sending this, as you see, at the last last moment while the old year is in the very act of turning up his toes. I wish I could explain why I have not written to you for so long. It is not for lack of love. But such a black fit came over me in Paris when I realized that X-ray treatment wasn't going to do any more than it had done beyond upsetting my heart still more that I gave up everything and decided to try a new life altogether. But this decision was immensely complicated with 'personal' reasons, too. When I came to London from Switzerland I did (Sydney was right so far) go through what books and undergraduates call a spiritual crisis, I suppose. For the first time in my life, everything bored me. Everything, and worse, everybody seemed a compromise and so flat, so dull, so mechanical. If I had been well I should have rushed off to darkest Africa or the Indus or the Ganges or wherever it is one rushes at those times, to try for a change of heart (One can't change one's heart in public) and to gain new impressions. For it seems to me we live on new impressions – really new ones.

But such grand flights being impossible I burned what boats I had and came here where I am living with about 50–60 people, mainly Russians. It is a fantastic existence, impossible to describe. One might be anywhere, in Bokhara or in Tiflis or Afghanistan (except, alas! for the climate!). But even the climate does not seem to matter so much when one is whirled along at such a rate. For we do most decidedly whirl. But I cannot tell you what a joy it is to me to be in contact with living people who are strange and quick and not ashamed to be themselves. It's a kind of supreme airing to be among them.

But what nonsense this all sounds. That is the worst of letters; they are fumbling things.

I haven't written a word since October and I don't mean to until the spring. I want much more material; I am tired of my little stories like birds bred in cages.

Goodbye, my dearest cousin. I shall never know anyone like you; I shall remember every little thing about you for ever.